AGENT OF CHANGE

A LIADEN UNIVERSE® NOVEL

THIRTIETH ANNIVERSARY EDITION

SHARON LEE & STEVE MILLER

BAEN

AGENT OF CHANGE

This is a work of fiction. All the characters and events portrayed in this book are fictional, and any resemblance to real people or incidents is purely coincidental.

A Baen Book

Baen Publishing Enterprises
P.O. Box 1403
Riverdale, NY 10471

ISBN: 978-1-4814-8364-3

Cover art by Sam Kennedy

Baen paperback printing, November 2018

Distributed by Simon & Schuster
1230 Avenue of the Americas
New York, NY 10020

Printed in the United States of America

10 9 8 7 6 5 4 3 2 1

INTRODUCTION
Thirtieth Anniversary Edition

IT'S AN HONOR to have been asked to write the introduction to the thirtieth anniversary edition of the timeless science fiction novel *Agent of Change*, by Sharon Lee and Steve Miller.

Our acquaintanceship spans decades; in fact Lee and Miller is our closest colleague in the field. It is tempting to say that we know the author as ourselves, but that would be deceptive.

Or at least misleading.

Lee and Miller began writing in 1980. The first work published under the author's byline, in 1983, was a short story, "The Naming of Kinzel: The Innocent." The second, also published in 1983, was another short story, set in the same fantasy universe, "The Naming of Kinzel: The Foolish." A few more short pieces followed but Lee and Miller was after bigger game.

In February 1988, space opera classic *Agent of Change* was published, Lee and Miller's first novel.

The author's career after the publication of this first novel was erratic, occasionally terrifying, and sometimes short of food. Doubtless, the whole adventure would make compelling reading for those with a taste for tales of desperate derring-do, but that must wait for another opportunity.

Our topic today is the novel, *Agent of Change*.

It was a strange novel for its time; perhaps for any time. In form, it is indisputably space opera, that most exuberant of science fictional sub-genres. It is an action-adventure novel with overtones of the spy fiction of its day, the dialogue written in an often witty style with purposeful touches of melodrama. one famededitor called it "John Le Carre in space" as it was making the rounds of publishers. The human characters are warmly drawn, and deadly in context; the alien race is charming and whimsical, not merely comic relief; and the plot is downright quirky.

The world-building is notable: Multi-cultural. Gender equal. Textured.

The heroes of the piece, Val Con yos'Phelium and Miri Robertson, are a study in contrasts. Val Con is Liaden, human, though not "Earth human;" the child of a wealthy clan seated on a wealthy world that has long dominated trade. Liaden society is privileged and proud; dismissive of "lesser" peoples and their cultures. The native tongue is chorded, tonal; sweet on the ear but difficult for non-natives to learn.

Val Con himself is educated, cultured, refined; fastidious, reminiscent at times of upper ton characters drawn by Georgette Heyer, the doyen of Regency Romance, whose influence can be seen more fully in later Lee and Miller work.

Hewing to the traditions of the science fiction genre,

harking back to the vintage space opera of Andre Norton, and James H. Schmitz, Val Con is an assassin; a spy . . .

. . . and an agent of change.

Co-hero Miri Robertson, late of the Gyrfalks Mercenary Unit, is Val Con's apparent opposite. She escapes the ghetto world of her birth by joining a mercenary unit as an apprentice soldier. By the time she and Val Con meet, in a firefight, true to the story's space opera roots, she is a master sergeant, lethal, humorous; a hard-edged realist; a true friend. . .

. . . and an agent of change.

Miri is worth some further attention, as a character and as a marker of Lee and Miller's intent in creating this fictional universe.

In the 1980s female soldiers were not precisely thick on the ground—in real life or in fiction. And yet here is Miri Robertson: efficient, unflappable; a thorough professional, and a fully realized character.

This is one of the hallmarks of Lee and Miller's work: We see male and female (and later, alien and AI) characters in a variety of roles: soldiers, caretakers, pilots, card sharps, security guards, mechanics, bartenders, scholars, planetary administrators—heroes, villains, and ordinary citizens, going about their lives.

Lee and Miller made another radical storytelling decision, which reverberates throughout *Agent of Change,* and the stories that follow. It was this notion that, though people are competent, no one thrives in isolation. Throughout the narrative, the author makes the argument that people, all people, need people; they need comfort, assistance, companionship.

As much as it is, very firmly, space opera, *Agent of Change* is also a discussion of what it is to be human, and to be a full partner in a relationship.

By turns, and sometimes simultaneously, *Agent of Change* is gripping, moving, and funny; a novel which has not only endured for thirty years, but which provided the launch pad for twenty more novels and dozens of short stories, all set in what is now dignified as the Liaden Universe®, Lee and Miller's lifework—which is still growing.

We hope you enjoy reading *Agent of Change*.

Sharon Lee and Steve Miller
Cat Farm and Confusion Factory
April 2018

AGENT OF CHANGE

A LIADEN UNIVERSE® NOVEL

✧ CHAPTER ONE ✧

THE MAN WHO was not Terrence O'Grady had come quietly.

And that, Sam insisted, was clear proof. Terry had never done anything quietly in his life if there was a way to get a fight out of it.

Pete, walking at Sam's left behind the prisoner, wasn't so sure. To all appearances, the man they had taken *was* Terrence O'Grady. He had the curly, sandy hair, the pug nose, and the archaic black-framed glasses over pale blue eyes, and he walked with a limp of the left leg, which the dossier said was a souvenir of an accident way back when he'd been mining in the Belt of Terado.

They stopped at a door set deep into the brick wall of the alley. Up in front, Russ raised his fist and struck the heavy kreelwood twice.

They waited, listening to the noises of the night city beyond the alley. Then the door opened silently on well-oiled hinges, and they were staring down a long hallway.

As he stepped over the threshold, Pete gritted his

3

teeth and concentrated on the back of the man before him. The man who was not Terrence O'Grady. Maybe.

It was in no way a remarkable back: slightly stoop-shouldered, not quite on a level with Pete's own. Terrence O'Grady, the dossier noted, was short and slender for a Terran, a good six inches below the average. This made him a valuable partner for bulky Sam, who handled the massive mining equipment effortlessly, but was not so well suited to exploring the small gaps, craters, and crevices where a rich vein might hide.

Sam and Terry made money in the Belt. Then Terry quit mining, bought himself some land with atmosphere over it, and settled into farming, child raising, and even politics.

Eight years later Sam got a bouncecomm from Terry's wife: Terrence O'Grady had disappeared.

Sam went to talk to wife and family, as an old friend should; he asked questions and nosed around. No corpse had been found, but Sam declared Terry dead. He'd been too stubborn a dreamer to run out on all of them at once. And, given Terry's luck, someone would have had to kill him to make him dead before old age.

Sam said Terry had been murdered three years ago.

But recently there had been rumors, and then this person here—wearing a dead man's face and calling himself by a dead man's name.

Pete shook himself as they rounded a sharp corner and barely avoided stepping on the prisoner.

"Look sharp!" Sam whispered harshly.

They turned another corner and came into a brightly lit, abandoned office.

The man who was not Terrence O'Grady nearly smiled.

From this point on, he knew the layout of each of the fourteen suites in this building, the voltage of the lighting fixtures, the position of doors and windows, the ambient temperature, and even the style and color of the carpets.

Within his mental Loop, he saw a number shift from .7 to .85. The second figure changed a moment later from .5 to .7. The first percentage indicated Chance of Mission Success; the second, Chance of Personal Survival. CMS recently had been running significantly above CPS.

His escort halted before a lift, and both numbers rose by a point. When the lift opened onto an office on the third floor, the Loop flickered and withdrew—the more imminent the action, the less precise the calculations.

THE DESK was beautiful, made of inlaid teak and redwood imported from Earth.

The man behind the desk was also imported from Earth and he was not beautiful. He had a paunch and an aggressive black beard. Soft hands laced together on the gleaming wood, he surveyed the group with casual interest.

"Thank you, gentlemen. You may stand away from the prisoner."

Russ and Skipper dropped back, leaving the man who was not O'Grady alone before Mr. Jaeger's desk.

"Mr. O'Grady, I believe?" Jaeger purred.

The little man bowed slightly and straightened, hands loose at his sides.

In the depths of his beard, Jaeger frowned. He tapped the desktop with one well-manicured finger.

"You're not Terrence O'Grady," he said flatly. "This readout says you're not even Terran." He was on his feet with a suddenness surprising in so soft an individual, hands slamming wood. "You're a damned geek spy, that's what you are, Mr.—O'Grady!" he roared.

Pete winced and Sam hunched his shoulders. Russ swallowed hard.

The prisoner shrugged.

For a stunned minute, nobody moved. Then Jaeger straightened and strolled to the front of the desk. Leaning back, he hooked thumbs into belt loops and looked down at the prisoner.

"You know, Mr. . . . . O'Grady," he said conversationally. "There seems to be a conviction among you geeks—all geeks, not just humanoid ones—that we Terrans are pushovers. That the power of Earth and of true humans is some kind of joke." He shook his head.

"The Yxtrang make war on our worlds and pirate our ships; the Liadens control the trade economy; the turtles ignore us. We're required to pay exorbitant fees at the so-called *federated* ports. We're required to pay in cantra, rather than good Terran bits. Our laws are broken. Our people are ridiculed. Or impersonated. Or murdered. And we're tired of it, O'Grady. Real tired of it."

The little man stood quietly, relaxed and still, face showing bland attention.

Jaeger nodded. "It's time for you geeks to learn to take us Terrans seriously—maybe even treat us with a little respect. Respect is the first step toward justice and equality. And just to show you how much I believe in justice and equality, I'm going to do something for you,

O'Grady." He leaned forward sharply, his beard a quarter-inch from the prisoner's smooth face. "I'm going to let you talk to me. Now. You're going to tell me everything, Mr. O'Grady: your name, your home planet, who sent you, how many women you've had, what you had for dinner, why you're here—everything." He straightened and went back around the desk. Folding his hands atop the polished wood, he smiled.

"Do all that, Mr. O'Grady, and I might let you live."

The little man laughed.

Jaeger snapped upright, hand slapping a hidden toggle.

Pete and Sam dove to the left, Russ and Skipper to the right. The prisoner hadn't moved at all when the blast of high-pressure water struck, hurling him backward over and over until he slammed against the far wall. Pinned by the torrent, he tried to claw his way to the window.

Jaeger cut the water cannon and the prisoner collapsed, chest pounding, twisted glasses two feet from his outflung hand.

Russ yanked him up by a limp arm; the man staggered and straightened, peering about.

"He wants his glasses," Pete said, bending over to retrieve the mangled antiques.

"He don't need no glasses," Russ protested, glaring down at the prisoner. The little man squinted up at him.

"Ah, what the hell—give 'em to him, then." Russ pushed the prisoner toward the desk as Pete approached.

"Mr. Jaeger?" he ventured, struck by an idea.

"Well?"

"If this ain't O'Grady, how come the water didn't loose

the makeup or whatever?" To illustrate, Pete grabbed a handful of sandy curls and yanked. The little man winced.

"Surgery?" Jaeger said. "Implants? Injections and skintuning? It's not important. What's important—to him and to us—is that the readout says he's a geek. Terry O'Grady was no geek, that's for sure." He turned his attention to the prisoner, who was trying to dry his glasses with the tail of his saturated shirt.

"Well, Mr. O'Grady? What's it going to be? A quick talk or a slow death?"

There was a silence in which Pete tried to ignore the pounding of his heart. This was a part of the job that he didn't like at all.

The little man moved, diving sideways, twisting away from Russ and dodging Skipper and Sam. He hurled a chair into Pete's shins and flung himself back toward the desk. Sam got a hand on him and was suddenly airborne as the little man threw his ruined glasses at Jaeger and jumped for the window.

Jaeger caught the glasses absently, standing behind his desk and roaring. The former prisoner danced between Russ and Skipper, then jumped aside, causing them to career into each other. He was through the window before Pete caught the smell of acronite and spun toward the hallway.

The explosion killed Jaeger and flung Pete an extra dozen feet toward safety.

✦ CHAPTER TWO ✦

DRIPPING, he kept to back streets, passing silently through the deepest shadows. Sirens shrilled distantly in the west, but he had not seen a police car for several blocks.

He ghosted down a side street and vanished into a dark vestibule. Two minutes later he opened the door to his apartment.

The telltales had not been altered, and the little man relaxed minutely. The landlord had seen nothing odd in his story of needing a place for "an occasional night out, for when a man wants a little variety." He'd been more interested in the prospect of earning a few untaxed bits.

The lights came up as the man crossed into the bedroom. He pulled the shirt over his head, unlaced the belt from his waist, and headed for the bathroom.

He let the water run in the shower as he stripped off boots and trousers. Naked and shivering slightly, he opened the box by the sink and fished out three vials.

The Loop showed a gratifying .9 on the CPS now that the mission was a success. He sighed and upped the odds by opening the first vial.

He worked the smelly purple goo into his sandy curls, wincing when he pulled knots, nose wrinkled in protest. Carefully, he coated both eyebrows and resealed the tube with relief.

He looked at the second vial with loathing. Leaning toward the mirror, he stared into the wintery blue eyes beneath the purple eyebrows for a dozen heartbeats before taking up the dropper-topped bottle and reluctantly breaking the seal. He administered two quick drops to each eye, hand steady, breath hissing between his teeth.

Tears ran down his cheeks as he counted and blinked. After his vision cleared, he bent to the mirror again, reaching a probing finger into his mouth. From inside each cheek came a curve of flexible material; he worked the caps from his teeth and spat them out before beginning on the brace that had squared his chin. That out, he gingerly adjusted ears and nose, pleased to see the normal shapes reappear.

He carried the last vial into the shower with him. The contents of this were green and sticky and even more foul smelling than the other chemicals. He rubbed the goo over every bit of skin, trying not to breathe as he coated his face. On the count of five he stepped into the dash of steaming water, gasping at the ache in cheeks, chin, and nose.

Ten minutes later he was toweling himself dry: a slender young man with straight dark hair and green eyes set deep in a high-cheeked, golden face. He finger-combed his hair and went quickly into the bedroom, shoulders level, carriage smooth and easy.

He dressed in dark leather trousers and vest, cloth shirt, and high, soft boots; ran the wide belt around his waist and checked the holstered pellet gun. The most important blade he slid into his left sleeve; the throwing knife went into the sheath at the back of his neck. The belt pouch contained sufficient funds and convincing papers; he snapped it shut and looked around.

Terrence O'Grady's papers and the depleted chemicals were disposed of with a hand incinerator. He bundled up the used clothing, but a wary glance at the smoke detector convinced him to dispose of the clothing differently.

Another quick tour of the tiny apartment satisfied him that all was in order. It was time to move on, if he intended to catch the late shuttle to Prime Station.

He dropped tenbit on the counter for the landlord to find, gathered up his bundle of clothes, and turned out the lights.

Three blocks closer to the Port he stepped firmly through a pool of light, to all appearances a night-guard or a shuttle-ape on his way to work. The clothes had been scattered in three separate alleys, and he felt confident that, on such a world as Lufkit, they would not remain ownerless long.

The night was very quiet; the street he walked, empty. Abruptly, he chose a side street. His hunch had it that things were unnaturally quiet in the area. Noting that the vehicle parked at the far end of the street bore a strong resemblance to a police cruiser, he melted into the shadows and turned down the next alley, striking diagonally for the Port.

The way was twisty and unlit, the glow from the Port cut off by towering warehouses. Relying on his ears and an excellent sense of place, the little man proceeded soundlessly, if not quickly.

He froze at the first sound of pellet fire, sorting echoes and waiting for a repeat. It came. There was more than one shot: a fusillade, coupled with shouts. He drifted toward the ruckus, hand on gun.

The alley twisted once more and widened into bright spaciousness, showing him a loading dock and five well-armed persons protected behind shipping containers and handtrucks. Before the dock a red-haired woman held a gun to the throat of a Terran, using his body as a shield between herself and the five others.

"Please guys," the hostage yelled hoarsely. "I'll give you my share—I swear it! Just do like she—"

One of those behind the containers shifted; the hostage stiffened with a throttled gasp, and the woman dropped him, diving for the scant cover of a wooden crate. Pellets splintered it, and she rolled away, the fleeing hostage forgotten, as one of the five rose for a clear shot.

The little man's gun spat once, and the assassin slumped over his erstwhile concealment, weapon sliding from dead fingers.

"Over there!" one of the hidden men screamed. "There's someone—"

A pellet whined over the little man's shoulder and he jumped for cover, swearing alike at reactions and hunches. At the dock, the woman had come to her feet, accounting for another of her opponents with casual efficiency. The little man found himself the recipient of an assassin's sole attention and calmly put three holes through the container sheltering her. There was a scream—and then nothing.

Suddenly, the two remaining assassins were up, rushing the red-haired woman and firing wildly. She dodged behind a container and fired, but they came on, though a red stain had appeared on the lead man's sleeve.

The little man took careful aim. The leader dropped. Half a heartbeat later, the woman's shot accounted for the last of the five.

Warily, the man came out from his cover, beginning to salute the woman.

The blow that knocked him unconscious took him entirely by surprise.

ONE HAD GOTTEN AWAY, which was not good.

The red-haired woman came back down the alley and stooped to run probing fingers over the dark head and touch the pulse at the base of the slim throat. She froze, counting the rhythm for a full minute, then settled back on her heels, hands hanging loosely between her knees.

"Ahhh, damn."

She stared at the dark lump of the stranger, willing him to come to, pick up his gun, and go away.

No luck today, Robertson, she said to herself. Man saved your life. You gonna leave him here?

Cursing herself for a seven-times fool she scooped up the fallen weapon and stashed it in her belt. Then she bent to get a grip on the stranger and heaved.

THANK THE GODS for robot cabs, she thought

sometime later, letting her burden slide to the shattered tile floor. Thanks be, too, for sheer, dumb luck—the street had been empty when the cab pulled up, and had remained empty while she maneuvered the man's body across the walk and into the building.

She sighed now, stretching back and shoulder muscles and acknowledging in advance the stiffness she'd feel tomorrow. She hadn't expected such a little guy to weigh so much, though at that he was bigger than she was. *Everybody* was bigger than she was.

Bending, she worked the catch on the man's pouch and pulled out a sheaf of papers. She whistled soundlessly at the verification of the obvious and refolded the sheaf, eyes on his unconscious face.

She saw high cheeks curving smoothly to a pointed chin, a generous mouth, straight brows above the shuttered eyes, thick, glossy hair tumbling across a smooth golden forehead—a boy's face, though the papers claimed thirty Standards for him. Liaden citizen. Damn, damn, damn.

She replaced the papers and snapped the pouch, then moved a safe distance away, folded her legs, and sat on the floor. Absently, she unpinned the braid wrapped around her head and began to unweave it, eyes sharp on the still figure of the man.

VERY LIKELY, he told himself, your skull is broken. More likely, his money was gone, as well as his gun and his knives—which was a damned nuisance. If his Middle River blade were lost, he'd have a hard tale to tell. Still, he thought, keeping his eyes closed, having a chance to wake up is more luck than a man with a broken skull and no brains at all should expect.

He opened his eyes.

"Hi there, thrill-seeker."

She was sitting cross-legged on the blasted tiles, weaving her copper-colored hair into one long braid. Her leathers were dark, like his own; her white shirt was loosely laced with silver cord. A black scarf was tied around one forearm, and the gun strapped to her thigh looked acceptably deadly.

She grinned. "How's the brain-box?"

"I'll live." He sat up slowly, noting with surprise that the knife was still in his sleeve.

"Interesting theory."

He regarded her blandly, noting the set of her shoulders and the deceptively gentle motion of her hands as she braided her hair, and recalling her efficiency during the fire-fight. The Loop indicated that he could take her— if he had to. But he'd have to kill her to be sure; she meant business, and no simple rush to disable would suffice.

He let the calculation fade, mildly astonished to find that he was disinclined to kill her.

Sighing aloud, he crossed his legs in deliberate reflection of her pose and rested his arms along his thighs.

She grinned again. "Tough guy." It seemed a term of admiration. She finished her braid, put a knot at the end, and flipped the length behind her shoulder, one slender hand coming to rest on her gun.

"So, tell me, tough guy, what's your name, what're you doing here, who do you work for?" She tipped her head, unsmiling. "Count of ten."

He shrugged. "My name is Connor Phillips, Cargo Master, formerly of free-trader *Salene*. Presently I am between berths."

She laughed, slid the gun free, and thumbed the safety.

"I got a weakness for a pretty face," she said gently, "so I'm gonna let you try it again. But this time you tell me the truth, tough guy, or I blow the face to the fourteen prime points and you along with it. *Accazi*?"

He nodded slowly, eyes on hers.

"Go."

"My name—" He stopped, wondering if the blow to the head had scrambled his brain. The hunch was so strong. . . .

"My name is Val Con yos'Phelium. I am an agent for Liad. I am here because I have recently finished an assignment and was hurrying to catch the shuttle when I happened by a loading dock where there was a lone woman and some others having a disagreement." He lifted an eyebrow. "I assume the shuttle has lifted?"

"Quarter hour ago." She stared at him, gray eyes expressionless. "An agent for Liad?"

He sighed and tipped his hands out, palms up, in his own gesture. "I think you might call me a spy."

"Oh." She thumbed the safety, slid the gun back home, and nodded at him. "I like that one. I like it a lot." Yanking his weapon from her belt, she threw it to him, then jerked her head at the door. "Beat it."

His left hand flashed out, snagging the gun. As he slipped it into its holster, he shook his head.

"Not a return introduction? Who you are, what you

do, for whom?" He smiled suddenly. "The headache I suffer for you. . . ."

She pointed at the door. "Scram. Get out. Begone. Leave." The gun was back in her hand. "Last chance."

He bowed his head and came to his feet with swift fluidity—to find her standing, her gun steady on his gut.

A most business-like lady, indeed, he thought with a smile. "You wouldn't have a shuttle schedule, perhaps? My information seems out of date."

She frowned. "No. Just get moving, tough guy. Schedule's carried in every infobooth in this rathole." The gun moved infinitesimally toward the door. "I'm tired of your company, accazi?"

"I understand," he murmured. He bowed as between equals. Then he was through the door and out, seeking location, listening to the night.

In a moment he had his bearings; the heavy glow to the—east, it was—that was the shuttleport. It was rather farther away than it had been before he'd taken his impromptu nap; he thought he was close to the area where Terrence O'Grady had rented his second apartment.

The sounds from behind the door spoke of someone efficiently in motion. He recognized the movement pattern of a person with no time to waste, acting with rapid, purposeful calm, and his respect for the red-haired woman increased.

He turned his attention to the street. Halfway down the block two men stood beneath a street lamp, heads together. From the breezeway to his right came the sound of two unhurried sets of footsteps: friends strolling.

He left his shadowed wall and went down the street at a brisk walk, a man with a destination, but without urgency.

The men under the streetlight seemed to be discussing the betting on a sporting event, comparing official odds against their own notions. He passed with barely a glance, heading for the blue glow of an infobooth at the end of the block. Another pair of companions passed him, walking arm-in-arm toward the building he'd recently left.

He went on, and presently his ears told him that a set of quiet footsteps paced his own silent ones. The Loop flickered into being, diagramming the chances of an imminent attack—.98 surety. His outlook for survival over the next ten minutes was .91.

The infobooth loomed to his right, its blue dome light making garish ghosts in the evening mist. He turned firmly in that direction, quickening his pace. The escorting steps quickened, as well, attempting to overtake him.

He reached the door and fumbled with the catch. A hand fell on his shoulder and he allowed himself to be spun around. His hands moved with deadly precision.

The man dropped without a sound. Val Con went to one knee, made sure that the neck had broken, and was on his feet, running back the way he had come.

He streaked by the abandoned streetlight and dived for the deeper shadow the light created, smelling clean night air and a touch of heavy cologne.

They were grouped in a rough semicircle before the building, emulating the approach that had been so disastrous earlier. One pair was near the fence by the alley, while three more stood wide, farther from the light. The shifting shadow of the man who wore cheap cologne was at the door itself, in position to either slay her as she left, or surprise her if she ran.

Val Con did not think she would run.

He dropped to one knee, waiting for the watchers to take action, hoping that the woman had anticipated this much trouble and prepared another exit. Perhaps she was already in another safe place and would laugh if she knew he had returned.

Would she have sent him out to die—to be a diversion while she escaped? He wondered and then forgot, for the door opened and she stepped out.

He flashed to his feet, running soundlessly.

She closed the door and the assassin in the shadows moved. Something—a noise? a motion in the dim light? a thought?—betrayed him an instant too soon and she dove, hitting the ground on her shoulder and rolling. Her gun flashed up too late. The man was nearly on top of her—

He gasped, dropping his weapon and clutching at his throat with clawed hands as she continued her roll, gun coughing twice in quick succession, counting a pair of slow-moving men among the dead. Distantly, she heard three sharp cracks and knew without doubt that three more lay dead nearby.

To the right, two dead; to the left, three huddled lifelessly against a fence as a fourth stood upright, hands held out at waist level, palms toward her.

She stood warily in the shocking quiet and motioned him over with a wave of her gun.

"Hey, tough guy." Her voice was a raspy whisper.

He came, hands empty at his sides, and walked within grabbing distance. She stepped back, then laughed and took a half-step toward him.

"Thanks," she said, and her voice was stronger. She slid her gun away and nodded at the single assassin.

"What's with him? Thought for sure he had me. Then he just falls over!"

Val Con moved past her and knelt by the dead man, avoiding the pooling blood. She came and stood by his shoulder, bending forward with interest.

He turned the man over and pulled the hands from the sticky throat.

"Knife," he murmured, slipping it from its nesting place and wiping it clean on the dead man's shirt.

"Not even a laserblade," she said, wondering. "Unusual toy, ain't it?"

He shrugged and slid the blade into its neck sheath.

She wrinkled her nose at the dead man. "Messy." She felt him tense beside her and shot a glance at his face. "More company?"

"You seem to be a popular young lady." He offered her his arm. "I suggest you have dinner with me," he said, smiling. "We can lose them."

She sighed, ignoring his arm. "Right. Let's move."

A moment later the dead had the street to themselves.

⟡ CHAPTER THREE ⟡

THE BARGRILL was near the shuttleport, a smoky, noisy place crowded with grease-apes, shuttle-toughs, fuelies, and any number of local street-livers. Two women played guitars, providing music of the driving, inane variety and eating and drinking their wages between sets.

The red-haired woman settled a little more comfortably against the wall, hands curved around a warmish mug of local coffeetoot, watching her companion watch the crowd. They had arrived here via the appropriation of three robot cabs, as well as several private cars. As self-appointed lookout, she was sure they'd lost their pursuers, but apparently the man beside her was taking no chances.

"Now," he murmured, eyes on the room, "you may begin by telling me your name, and continue down the list."

She was silent, drinking 'toot, and he turned to look at her, his face smooth, green eyes expressionless. She sighed and looked away.

Two fuelies were rolling dice at a corner table. She watched the throw absently, automatically counting the sides as they flashed.

"Robertson," she said in a cracking whisper. She cleared her throat. "Miri Robertson. Retired mercenary soldier; unemployed bodyguard." She flicked her eyes back to his face. "Sorry 'bout the bother." Then she paused and sighed again, because this was much harder to say—something she did not say often. "Thanks for the help. I needed it."

"So it seemed," he agreed in his accentless Terran. "Who wishes you dead?"

She waved a hand. "Lots of people, it seems."

The green eyes were back on hers. "No."

"No?"

A muscle twitched near the corner of his mouth. He stilled it and resumed his constant survey of the bar.

"No," he said softly. "You are not stupid. I am not stupid. Hence you must find another way to lie to me. Or," he added, as one being fair, "you might tell the truth."

"Now why would I do that?" she wondered and drank some more of the dreadful 'toot.

He sighed. "You owe me a debt, I think?"

"I knew you were gonna bring that up! You can forget that stuff right now, spacer. *You're* the Liaden in this skit. Terrans don't count coup."

She almost missed his start; she snapped her eyes to his face, only to find him expressionless, watching the patrons of the bar.

"What?" she demanded.

"It's nothing." He shifted his shoulders against the

wall. "A better reason, then. Whoever wishes to kill you most likely has us linked by now, and so hunts us both. Is my new enemy one individual with the means to buy service? Or a group, most of whom we have dispatched already? Can I safely go off-planet, or will I find assassins around my Clan fire when I return home?" He paused. "Your danger is my danger. Your information may save my life. I wish to stay alive. It is dishonorable for a soldier not to know the enemy!" He turned his head to look at her, one eyebrow askance. "Is that reason sufficient?"

"Sufficient." She drank off the rest of the 'toot and set the mug on the table. Eyes on the cracked blue plastic, she resettled against the wall.

"Half a Standard ago I left the Merc," she began, voice perfectly even. "Felt like I wanted to settle down, I guess, learn about one world . . . relax . . . Got a job as a bodyguard on this place called Naome. Lot of rich paranoid types go there to retire. All of 'em got bodyguards. Status symbol.

"Anyhow, I was hired the third day on the Lists by a man who called himself Baldwin. Sire Baldwin. Paid me three months in advance. To demonstrate good faith." She shook her head.

"He needed help, okay. I worked for him five—six local months. Used to wonder once in awhile what he used to do that made him need so much protection now. . . ."

She let her voice drift off as the waiter came and refilled the cups, hers with more 'toot, Val Con's with tea.

"And?" he prompted as soon as the waiter was away.

She shrugged. "Turned out Sire Baldwin had been

somebody else before. Somebody who'd worked for the Juntavas. You savvy the Juntavas, tough guy?"

"Interplanetary crime net," he murmured, eyes on the room. "Drugs, gambling, prostitution, contraband." He flicked his eyes to her face. "Bad trouble."

"You're the one wanted to know."

"Yes. What happened next?"

"He got tired of the work, I guess. Resigned without paying his severance money. Took some cash and some confidential info—guess a man's gotta eat. . . ."

"It was the people from his old unit I'd been protecting him from. They'd tracked him down and were asking for 'restitution.'" She took a swallow of 'toot that she didn't want, then shook her head.

"Baldwin told 'em to come ahead, that he was tired of hiding out and wanted to make everything square. He invited 'em to come to the house on Naome."

She paused, staring into the depths of the mug.

The pause lengthened. Stifling an impulse to touch her shoulder, Val Con tried a soft "And?" When a second "And?" brought no response, he snapped his voice like fingers in her face.

"Miri!"

She started and looked at him, face wry. "It was a doublecross. A bamboozle. Baldwin called the house staff together, from the cook to the upstairs maid. Told us we were being invaded. That we'd have to fight.

"The whole staff fought—and most of 'em had never carried a gun before! We refused Baldwin's buddies entrance, and when they insisted, we insisted right back. Bad, seeing untrained people fight that way . . . When it was sure we couldn't hold it, I went off loyally looking for my boss so I could perform my last duty—I *was* his bodyguard, wasn't I?" She shrugged and drank some 'toot.

Val Con looked at her.

"Don't you see? Gone. Bolted. Flew the coop. Left us to fight and die. I *think* five of us got away. Means fourteen didn't. Gardener didn't. Maids didn't. Cook—I don't know. He looked pretty bad, last time I saw him." She moved her shoulders again in a gesture that was not quite a shrug.

"Don't know who else they might've tracked down, but I was his bodyguard, all legal and certified and recorded. Took 'em about two hours to get on my trail."

She looked hard at nothing for a couple of minutes, then took another slug of her drink. "I came here 'cause there's a man who owes me money and a friend who's keeping some—things—for me. I better take everything. Not sure I'll get back in this Quarter again. . . ."

The man beside her was quiet. She relaxed deliberately, her thoughts touching people she'd known as she sipped the 'toot for something to do and wondered where she might spend the night, now that she had one to spend.

The bench creaked, and she looked up into decisive green eyes.

"You come with me," he said in the tone of someone who has weighed odds and reached a decision.

"I do what?"

He was fishing in his pouch. "You come with me. You will need new papers, a new name, a new face. These will be provided." He raised a hand to cut off protest.

"Liadens count coup, remember? The debt runs in two directions."

He scattered a handful of Terran bits on the table to pay for the meal, then rose and moved off, not waiting to see if she followed.

After a moment, she did.

THE CAB DEPOSITED them before a modestly lit whitestone building in the affluent side of town. The door to the lobby swung open on silent hinges, and Val Con moved across a wilderness of Percanian carpet, his reflection keeping pace in the mirrored walls.

Miri paused just inside the door, mistrusting the light. Cursing herself for more of a fool, she set off across the carpet and arrived at her companion's shoulder as he removed his finger from the keyslot and said "Connor Phillips" into the receptionist's mike.

The desk hummed as a slot slid open and a large, ornate key emerged. Val Con crooked his left index finger in the loop and half-smiled at her.

"Two floors up," he murmured, moving toward the bank of sliding doors.

Miri trailed by half a pace, letting him summon the lift, enter it before her, and exit the same way when it stopped.

This hall was somewhat dimmer than the lobby and he paused, listening, she thought, before moving on. His head swung to the left and to the right, some of the tension leaving his shoulders as he used the ridiculous key on the second door on the left.

The door sighed open and lights came up in the room

beyond as they stepped through. Miri stopped just over the threshold, hand dropping to her gun.

The door sighed shut behind her.

Halfway into the room, the man turned to look at her, one eyebrow raised, empty palms up. "I won't hurt you." He dropped his hands. "I'm too tired."

She stayed where she was, surveying the room.

Before her, a large double window showed the city night; a pillowed couch sat to one side, opposite two soft chairs and a table. To her right was an omnichora, its keyboard covered against dust. Beyond that, surrounding a closed door, were floor-to-ceiling shelves lined with tape boxes, and a comm unit—an oasis of practicality.

To her left were more shelves, filled with tape boxes interrupted here and there with figurines and bric-a-brac. Beyond the unit bar and its two upholstered stools was another closed door, and past that, through an elliptical archway, she caught the shine of kitchen tile.

"Pretty fancy for a cargo master."

He shrugged. "It was a profitable ship."

"Um." She gestured vaguely behind her. "That the only way out?"

He tipped his head at the windows, moved to the right, pulled open the door, and waved her inside.

A bedroom—with a sleeping platform adequate for the demands of a small orgy—connected to a bathroom that included wet and dry cleaning options and a valet for care of clothes. There were no windows.

She stepped out and the man guided her across the central room to the second door and a suite that was a mirror twin to the right-hand bedroom.

In the kitchen there was a small, high window, and another door.

"Beyond is a service corridor, which empties into another, which ends in a staircase, which—"

"Gets me to the cellar?" she guessed.

He smiled, moving back into the big room. "Would you like something to drink?"

"Would I. And then a shower. And then about twelve hours' sleep. Or maybe sleep and then shower—kynak," she said to his lifted brows, naming the mercenary soldier's drink.

He frowned at the display. "The bar appears to be understocked," he apologized. "I can offer Terran Scotch?"

"Scotch?" she repeated, voice keying upward.

He nodded, and she sat gently on one of the stools.

"Scotch'll be fine," she told him. "Don't put ice in it. A religious experience shouldn't be diluted."

He punched the button, then handed her a heavy glass half full of amber liquid.

Eyes closed, she sipped—and was utterly still before exhaling a sigh of soul-satisfaction.

Val Con grinned and punched in his own selection.

"What's that?" Her eyes were open again.

He swirled the pale blue liquid in the delicately-stemmed goblet. "Altanian wine—misravot."

"Limited selection on this model, ain't it?"

"It's not so bad, for a rental unit."

"Well," she conceded, playing it straight, "but when you go to buy, remember it's things like these cut-rate bars they try to stick you with every time. Put 'deluxe' on it in gold letters and stock it with grain alcohol."

"I will remember," he promised solemnly, moving around the bar and heading for the window. He stopped before he got there, settling instead into a corner of the couch and nearly sighing as the cushions molded themselves to his body. He sipped wine and *did* sigh. His head hurt abominably.

Miri moved behind him. He let his head fall back on the cushion. Glass in hand, she bypassed the couch at a cautious distance, circled the chairs, and approached the window from the side. Standing back, she looked out at the street, now and then tossing Scotch down her throat with well-practiced smoothness.

Tired, he thought suddenly. No way to know how long she's been running. And I'm too tired for any more questions. He half-closed his eyes. The effort of trusting another person was not best made in the teeth of headaches and exhaustion.

She turned from the window, surprise flickering over her face as she saw him lounging half-asleep on the cushions, long lashes shielding green eyes, throat exposed.

She sees me vulnerable, he thought, and the phrase struck something within his aching skull. He moved his head and opened his eyes.

"I'm beat," she said quietly. "Where's to sleep?"

He waved a hand. "Choose."

After a moment, she nodded and went off to the right. As she reached the bedroom door, she turned back to look at him.

"Good night." She was gone before he could reply.

He sighed as the door closed, and took a deeper sip of wine. He should go to sleep, as well.

Instead, he snapped to his feet and moved to the window as a free man would, gazing out as if he were safe and had no enemies to watch for.

The street was brightly lit and empty; a fledgling breeze tossed an occasional bit of plastic trash about.

It's good, he thought, that this place has not been found. I need a rest, need not to be O'Grady or Phillips or whoever. I need time to be—me.

He raised a hand to comb fingers through the lock that fell across his forehead, and in a moment of aching clarity recognized the gesture as one of his own. Unexpectedly, the Loop loomed in his vision, blocking out the street before him. CMS was .96. CPS flickered and danced, then flashed a solid .89 the instant before it faded away.

He swallowed wine and again stroked hair away from his eyes. Val Con yos'Phelium, Clan Korval; adopted of the Clan of Middle River. . . . He thought every syllable of his Middle River name, as if it were a charm to hold thoughts at bay.

The face of Terrence O'Grady's wife intruded, sharpening and fading to the echo of the battering music from the bar he and Miri Robertson had been in.

He drank the rest of the wine in a snap that did it no justice. How many faces had he memorized, how many men had he been, in the last three Standards? How many gestures had he learned and then cast off, along with the names and faces of lovers, parents, children, and pets?

How many people had he killed?

He tuned sharply from the window, moving blindly across the room, seeking the omnichora.

The light on the keyboard came up as he touched the

pressure plate. He found the echo of the bar music in his head, picked it up in his fingers, and threw it into the 'chora with a will, driving out the face of the woman who was not *his* wife and replacing it with the vision of the song.

His fingers fluttered up and down the scales an instant, then found the harsh beat again and filled the room with it, the sound echoing in his throbbing head. His hands fumbled, then recovered. He captured the rhythm with his right hand and began to weave melody around it with his left. He increased the tempo, found a suggestion of an older rhythm, moved into that *there*. . . .

His right hand left the beat for a moment, switching stops and ranges, intensifying sound. The images drew back from him. The names of the dead he'd known and the faces of those who'd died nameless lay back down, battered into restless submission, into uneasy sleep, by the force of the music.

There came another recognition, almost lost in the music's swirl: *this* was a talent that belonged to Val Con yos'Phelium, learned and nurtured from joy, not from need.

The driving beats slowed into others; he played what his fingers found and realized that he was playing a lament from a planet he had visited in his early Scouting days. He added to it; he dropped it to its sparest bones, and slowed it even more. He reached an end of it and found that his hands had stopped.

The sound remained in the room for a few moments more as the 'chora slowly let the dirge go, then he dropped his head against the stopfascia, drained. Emotionless.

Bed, he thought with crystal clarity. Rest. Go now.

He stood and she was there, the stranger who had saved his life, standing at the open door to the bedroom, red hair loose, vest and gun gone, shirt unlaced. Her gray eyes regarded him straightly. He did not recognize the expression on her face.

She bowed slightly, hands together in the Terran mode.

"Thank you," she said, and bowed again, turning quickly to enter her room.

"You're welcome," he said, but the door was closed.

He walked carefully across the room to the second closed door. He did not remember passing through or lying down to sleep.

✧ CHAPTER FOUR ✧

MIRI WOKE and stretched slowly, eyes focusing on the clock across the room. Ten hours and change had passed since she'd lain down to sleep. Not too bad. She rolled out and headed for the shower.

Half an hour later, sun-dried and refreshed, she pulled her gun from beneath the pillow, slipped it into the deep pocket of the coverall the valet had supplied, and went in search of protein, carbohydrates, and ideas.

What she found first in the kitchen was coffee! Brewed from real Terran bean, this beverage sat steaming at her right hand as she ordered food and then dialed up the mid-morning local news on the screen set into the table.

The lead story bored her. Something about an explosion at local Terran Party headquarters. One man killed, two injured, one Terrence O'Grady sought in the apparent bombing. An image of O'Grady appeared—it bored her, too, and she hit the REMOVE key in search of something useful.

Transport crash. No lives lost. Robotics Commission

to convene today. . . . REMOVE, she said to herself and punched the key.

She took a sip of coffee, savoring it as much as she had the previous night's liquor. Some people get the right jobs, she thought. Scotch and coffee . . .

She canceled three more articles in rapid succession, then paused to scan the brief story about six bodies found in an alley in the warehouse district. Juntavas work, police speculated.

A little farther on she stopped the text to read about a rash of vehicle thefts, including four robot cabs. All the cabs had been found in a lot at the spaceport, engines running, memories wiped. She smiled—he hadn't told her where he'd sent them—and hit REMOVE. The paper scrolled across the screen, through Obits and into Classified, as she continued with breakfast.

Juntavas work.

It was unfortunate that anyone had connected the incident to the Juntavas. If she'd been found dead by herself, it would just have been an unsolved murder. Something was going to have to be done about her not being found dead in the near future.

The tough guy seemed to think he had the pat answer for that. A quick and total overhaul, courtesy of Liad: new papers, new name, new face, new life. Good-bye Miri Robertson. Hello—well, did it matter?

Somehow, she admitted to herself, it does. She finished her coffee, leaned to place the cup on the table, and froze, eyes snagging on a familiar phrase.

WANTED: CARGO MASTER. Expd only, bckgrd with

exotic handcrafts, perfumes, liqueurs, xenonarcotics. Apply Officer of the Day, Free Trader *Salene*. No xenophobes, no narcoholics, no politicians. Bring papers. All without papers stay home.

SHE WAS STILL staring at the screen when Val Con entered the kitchen a full two minutes later.

"Good morning," he told her, moving to the chef panel and making a selection.

Miri leaned back in the chair, eyes on the screen. "Hey, you. Tough Guy."

He came to her elbow. Without looking up, she waved her hand at the ad. Arm brushing hers, he bent forward to see, exhaling softly as he straightened, his breath shivering the gossamer hairs at her temple. He sat on the edge of the table and took a sip of milk, swinging one leg carelessly off the floor. She noted that the pockets of his coverall were flat. Gunless.

He raised an eyebrow.

She hit the table with her fist, clattering the empty coffee cup, and glared up at him.

"Who *are* you?" The question was gritted out against clenched teeth. She felt her heart pounding and forced herself to relax back into the chair.

He drank some milk, his eyes steady on her face. "My name is Val Con yos'Phelium, Second Speaker for Clan Korval. I work as an agent of change. A spy."

She pointed at the screen. "And that?"

He shrugged. "A tissue of lies tears much too easily. There must be meat and bone beneath." He paused to sip his milk. "I came to this world as Cargo Master on *Salene*.

My papers said I was Connor Phillips, citizen of Kiang. When *Salene* took orbit, Connor Phillips had an argument with the Chief Petty Officer and as a result of this sudden feud tendered his resignation, effective off-loading of all local cargo. In the meantime, for the sake of ship's morale, he rented this place while he searched for a more convivial berth. And so we have this comfortable refuge in a time of stress." He offered her a smile. "Not too bad a sort, Master Phillips."

She closed her eyes. Every time you get the world by the tail, she thought, you gotta remember there's teeth on the other end.

"Where'd a spy learn to play the 'chora like that?"

His brows twitched together in surprise, and he answered carefully. "My kinswoman, Anne Davis, taught me. It gave her joy to see that I had the talent, when none of her own children did."

"Your *kinswoman.*" She wasn't sure she'd meant it as a question, but he answered it.

"Yes. My—is it aunt? The wife of my father's brother?"

"Aunt," she agreed, puzzled by this lapse in his smooth command of Terran.

"More," he said thoughtfully. "She was my—foster-mother. After my mother died I went into her home, was raised with her children."

"Is this any more—or less—real than Connor Phillips?" she demanded. "Do you really know who you are?"

He looked at her closely. "If you are asking if I'm insane, which of the answers I may give will comfort you more? I know who I am, and I have told you. Even when I am on assignment, I know who I really am."

"Do you? That's comforting." She said it without conviction, aware that she was tensing up again.

"Have you a problem, Miri Robertson?"

"Yeah. I do. The problem is that I don't know why you're helping me. Your logic don't hold up. If you *were* Connor Phillips, why can't you *be* him again, find a ship, and go away? You can get out of it! The Juntavas don't know who you are—what kind of description can they have? That you're short? Skinny? Dark?" She moved her shoulders to throw off some of the tension.

"The clincher is that you're with me. Without me they look—" She spread her arms. "—and they look away."

The equation had formed in his head, showing him how he might get away, her death balancing his escape. She knew much about him and could be a danger. In fact, he thought, if I—no! He forced the Loop back and down, refusing to know how useful she would be, dead.

Setting his empty glass aside, he began to read the breakfast selections.

She studied his profile, but saw nothing more than polite interest in the information imparted by the selection grid.

"Well?" she demanded.

He lifted a slender hand to select an egg dish, then glanced at her. "I think that last night's reasoning is sound. The Juntavas may have an imperfect description of me. Or they may have a photo image. I cannot afford to ignore that possibility."

Another equation showed itself, this one concerning not her death, but her betrayal. It noted that it was an approximation; the odds were good that her life would buy his own from the Juntavas.

The long lashes dropped over his eyes and he turned back to the panel, choosing hot bread and a fruit. Gathering the plates from the dispenser, he moved back to the table and took the seat across from Miri.

She got up silently, selected a slightly stronger brew of Terran coffee, and returned to her chair.

"So where does that leave me? Instead of wanted by the Juntavas, I'm a political prisoner of Liad, right?"

He shook his head, attention seemingly more than half occupied by slicing a ripe strafle into two equal portions. He offered her half. When she made no move to take it, he placed it on the table by her hands. "Where does that leave things?" she insisted, an edge in her voice.

"I think," he replied, swallowing a mouthful of eggs, "that it leaves things where they were in the beginning. We are thrown together. We wish to live. Already each of us has brought something useful to the task of surviving. If we are fortunate, we shall live through the experience. In fact, we make our own fortune simply by doing what must be done, as it needs to be done."

He took a bite of bread, frowned as he reached for the glass that wasn't there, and combed a hand through his forelock, sighing.

"Mutual survival being the goal, I think you should tell me about these people—the man who owes you money and the friend who keeps your things—so that we may plan usefully."

He pushed back his chair and went to ask the chef for more milk.

Miri drank coffee, acutely aware of the weight of the gun in her pocket. She understood about mutual survival: it was why so many of the Gyrfalks had partners. Trust wasn't something that came easily to her; still it was obvious that her companion knew what he was doing in a tight spot.

"Okay," she said slowly. "The man who owes me money—that's Murph. Angus G. Murphy. The third. He was in my unit in the Merc. Decided he couldn't take all the killing." She smiled at the man across from her. "Thought there'd be lots of glory and romance. Anyhow, he wanted out, and it was safer to have him out, if he felt that way about it."

Val Con ate, watching her face as she spoke.

"So, I lent him most of his severance money," Miri continued, "with the understanding that he'd pay it back with interest in three Standards. Been damn near four."

She leaned farther back in the chair, leaving the untouched fruit between them like a challenge. He did not appear to see it.

"Murph is recalcitrant?"

"Absent," she corrected. "Address listed in the poploc. Nobody home." She shook her head. "I didn't have time to buttonhole all the neighbors. Somehow, from the way I remembered him, I figured he'd be home." She sipped her coffee.

"The friend who's keeping my things is Liz. Friend of my mother's, first. Lives closer to where we met than where we are now. Plan is to call her, make sure she's home and gonna stay there so I can drop by and pick up my box."

"And then pursue the search for the absent Murph?"

"Say!" she said, opening her eyes wide and smiling. "You've got almost as many smarts as a *real* person!"

To her surprise, he laughed—a sound oddly at variance with his tightly controlled face and unemphatic voice. There was *joy* in his laugh. Miri filed that information away with the echoes of the music he'd pulled from the 'chora.

"The best course," he said, "is for you to call your friend Liz and explain that you will need your things. Explain also that you will not be coming yourself but will be sending an associate—"

"Wrong."

He shook his head. "Consider it. The risk is less—they *may* know me; they *do* know you. And in the time it takes me to accomplish the errand you may be profitably employed in locating Murph." He waved his hand toward the common room.

"The comm is quite adequate. The planet is at your disposal."

She stared into the dregs of her coffee, considering it. Her own life was one thing, but to gamble Liz on the feeling that an undoubtedly deadly stranger meant her well? A Liaden stranger, just for fun. Liadens were known for playing deep: it seemed a source of racial pride. Miri closed her eyes.

Judgement call, Robertson, she said to herself. You trust him at your back or you don't.

She opened her eyes. "Liz hates Liadens."

The straight brows pulled together, his mouth nearly twisted, and he thumped the half-full glass on the table.

"It seems that all the galaxy hates Liadens," he said. He pushed his chair back to balance on two legs, taking a sharp bite out of his strafle.

Somehow, that decided it. Miri rose, deposited her cup in the clean-up slot and headed to the big room.

"I'll call her," she said over her shoulder.

Liz was at home. She was also unhappy to learn that Miri would be sending her "partner," rather than coming to collect the box herself.

"Since when have you had a partner, anyway?" she wanted to know, brown eyes shrewd. "You always played single's odds."

"Times change," Miri told her, trying to sound as if they had.

Liz snorted, eyes softening. "How much trouble you in?"

"More'n last week, less than next. You know how it goes."

Liz did know; she'd been a mercenary herself, after all.

"It can stay here, you know. Might slow you down if you need to get a move on."

"That's so," Miri said. "But I'm going on the Grand Tour. No telling—"

"When you'll be back," Liz finished for her. "Okay, send your partner around. Description? Or do I just hand it over to the first slob says they're here for Redhead's box?"

She grinned. "Short, I guess. Skinny, maybe. Brown hair—needs to be cut. Green eyes. Male." She bit her lip and looked Liz full in the face. "Liaden."

But, to Miri's surprise, Liz only nodded. "I'll be watching for him. Take care of yourself, girl." Her image faded.

Miri turned away from the comm to see Val Con behind her, positioned so that he could see the screen, yet not be seen himself. He had exchanged his coverall for dark leathers and dark shirt. A worn belt was around his waist; equally well-used boots were on his feet.

He did not appear to be armed.

Miri opened her mouth, remembered the primitive little blade that had saved her life, and closed her mouth without comment.

"Your friend expects me."

"You heard it." She hesitated. "Make sure nobody follows you there, okay? Liz and my mother . . ." She moved her hands, shapelessly. "Liz is all the family I got."

His smile flickered into being. "I will be careful." He gestured, enclosing the apartment in a hand-sweep.

"This is a secure place. There is no need for you to leave. No need for you to let anyone in. I let myself out and let myself back in. You are free to search for Murph via the comm. It is scrambled and traceless."

She tipped her head to one side. "You're telling me I'm safe?"

He half-smiled, shoulders dipping in a gesture she was unsure of. "Forgive me," he murmured, "but, yes, I think so."

She grinned, shaking her head as she turned back to the comm.

"Just get me that box without getting killed, okay? I'll have Murph nailed by the time you get back."

"Okay."

She turned in time to see the door to the hallway closing behind him.

THE CALL to the residence of Mr. Angus G. Murphy III was less than satisfying. Mr. Murphy's direct-comm had been temporarily disconnected, the visual told Miri, and messages might be left at another number. She dialed that number, found it to be an answering service, and broke the blank-screen connection instantly.

"Don't call me, I'll call you," she muttered, frowning. It would be best if he didn't know she was on-world.

Well, it would have to be the neighbors, then, though she disliked that tack. With her luck, the next-door neighbor would be a local Juntavas boss, with her picture on his desk. She could blank the screen, of course, but who would give info to a blank screen?

Blank screen was out, she decided. But her own face was also out.

She snapped forward in frowning study of the commboard. Fancy, she decided, after a few minutes. Sire Baldwin had had no better in his palatial home. Leaning back and letting her eyes rest on the understated luxury of the room around her, she was reminded that money and taste were very different matters. After all, look at the lovers Baldwin would bring home.

Suddenly grinning, she bounced to her feet and ran to her sleeping quarters.

Standing before the floor-to-ceiling mirror in the valet-room, she let down her hair and combed it straight. A few moments later the valet supplied a quantity of glittering jeweled pins and nets to confine the whirls, knots, and bunches the copper-colored mass had assumed. Likewise, she obtained cosmetics, gilded earbobs, rings of eight different sizes and metals, and a necklet of glazed silver flowers.

After some thought, she decided the coverall was just right for the occasion, but she unsealed the neck seam a little farther—and a little farther again, after consulting the mirror. She grinned at her reflection, paused to add just a dash more emphasis under each eye, and headed back to the comm.

SHE CHOSE a firm with its single office in the most prestigious of high-rent facilities. Setting her face into what she hoped was simpering unease, she punched up the code.

"Mylander and Zanthal Collections," the receptionist told her.

Miri stretched her mouth in a closed-lip smile. "Good afternoon," she said in her best Yark accent. "I'd like to talk to somebody about—'bout this guy, see? He owes me a bundle an' won't pay."

The receptionist blinked, then recovered. "Why, surely. I'm certain that our Mr. Farant would be delighted—"

"Naw," Miri said. "Naw. Look, honey, this is—delicate, y'know? You got a woman up there can talk to me?" She stretched her mouth into the unsmiling rictus again. "Girl stuff, honey. *You* know."

The receptionist swallowed. "Well, there *is* Ms. Mylander."

"Aw, geez," Miri protested. "Not the boss herself?"

"Not exactly," the receptionist admitted, shakily. "Ms. Susan Mylander is Ms. Lavinia Mylander's granddaughter."

"Oh! Well, hey, that's great! I'd be real pleased to have a little girl-talk with Susan, honey. You just tell her Amabel Gleason's on the screen, okay?"

"Certainly, Ms. Gleason," the receptionist said, falling back on the comforts of training. "If you'll hold just one moment—" The screen offered an abstract in soft pastels to soothe Miri's eyes while she waited. She moved a hand, pushed two keys, and settled back into an attitude of watchful expectation.

The screen cleared after a time sufficient for the receptionist to have located Ms. Mylander and imparted all the details of her caller's manner, with embellishments. Miri performed her smile for the dark young woman in sober business attire.

"Ms. Gleason?" the young woman asked. Her accent was the cultivated drawl of the elite.

Miri ducked her head. "Ms. Mylander, it really is nice of you to talk to me and everything. I just didn't know where to turn, y'know, and when that pretty young lady who answers your phone said you were in—" She fluttered her jeweled hands, rings flashing. "Some things you just *gotta* talk to another woman about."

"Indeed," the other woman said. "And just what did you wish to speak with me about, Ms. Gleason?"

"Well, Ms. Mylander. I—could I call you Susan? I mean, you're so friendly and everything—" Miri leaned forward, jumpsuit gaping.

The woman in the screen took a deep breath. "If it makes you feel better, Ms. Gleason, by all means call me Susan."

"Thanks. So, Susan, there's this guy, y'know." Miri waved her hands again, rolling her eyes. "There's always a guy, ain't there? Anyway, we date for awhile and he likes me and I like him okay—I mean, he's got some money, an' a steady job on the shuttle as a grease-ape. Don't mind buying a girl a few presents, taking her out to nice places. . . ." Miri shrugged, taking her time about it. "Asks me to marry him—standard hetero contract; progeny clause says he'll take care of any kids we have while we're married, even if we don't re-up." She paused.

"I am familiar with the standard co-habitation/progeny contract, Ms. Gleason. Did you sign it?"

"Well, yeah, we did. I moved into his place. 'Bout three months later, shows I'm pregnant. I figure everything's okay, 'cause of the progeny clause—" She broke off, bowing her head sharply and raising a hand to wipe at her eyes. "Bastard walked out on me."

There was a short silence. Miri raised her head again, bravely displaying her smile.

"I don't quite understand, Ms. Gleason, what this has to do with Mylander and Zanthal," Susan Mylander said with professional puzzlement.

"I'm gettin' to that," Miri said, visibly getting a grip on herself. "It's that he left. Contract had three years to run. I have the baby and he says forget it, contract's no good, 'cause it ain't his kid!"

"Is it?" Ms. Mylander asked, staring in what seemed to be fascination.

Miri wriggled her shoulders. "I *think* so. 'Course, there's a problem with it being so close to the time we signed and all. I didn't know he was gonna propose contract and—well, I ain't *dead,* y'know, Susan. An' grease-apes work the shuttle two weeks on, two weeks off."

"I'm still not sure I understand why you need a collection agency, Ms. Gleason."

"He owes me *money,*" Miri cried, voice rising. "He signed a contract said he'd pay for any of his brats I had while we were married. Could've been his as much as anybody else's. An' we were *married.*" She took a deep breath and let her voice even out a little. "He owes me a bundle of cash. An' he says he won't pay. That's why I need a collection agency, Ms. Mylander. To get my money for me."

"I—see." Ms. Mylander paused. "Ms. Gleason, I'm afraid that you do not need a collection agency at this point. What I advise you to do is engage legal counsel. If you speak to a lawyer, and he deems it proper for you to bring suit against your husband for breach of contract, wins the case for you and has your husband ordered to pay you a specified sum, and if your husband then refuses to pay that sum, Mylander and Zanthal will be happy to assist you." She steepled her fingers under her chin. "You must really engage counsel first, though, Ms. Gleason, and abide by the judgment of the courts as to whether your husband is responsible for your child or is liable for voiding the contract. We are not able to help you with those matters."

"Oh," Miri said, bright mouth turning down at the

corners. She forced another horrible smile, though her face was beginning to ache. "Well, that's fine, then, Susan. I know a couple lawyers. Real go-getters." She bent to the screen once more and reached out as if to touch the other woman's hand.

Ms. Mylander was made of stern stuff. She did not flinch from the impossible caress, though her mouth tightened.

"Thanks an awful lot for your help, Susan," Miri cooed, and hit DISCONNECT.

She laughed for five minutes, leaning back in the embracing cushions and howling, tears running out the corners of her made-up eyes. When she was sure she could navigate, she went to the kitchen for a cup of coffee.

Resuming her seat in front of the comm, she began to edit her tape.

LIZ ANSWERED THE DOOR herself and stood looking down at him.

Val Con made the bow of youth to age, straightening to find her still frowning at him from her height.

"I am here," he said softly, "for Miri's box."

Wordless, she pulled the door wider and let him in. After making sure the locks were engaged, she led him down a short, dark hallway to a bright living room. He stood in the entranceway as she moved to what seemed the only chair—indeed the only surface—not piled high with booktapes.

"Come here, Liaden." It was a command, delivered harshly.

He made his soundless way across the room and stopped before her, hands folded loosely.

She surveyed him silently and he returned the favor, noting the dark hair shot with gray, the lines about mouth and eyes, the eyes themselves, and the chin. This was, he saw, a person used to command, who knew command as responsibility.

"You're here for Miri's box."

"Yes, Eldema," he said gently, giving her the courtesy title of the First Speaker of a Clan.

She snorted. "Tell me Liaden: Why should I trust you?"

He raised his brows. "Miri—"

"Trusts you," she cut in, "because you're beautiful. It's a fault comes with growing up where nothing's beautiful and everything's dangerous—real different from sunny Liad."

He stood at rest, waiting.

Liz moved her head sharply. "So, you grow up on a world like Surebleak, manage, somehow, to get off, finally encounter beauty. And you want to give it every chance. You don't want to believe that a pretty rat's still a rat. That it'll bite you, just as sure." She clamped her mouth into a straight line.

Val Con waited.

"I don't care if you got three heads, each one uglier than the next," she snapped. "I want to know why *I* should trust you."

He sighed. "You should trust me because Miri sent me here. You must judge whether she would do so—besotted as she must be with my beauty—were I a danger to you."

She laughed. "A little temper, is it? You'll need it." She sobered abruptly. "What kind of trouble's she in, she needs to send you at all? Why not come herself?"

"It is not the kind of trouble it is safe to know by name," he said carefully. "It is only . . . trouble."

"Ah. So we all get in that kind of trouble once, now, don't we?" There was no particular emphasis; he thought she spoke to herself. Yet she continued to stare at him until Val Con wondered if he *were* growing another head.

"You're going with her when she leaves? Eh? To guard her back? She called you her partner."

"Eldema, when we go, we go together. I think it very likely that we will outrun the trouble. Lose it entirely." There was no flicker of the Loop, giving the lie to this piece of optimism, for which he was grateful.

She nodded suddenly, then reached to the overflowing table at her side and produced a black lacquer box from amidst a pile of tapes. It was a double hand's width of his small hands wide and twice that long—too odd-shaped to fit comfortably into pocket or pouch.

Liz frowned and fumbled further on the table, locating a less-than-new cloth bag with a drawstring top. She slid the box inside, drew the string tight, and handed him the sealed package.

He stepped forward to claim it, slipping the string over his shoulder.

"Thank you." He bowed thanks. When it became apparent that she had no more to say to him, he turned to go.

He was nearly to the hall when she spoke. "Liaden!"

He spun in his tracks, quick and smooth. "Eldema?"

"You take care of Miri, Liaden. None of your damn tricks. You just take the best care of Miri you can, as long as you can."

He bowed. "Eldema, it is my desire to do just that."

He turned on his heel and was gone.

Liz sighed. She had had nothing else to say, except— but the girl knew that. Didn't she?

She heard him work the lock; heard the door open and close, gently.

After a while, for old times' sake, she went to make sure he'd locked the door on his way out.

MRS. HANSFORTH was excited. It had been years since she'd received a ship-to communication, but still the circuit was as she remembered it: a little scratchy, with occasional odd delays and the constant feeling that the mouth wasn't quite saying what it looked like it was saying.

Of course, it was disappointing that the beam wasn't meant for her, but disappointment was outweighed by the excitement of the event and the chance to gossip.

Yes, she told the dark-haired and serious young lady in the screen, she knew Angus quite well. A nice boy, not given to wild parties or exceptional hours. And his fiancée was a lovely girl. It was really a shame he wasn't in town to receive the message himself. . . .

Where? Oh, with the students off at the University, he and his fiancée had taken several weeks to go to Econsey. They'd wanted some time alone and hadn't had the calls forwarded. Surely, they couldn't have been expecting. . . .

Hadn't known she was going to be in-system? Oh,

such a shame . . . But Mrs. Hansforth got no further; after all, this was ship-to, and such things were fabulously expensive. The serious young lady said something about some research Angus had done in his traveling days. Well!

Mrs. Hansforth asked the young lady to leave a message, and was so sorry to find that she'd only be on planet for a few hours. The chance of reaching Angus in that time did seem very small. . . .

Perhaps on the return trip there would be time, Mrs. Hansforth heard. Or perhaps Ms. Mylander would be able to beam ahead next time. But research—you know how it *does* take one about. . . .

Mrs. Hansforth agreed, though she'd never been off-planet, herself.

When the connection was cut, Mrs. Hansforth was sorry. But, still, a ship-to! Why, Angus must be more important in his field than she had realized. Imagine!

MIRI LEANED BACK in the chair, flipping switches and smiling slightly. Engineering the delay hadn't been hard at all—simply a matter of bouncing her signal off seven different satellites and across the single continental landline about three times. Her new partner had called the unit "adequate." She wondered if understatement was his usual style.

Now, sipping some exquisite coffee, she considered the information gathered. Not much, but maybe something. Flipping another series of toggles, she tapped "Econsey" into the query slot.

The door cycled at her back and she was up, spinning, hand on the gun in her pocket, as Val Con entered, a blue drawstring bag slung over one shoulder. He stopped just inside the room, both eyebrows up and a look of almost comic horror on his face.

She pouted and took her hand off the gun. "You don't like my makeup!"

"On the contrary," he murmured. "I am awestruck."

He slid the string off his shoulder and held the bag out. She nearly snatched it away from him, plopping crosslegged to the floor by the 'chora. The box was out in a flash, and she ran her pale fingers rapidly over the shiny black surface before cradling it in her lap and looking at him.

"How'd Liz do?"

"On the whole, I'd say she came off better than I did," he returned absently, staring at her as he drifted forward to sit on the 'chora's bench.

The hair. Was it really possible to twist, torture, and confine one head of hair into so many unappealing knobs and projections? But for the evidence before him, he would have doubted it. She'd also smeared some sort of makeup on her face, imperfectly concealing the freckles spanning her nose, and done something else to her eyes, making them seem larger than usual, but exquisitely lusterless. The color of her cheeks had been chosen with an unerring eye to clash with the color of her hair, and the blue on her lips was neon bright. Every piece of jewelry— and there was far too much of it—vied with the other for gaudery. He shook his head, lost in wonder.

She caught the headshake and smiled a ghastly smile that consisted only of bending her sealed lips and creasing her cheeks.

"You *do* think I look nice, doncha?"

He folded his arms on top of the 'chora and nestled his chin on a forearm. "I think," he said clearly, "that you look like a whore."

She laughed, clapping ring-laden hands together. "So did the woman at the collection firm!" She sobered abruptly, slanting lusterless eyes at him. "Your face was wonderful! I don't remember the last time I saw somebody look so surprised." She shook her head. "Don't they teach you anything in spy school?"

He grinned. "There are some things that even spy school cannot erase. I was raised to be genteel."

"Were you?" She regarded him in round-eyed admiration. "What happened?"

He ignored this bait, however, and nodded toward the comm. "Murph?"

She sighed. "On vacation with his fiancée in some place called Econsey—southern hemisphere. That's what I know. I was gonna see what else the comm knew when you came in and insulted my hairdo."

"Econsey is situated on the eastern shoreline of the southern hemisphere," he told her, singsonging slightly as he read the information that scrolled before his mind's eye. "It sits at the most eastern point of a peninsula and is surrounded on three sides by the Maranstadt Ocean. Year round population: 40,000. Transient population: 160,000, approximate. Principal industries: gambling, foodstuffs, liquors, hostelries, entertainment, exotic imports." He paused, checking back, then nodded. "Juntavas influenced, but not owned."

Miri stared at him; whatever expression may have been in eyes and face was shielded by the makeup.

"Mind like that and it's all going to waste."

Irritation spiked from nowhere and he frowned. "*Will* you go wash your face?"

She grinned. "Why? You think it needs it?" But she rolled to her feet, box in hand, and headed for her room. Behind her, Val Con flipped open the cover and touched the keyboard plate.

In the bathroom, Miri stripped the rings from her fingers and the bobs from her ears, jangling them along with the necklet and hair jewelry into the valet's return box. A glance at the readout showed that her leathers were at long last clean and the jumpsuit joined the gaudy jewelry. She closed the lid, hit the return key, and turned to the sink.

It took longer to scrape the gunk off her face than it had to put it on—the eyeshadow was especially tenacious—but a clean face was eventually achieved and, moments later, a braid was pinned in a neat crown around her head.

Her leathers slipped on smoothly, sheathing her in a supple second skin; she stamped into her boots, tied the knot in the arm-scarf, and carried the belt with its built-on pouch back to the sleeping room.

Sitting on the edge of the tumbled platform, she picked up the lacquer box and spun it in her hands like a juggler, hitting each of the seven pressure locks in unerring sequence. There was a *click*, loud over the soft drift of 'chora music from the other room. Miri set the box down and raised the lid.

Opening the belt-pouch, she pushed at the back bracing wall until she coaxed the false panel out, and laid it aside.

From the box she took a key of slightly phosphorescent blue metal, a thin sheaf of papers, a badly-cut ruby the size of a Terran quarter-bit, a loop of pierced malachite, and a gold ring much too big for her finger, set with a cloudy sapphire. She stowed each item in the secret space in the pouch. Then she removed the last object, frowned, and sat balancing it in her hand.

The room's directionless light picked out a slash of red, a line of gold, and a field of indigo blue. She flipped it to the obverse, and light skidded off the polished metal surface, snagging on the roughness of engraving. As she'd done a hundred times since she'd gotten the thing, she ran her finger over the engraving, trying to puzzle out the alien characters.

In the room outside her door, the comm unit buzzed once . . . twice.

Miri dumped the disk among her other treasures, sealed the hiding place, and was on her way to the door, threading the belt around her waist as she went.

VAL CON was on his feet and moving as the comm buzzed a second time. He touched BLANK SCREEN and GO.

His eyebrows shot up as he saw one of his four captors of the night before standing in the lobby below, a squad of six ranged at his back, and he shook his head to banish the feeling of creeping déjà vu.

"Mr. Phillips?" demanded the man he recognized.

"Yes," Val Con said, taking the remote from its nesting place atop the comm.

"Mr. *Connor* Phillips," the leader insisted. "Former crew member on the *Salene?*"

Val Con strolled across the room to the bar. "It would be useless to deny it," he told the remote. "I was Cargo Master on *Salene*. To whom am I speaking? And why? I left instructions that I was not to be disturbed." He set the remote on the shiny bar top and activated the refreshment screen.

"My name is Peter Smith. I'm working with the police in the investigation of the explosion that took place at Terran Party Headquarters last night."

Val Con dialed a double brandy from the selection list "I am unenlightened, Mr. Smith. Unless I understand you to say that I am suspected of causing an explosion in— where was it? Terra Place?"

"Terran Party Headquarters." There was a real snarl in that correction, then a pause, as if for breath. "We're looking for a man named Terrence O'Grady, who caused the explosion and disappeared. We're asking everybody who's come on-world during the last fifteen days to answer a few questions about the—incident. Refusing to assist in a police investigation, Mr. Phillips," Pete said, with a very creditable amount of piety, "is a criminal offense."

Val Con dialed another brandy. "I am chastised."

Across the room, the door to Miri's bedroom opened and she came out, buckling her belt as she walked. She paused briefly in front of the comm screen before continuing on to the second bedroom.

"Mr. Smith," Val Con said, dialing yet another brandy. "It is really of no interest to me whether or not you catch this—individual—who blew up these headquarters. However, since you have already disturbed me, and since

I have no wish to be treated as a criminal, you may as well ask your questions."

"That's fine," Pete said. "Now, if you'll tell the receptionist to let us up, we'll just take a few minutes of your time—"

"Mr. Smith, please. I said you may as well ask your questions. I did not say that I would welcome you into my home. The presence of a police representative would place me in a very awkward negotiating position at this moment."

Miri laid his gun silently on the bar and was gone, vanishing into the kitchen. Val Con dialed a brandy, clipped gun to belt, and waited.

After a pause, Pete's voice came again. "Okay, Mr. Phillips, if that's how you want it. Where were you last night between 10:45 p.m. and midnight?"

Miri reappeared, raised her brows at the row of brandy snifters on the bar, and passed silently on to survey the comm screen.

"Last night," Val Con said easily, "I was engaged with friends. There was a party, with fireworks and conversation." He dialed another brandy.

"I see. You can, of course, supply the name and address of your friends," Pete said. In the lobby, he jerked his head and two of his squad moved toward the elevators. Miri walked back to the bar.

"I can," Val Con was saying. "I won't. But I can."

"I see," Pete said again. "Mr. Phillips, do you know a man named Terrence O'Grady?"

"No." Val Con handed two brandies to Miri and waved toward her bedroom. She stood still, frowning; he reached into the depths of the bar, produced a flamestick, and tucked it in her belt. Enlightenment dawned with a grin of delight, and she departed on her mission.

"Mr. Phillips, I'm going to have to insist that I see you."

"Mr. Smith, I'm going to have to insist that you produce a legal document giving you the right." Miri was back for two more brandies, which she carried into the other bedroom. Smoke was beginning to waft from the doorway across the room.

"Have you any other questions?" he asked Pete.

"Why did you leave your post on the *Salene*?"

"It was not as profitable an association as I had hoped for, Mr. Smith. But I fail to see what that has to do with your problem. *Salene* did not ship explosives. I met no one there named O'Grady. I have met no one named O'Grady since I have been on Lufkit. I doubt if ever in my life I have met anyone named O'Grady, but I give you leave to explore the possibility." Smoke wisped sweetly from his former bedroom to billow with the smoke from Miri's.

He stopped dialing brandies and splashed the contents of one of the remaining snifters on the carpet around the bar. Miri appeared, picked up two more glasses, and carried them to the comm chair and the sofa, touching the flamestick to the cushions.

"Mr. Smith?" Val Con asked the remote.

Miri came back for the remaining snifters and began to splash the carpet.

"What?" Pete snapped.

"Have you other questions? I really must return to my

own business." He held up a hand, stopping Miri from igniting the carpet.

"Any other—yeah, I do." Pete took an audible breath. "Are you a geek, Mr. Phillips?"

"Are you a horse's ass, Mr. Smith?" Val Con hit DISCONNECT. Miri touched the flamestick to the carpet.

Somewhere within the building, bells began to ring; a hiss of water striking flame came from Miri's bedroom as the sprinkler system activated itself. There were shouts from the hallway.

Miri and Val Con were already through the kitchen escape hatch. He slammed it to, twisted two knobs, and spun to find her shaking her head.

"Real genteel."

He grinned. "Thank you."

Then they were moving without haste down the small service corridor, toward the larger world beyond.

✧ CHAPTER FIVE ✧

HE WAS MALE, though that rarely mattered to him. Indeed, he was hardly male at all, in the sense of lyr-cat, bearded Terran stud, or mouse. What mattered more to him was his name, which might take up to three hours of introduction when spoken to humans and, spoken fully, might consume nearly twelve hours. For purposes of the visas and other official papers that hasty humans required of one, there were several short forms of his name, which pleased him.

He was regal, as befitted a *T'carais* and a being more than nine hundred Standard Years old, though among his race he was known for his occasional hasty action. On visas he was thus: Twelfth Shell Fifth Hatched Knife Clan of Middle River's Spring Spawn of Farmer Greentrees of the Spear-makers Den, The Edger.

Some few of the Clans of Men—Terran and Liaden separately they named themselves—knew him reasonably well as Edger. He enjoyed this informality; it reminded him of those early days of learning his trade and life role.

With him now traveled other functionaries of his Clan:

The Handler, The Selector, The Sheather, and, off-planet, The Watcher. Most of the Clan was home, growing knives in the cold, beautiful caverns of Middle River. His group of five had been sent by the Elders out into the wide universe to discover what knives were required. "Market research" his visa named this vast adventure, though Edger himself thought of it more fully as "Education." After all, one had to discover the uses and users of a knife before one could know what blade to grow, what edge to encourage, what handle to smooth, what sheath to mold. He never doubted that knives were needed, or that knives from the Knife Clan of Middle River were needed most of all.

So far, they'd been seven years on this hectic trip. Edger felt confident that another seven would yield all the information the Elders required.

Being relatively young, Edger did not regard himself as large; his twelfth shell had been still dangerously soft when they'd begun their journey, and even now was barely set. Yet people not of the Clutch regarded him with awe, for few of the working class traveled, and his four-hundred-pound bottle-green frame was fully one-third larger than the svelte and speedy persons the Ambassadorial Clans sent to human worlds.

Being young, Edger was fond of entertainment. In fact, it was for this purpose that he and his three companions were now moving with ponderous haste down the wide walkway of a neighborhood consisting of very tall, pastel-colored buildings. There was a piece of music to be performed in a building just a little farther down this street and then somewhat farther down the next. One could have argued that the briefness of the piece—barely longer than the speaking of Edger's full name in Terran—hardly justified walking such a distance at such a pace. But Edger's delight in music was well-known to his kin, and they were disposed to accompany him to this pleasure.

Thus they walked, taking care to keep to the strip of soft material Terrans lined their walkways with. And why not use stone, which endured at least a generation or two, demanded Selector, who had an acid tongue. Why use this—this *concrete*, which wore so quickly? Were the Clutch to use such material, nothing would be accomplished save the constant repaving of the roads.

Handler reminded Selector of the briefness of human lives. "Therefore, many of their own generations may walk upon this surface before it wears to nothing. And, in their hastiness, they may by then have decided upon the use of another material altogether so that it is not a waste for them, brother."

What reply Selector may have made to this gentle reproof was not to be known, for it was at that moment that the howl of a siren sounded behind them, echoed by another in front. Directly across the street from the group of Clutch members, a building chimed a shrill song to itself.

Edger stopped, enchanted.

The building continued its song while people gathered around it, each crying out in what could very possibly be some hasty new harmony. This was counterpointed by the screaming sirens atop the two bright red vehicles which had so recently arrived on the scene.

Edger left the walkway and moved across the crowded

street toward the building that sang. His Clan members, seeing him in the throes of his passion, followed.

They moved through the crowd at the entrance very like a herd of elephants moving through grassland, and they did not stop at the policeman's order. Possibly, he had not been heard. Or his voice might merely have been approved for its place in the song, the words disregarded in the present of the experience.

Rapt, Edger came into the lobby, kin trailing after. Here, he noted, the sound of the sirens was not so shrill; the rich counter-harmony of the singers faded to a primal growl over which the solitary, single-noted song of the building soared triumphant, nearly incandescent.

And there were other textures herein encountered, doubtless meant as a frame to the piece: the softness of the carpeting beneath his feet; the clearness of the colors; the harshness of the light reflected from the framed glass surfaces. Edger stepped deeper into the experience, opening his comprehension to the wholeness of this piece of art.

Patiently, his Clan members waited.

TOO DAMN EASY, Miri thought with habitual distrust of easiness. The service corridor formed a small cul-de-sac off the first-floor hallway, and they had loitered there until the evacuation team arrived and began knocking on doors and hustling people to safety. Val Con had stepped quietly into the group of refugees, Miri at his shoulder, and so they had gotten rescued, too.

When the group hit the lobby, he as quietly dropped out, slipping ghostlike into the foliage of an artificial oasis.

Intrigued by this return to complexity, Miri dropped out with him.

In the next few minutes, the situation in the lobby had grown noisier and more confused. Cops and firefighters were everywhere, yelling and pushing people around. Miri caught sight of two rescue workers shoving Peter Smith toward the door, and grinned.

"Tough Guy?"

"Hmm?" A gaggle of turtles had wandered into the lobby and he was staring at them, brows pulled together in a half-frown.

"*Do* you know Terrence O'Grady?"

The green eyes flicked to her face, his frown smoothing away to that look of bland politeness. Miri braced herself for a lie.

One of his eyebrows slid slightly askew and he took a deliberate breath, then released it.

"I don't *know* Terrence O'Grady," he said slowly. "But, for a few days, I *was* Terrence O'Grady."

The truth, after all. Miri blinked.

"I was afraid of that." She jerked her head toward the aliens in the lobby. "Friends of yours?"

He returned to his study. "It is difficult to be certain at this distance. They may actually be—kin."

She looked at him blankly and saw his face go from intent concentration to extreme pleasure as one of the Clutch began expounding incomprehensibly in its foghorn voice.

"That's Edger."

"It's *what?*" she demanded, dropping a wary hand to his arm.

"Edger," he repeated. "The big one in the middle is my brother Edger."

"Oh." She frowned at the group, and then at him. Maybe he's flipped, Robertson, she thought nervously. Don't look it, though.

The Clutch members were standing together, three of them waiting with visible patience, looking at nothing in particular, while the fourth—the loud one who stood a large head taller than his fellows—was in an attitude of animated attention. *Edger,* Miri reminded herself.

"Okay," she said, going with the gag for the moment. "What's he doing here?"

"I think . . ." He paused, eyes on the four aliens. "I think that he must be listening to the music."

Miri grabbed at the ragged edge of her patience. "*What* music?"

Her partner waved a slim hand, encompassing the pandemonium within and without. "Edger is a connoisseur of music. I met him when I was training as First-In Scout. I had a portable 'chora with me. . . ." He shook his head, eyes still on the Clutch members, face relaxed, lips half-smiling.

"He enjoyed my playing. After I—got to know him, he offered me a place in his household, as Clan musician." The half-smile became a full smile briefly. "He also offered to import a lifemate for me, or a series of pleasure-loves, so I wouldn't sicken for my own kind."

Miri was staring at him. "First-In Scout?" she repeated, in whispering awe.

His face closed like a trap, skin pulling tight over his

cheekbones and tiny muscles tensing around the eyes; the smile was gone as if it had never been.

Damn your tongue, Robertson! "What's next, boss?" she asked, fighting to keep her voice matter-of-fact.

He was already out of the tiny jungle. "Let us talk with Edger."

They moved quickly across the lobby, dodging firefighters and crowds of tenants being rescued. Val Con stopped before the largest of the Clutch people, Miri at his shoulder.

Slowly, hands hanging loose, he performed the bow of youth to age, as was proper when one who was yet shell-less would address the magnificence of one whose twelfth shell has set. He bent with the suppleness of a dancer until his forehead brushed his knee, then unbent as slowly and stood waiting to be acknowledged.

The measured pace of the bow, delivered with correct timing and in counterpoint to the frenziedness of the performance all about, drew Edger's eye. He studied the small figures before him: the brightly furred one standing in motionless respect, and the one who had performed the bow which had drawn the eye bearing a distinct resemblance to—

"By the first Egg of the first Clutch!" he boomed in joyful Trade. "It is my brother the musician! The dragonslayer! The stranger who teaches! Ahh, I had had suspicions, I will allow, but now they become certainties! Tell me, brother," he continued, lowering his voice to a mere bellow as he gestured about him with a three-fingered hand the size of a child's head. "This is yours, is it not?"

Val Con performed another slow bow, less profound than the first.

"I am honored that you recognize the workmanship," he murmured in soft Trade, "but I ask that you humor your soft brother. The work, which I had not known you might witness, is a specialty. It is to remain anonymous, known only to myself—and you, now, brother—and this lady, who assists me."

Edger sighed a tornado.

"What genius dwells within my brother! What nobility of purpose is his, who recognizes that art may be set free and allowed to pursue its own destiny and fulfillment!

"I am in your debt yet again, and I ask that you forgive my attention to the work which required you to bow such a bow. As your brother I ask that you not bow so to me again."

He paused to gaze at his brother the musician with wonder in his saucer-sized eyes.

"Frequently, I meditate upon that last work you played for the Clan, wherein you juxtaposed elements of the music of your people with the music of my own. That you could achieve such a thing without prior composition is a continuing astonishment to me. It is my opinion that most members of your race would rest, had they achieved such virtuosity upon an instrument. But you—I find you exploring other dimensions, tying the filaments of your work together with strands of discord and rhythm. . . ." He let this drift away in order to sample again the music happening *now*.

"It is I who must bow to you!" he announced suddenly,

nearly knocking over a passing firefighter as he attempted so do just that.

His brother waved his many-fingered hands, as if he would hold back the torrent of praise.

"It is too much—I thank you." The hands turned up to show the palms in his well-remembered gesture. "You permit?"

"Speak on. I permit all to such a brother, and such an artist."

"I would ask that you grant the boon of your company to myself and my companion for the space of a few days. It is that we must travel and there have been— hindrances. I feel we would be passed to our destination without molestation, if you grant us your cognizance." Val Con paused, head tipped slightly to one side.

"If you will," he continued slowly, "the art you see here is but part of a larger and more complex work we perform."

"It shall be done!" Edger declared, turning to his kin, who had been patiently standing by. "It shall be done!" he said in the highest of the Clutch dialects.

The others sketched quick bows, silently taking fresh note of Edger's lamentable haste. Still, a *T'carais* may have a brother, and who is to deny the brother of a *T'carais* when the request is reasonable?

"It is arranged," Edgar said in Trade. "A few days at the disposal of my brother. It is too little, yet it begins to repay the debt. I—"

"Will you damn turtles get the hell out of this lobby?" The policewoman who demanded it, stungun at the ready, was a towering, muscled brute, a scarred veteran of a multitude of riots and street fights. She loomed over Val Con like a mastiff over a lynx.

Edger looked down at her from his height, astounded by the temerity of such a small, soft person.

The small, soft person, blissfully unaware of her transgression, continued her tirade. "Don't you stupid reptiles know that this building's on fire, that there's a desperate criminal loose, that we're evacuating the tenants, and that *you* are obstructing *all* of it? You—" A jerk of the stungun at Val Con. "Who're you?"

"Linguistic Specialist Nor Ton yos'Quentl, of the—"

Miri closed her eyes briefly.

"You registered here?" the cop cut in.

"No, I'm with these—"

"Then, for the sake of Heyjus, get your butt *outta* here!" the cop yelled, tripping the safety on the stungun and waving it in emphasis. "And take this *zoo* with you; the building's being evacuated. If you wanna stand here and have the roof fall on you," she continued, as one suddenly struck by the brighter side of destiny, "I guess nobody'll be too upset over losin' a couple geeks and a herd of turtles."

She turned and strode away, slamming her gun into the holster as she went.

Val Con glanced up at Edger. "It is recommended that we make haste, my brother, before the roof falls on us with assistance from the local constables."

Edger sighed. "I had hoped to enjoy the last of your composition, but you are no doubt wise. It saddens me to find so many people unappreciative of art."

So saying, he turned in a wide circle—like a steamer

making a mid-ocean change of course, Miri thought—and set off for the door, one of the waiting trio at his side. The other two remained where they were.

Val Con caught Miri by the arm and pulled her with him as the second pair of turtles fell in behind, acting as escorts.

"What's going on?" she hissed at him in Terran as they moved toward the door. "Who in hell is Norton Quentin? Why are we—"

"Nor Ton yos'Quentl," he corrected, "is a Linguistic Specialist at the local—"

She jabbed him in the side with an elbow. "Listen you—you *turtle-brother!* This is crazy, all of it! First, you get us out of the room and into the lobby and nobody knows who we are. *Then,* you gotta attract attention to us by being related to some weird Clutch standing in the lobby—and *then* you're somebody else again! Damn chameleon, that's what you are."

He grinned at her, enjoying the sensation of looking down on someone with all the tall company around. "I'm your partner, just as you told Liz. A rose by any other name . . ."

For the next few minutes, he found out what kind of a vocabulary life in the mercenaries can foster in a young girl.

CLUTCH PEOPLE, Miri learned with surprise, were persons of consequence. Rooms for the two human members of Edger's party were bespoken and produced upon the instant at the hyatt where the marketing research team stopped. A private dining room was likewise provided, and, shortly, a meal of Clutch food and human food, with suitable beverages and utensils for each species. A concert-sized omnichora was shanghaied from some distant function room and placed also within the dining hall.

While they waited for the meal, and even before the beverages were poured out, Miri was formally introduced to Edger, Handler, Selector, and Sheather, each by his abbreviated, visa name.

"And your own?" Handler asked her.

Miri chewed her lip, working it out. "Miri Robertson Mercenary Soldier, Retired, Personal Bodyguard, Retired, Have Weapon Will Travel." She heard a small sound to her right, as if the other human member of the party had stifled a sneeze. Edger and Handler blinked solemnly.

"It is a well-enough name," the *T'carais* judged, "for one yet young."

Miri bowed in thanks, which pleased Edger, who thought her very pretty-behaved, and began to speak to her of music, asking, in his eventual way, if she played an instrument, as did his young brother.

She shook her head and confessed that, though she could pick out a tune, one-fingered and limp-timed, on a 'chora, it could not in justice be called playing. "I can sing some," she told Edger as they sat to dinner, "but Tough Guy says you're a connoisseur. My voice ain't anything special."

Edger paused, considering this message. Much of it was clear, but he was puzzled. "I believe I am unacquainted with this person who holds me in such esteem. My memory does not provide a face to match the name 'Tough Guy.' It is not often that I am so lax, and it troubles me."

"It is sometimes the custom among Terrans," Val Con explained, handing Miri a glass of wine and shaking his head at her, "to provide a person with what is known as a 'nickname.' This is most often suggested by a characteristic displayed by the person which seems very strong, yet is not touched upon by the person's official name." He paused and poured himself a glass of the canary before sliding into the seat between Edger and Miri. "For reasons best known to herself, Miri names me 'Tough Guy.'"

"I understand," Edger said, accepting in his turn a beaker of milky beverage from Sheather. "It pleases me that Terrans continue to adjust their names. It is not a tendency I have heretofore observed in them. But it is good to know of it." He quaffed his drink with apparent relish.

"I would be pleased," he continued, "if you and Miri would play and sing when the meal is done."

Val Con inclined his head and, after a slight hesitation, Miri copied the gesture.

The talk shifted to the mission of the four Clutch members. Miri let the conversation slide over and around her, not really listening to the words, but letting the slow voices, the grandiose phrasing and rolling periods, soothe her.

She broke a piece of bread from the loaf and buttered it leisurely. Edger's okay, she thought lazily. And Handler's sweet. And Selector—she grinned. As an ex-sergeant, she had a special feeling for Selector.

She became aware that shy, little—in a relative way, of course—Sheather was staring at her out of eyes the size of her salad plate, and smiled at him. He ducked his head and was suddenly very busy with his meal.

Miri ate her bread, luxuriating in the feeling of— safety? She sipped wine and decided that she liked the turtles.

"You will be pleased to know," Edger was booming to her partner, "that when you again come to us you will be able to eat of food and partake of drink designed for those of your kind. It was a source of shame to me that our Clan could provide you with naught but soups of which you must be unsure and which did not provide all the nutrients your body demands; and only water to drink, as our beer was too potent.

"To mitigate this shame, I have procured along our route foodstuffs prepared by your kind for your kind. And I am assured that these things are preserved for more than two hundreds of these standard years."

He paused, then, as delicately as the big voice could manage, asked, "Do you think you will return to us, as you promised, within two hundreds of years?"

Next to her, Val Con hesitated, and the glance Miri slanted at his face surprised an expression she recognized as sadness.

"Certainly before two hundred years," he said with strained lightness. "Liadens are not so long-lived as you." He lifted his glass and took a healthy swig of wine. "But how may I come to you at all, when you are adventuring around the galaxy?"

"Ah," Edger said, "but the expedition is nearly

complete! We will be back in the caverns of Middle River in less than seven Standard Years."

Val Con laughed. "I had no idea you were so close to the end," he said, and the talk passed on to other things.

PRESENTLY, it was judged time for entertainment. Bowing to their hosts, Miri and Val Con moved to the 'chora. He ghosted his fingers down the keys, releasing a shower of sound, and glanced at her from under long lashes. "What song, oh, Traveler?"

She ignored that, frowning in concentration. "You know 'Jim Dooley Blues'?"

His brows twitched together. "I am not certain."

She came around his side and leaned over to pick out the schmaltzy melody line. He listened for a bar or two, then his right hand began to pick up the rhythm; his left hand shifted further down the keyboard, grabbed her lagging melody, shook it firmly, and set it upon its feet.

Miri straightened. "Show-off."

Grinning, he flipped stops, adjusted frequencies, and slowed the lines she had shown him until they were obviously an introduction.

Miri turned toward the audience and begun to sing.

She sang well, he conceded, adjusting the 'chora to fill the spaces her voice left within the song. She did not have remarkable range, it was true, but she knew the limits of her voice, and the song she had chosen, with its overstated lament of the problems encountered by Programmer Dooley, fit her abilities perfectly.

The song ended at an even dozen verses, which he also appreciated.

The Clutch members sat motionless at the oversized table; Edger's eyes were glowing.

Val Con adjusted the stops and began the introduction to that ever-popular ballad of the spaceways, "Ausman Overboard." Miri laughed and nearly missed her first line.

The party lasted until very early the next morning.

✧ CHAPTER SIX ✧

THE STAFF of the hyatt in Econsey were even more impressed with the members of Edger's group than the staff at the City House, where they'd spent the previous night, had been. Of course, the Clutch had been staying at City House for several weeks—it was possible that the novelty had worn off.

A suite of rooms, arranged in a six-pointed star around a spacious common room, was provided. An omnichora, the stammering manager explained, was standard equipment in this apartment.

The suite was pronounced adequate, and the manager was requested to guide Handler and Sheather to the kitchens, where they could arrange the details of comestibles while Edger and Selector made a preliminary tour of Econsey's import shops.

Miri stared at Val Con and cleared her throat. "I'm gonna try the comm-net for Murph's registration," she said, jerking her head at the door to her bedroom.

He nodded wordlessly and drifted toward the 'chora.

✧✧✧

MURPH'S NAME WAS readily regurgitated by the net; the comm connected her with his hyatt's front desk immediately.

"Mr. Murphy and his guest have rented one of our island hideaways for a few days," the smiling young man at the Archipelago told her. "They should be back on the mainland—let's see . . . Yes. Tomorrow afternoon. Would you like to leave a message for him?"

"No, thanks," Miri said through gritted teeth. "My plans ain't fixed yet. I'll give him a call back when I know what I'm gonna be doing. I just thought, if he was free tonight . . ." She let it trail off, and the young man dimmed his smile by a kilowatt or two in professional sympathy.

She thanked him and broke the connection, seething.

Spinning slowly on her heel, she surveyed the bedroom. It was not, she thought, as luxurious as the apartment rented by Connor Phillips in Mixla City, though the private comm built into the desk was a nice touch. And the bed was *enormous*.

The bathing room offered a choice of wet or dry clean, as well as a sunroom; the valet was in a room of its own, flanked by floor to ceiling mirrors. On whim, because any occupation was better than thinking up ways to ruin Murph's nature, she called for the valet's catalog.

A low whistle escaped between her teeth as the pictures began to form in the screen. Hot damn, but you're in the wrong business! she told herself. A person didn't get rich being a soldier—not unless she got real lucky. And personal bodyguards didn't get rich either, unless the boss died grateful—of natural causes. Miri puzzled briefly, trying to figure out what line of work one could get into and afford to dress in the clothes offered by the hyatt's valet.

Sighing, she hit CANCEL. There was one thing for sure—any gimmick that let a person dress like that was not a gimmick that a mercenary from a ghetto world was likely to fall into.

That thought touched another, and then her fingers were working the catch on her pouch, pulling at the false wall. The enamel work of the disk was nearly blinding in the spotlights of the valet chamber, but extra illumination did not make the marks more meaningful.

She stood for a long moment, frowning down at the thing. Then, with a sharp nod, she went in search of her partner.

THE MANAGER of the second shop was appreciative. She turned the one knife they carried with them for such purpose—their "sample" Edger called it—this way and that, letting the light illuminate and obscure the crystal blade in artistic series.

"It's beautiful," she breathed, laying it with gentle care on the velvet pad she used for showing off fine pieces of jewelry. "I'm quite sure I could sell a few hundred every year. Why don't we start with an immediate shipment of fifty? In six months I'll have a better idea of how they're moving and be able to reorder." She looked up at the larger of the two aliens, who seemed to be the boss of the venture. "Will fifty percent up front and fifty percent on delivery be satisfactory?"

"Quite satisfactory," Edger replied politely. "But it

appears that I have not made myself perfectly clear. I am mortified to display such a lack of proficiency in your language. The case is this: 'Immediately,' as I understand you to mean the word, is not possible. It takes a space of time to encourage knives to grow in the desired form for the proper edge to be induced, for handles and sheaths to be formed and grown. . . ."

The manager frowned. "How long?"

Edger waved a hand. "For such a knife as that, do we notify those at home this day—twenty of these Standard Years."

"Twenty—" She swallowed and stared down at the lovely thing resting on the velvet. "What if you were to— ah, *encourage*—a smaller knife? Say one half as large as this? How long would that take?"

Edger considered. "Perhaps fifteen years. Some effort, you understand, cannot be hastened, though there is a saving in time due to the fact that the knife need not be encouraged to grow so large."

"There's nothing you can do to hurry the process a little? I mean—twenty Standards . . ." The bell rang in the front of the shop, announcing the arrival of another customer. *Two* customers, she saw around the curve of the silent turtle's shell, both well-dressed and cultured.

"Excuse me," she murmured to Edger and moved a bit down-counter. "Yes, sir? Is there something in particular you'd like to see?"

The older of the two smiled and flipped a hand. "Nothing particular. A birthday gift for my daughter. I'd like to look around, if you'd care to finish with those gentles."

She smiled and nodded. "Please take all the time you need. And if I can be of any assistance . . ." The phrase drifted off as she walked back to Edger and Selector.

"You must understand that it's not possible for a—a *human*—to wait twenty Standards for the filling of an order. Are you certain," she asked Edger very earnestly, "that there is nothing you can do to speed the process up?"

Edger moved his massive head from side-to-side in the gesture that he understood to mean negation. "I regret not. Were we to attempt such a thing—as has been done in the past, when knives were encouraged at a lightning pace—perhaps three Standards from thought to blade . . ." He sighed a huge sigh. "Such knives are flawed. They do not withstand the rigors we of Middle River Clan demand of our blades.

"That one before you—it will not shatter, no matter the provocation. Excluding, I should say, massive trauma, such as one would expect in the wreck of a land vehicle or collision of asteroid and starship. A flawed blade will shatter and be only dust upon the second strike against ordinary stone. We cannot, as craftpersons proud of our work, encourage a blade ahead of its time, knowing that it will perform as poorly as that."

He motioned, and Selector stepped forward to return the sample to its sheath of soft vegetable hide.

"Well," the manager said, putting her bravest face on it. "I'm sorry. I would've loved to have had some of your knives in the shop." She dredged up a smile. "Thank you for your time."

Edger inclined his head. "Our time has been well

given. My thanks for the gift of your own." He and Selector turned—carefully, in this place crammed with fragile things—and started for the door.

"Your pardon, Gentles," the elder of the two well-dressed men said. Edger paused. Behind him, Selector paused also, there being no place to go with his brother blocking the aisle.

The man made a slight bow, as would a resident prince upon greeting another traveling through his country. "My name is Justin Hostro. I could not help overhearing your conversation just now. Much that you have said interests me, and I believe I see a way in which we both may prosper. I would be very happy, were you to have time to walk with me to my place of business, so that we may discuss the matter more fully."

Edger was pleased. Forsooth, a human of beautifully polished manner and splendid turn of phrase. Further, one who wished to learn more fully of the knives of Middle River. He inclined his head.

"My brother and I are happy to learn your name and would be pleased to discuss our craft with you. Let us, as you say, walk to your place of business and speak."

Justin Hostro bowed once more. "I am delighted by your willingness. If I might beg the favor of an instant, while I complete the purchase of a gift for my only daughter?"

"It is well," Edger replied. "My kinsman and I shall await you and yours without."

If their new acquaintance tarried longer than the requested instant, it was not by so significant a time that either Edger or Selector noted the delay. Justin Hostro and his companion rejoined them quickly, the companion bearing a large and ornately wrapped box.

"Ah!" Edger exclaimed. "What delicacy you show in your choice! What supremacy of color—the so-bold yellow, how subtly tamed by the soberness of the black ribands! It is my belief that your daughter will be well pleased with such a gift."

The man carrying the object of this acclaim stopped dead, blinking at his leader. But Justin Hostro merely laid his hand upon Edger's forearm and turned him gently down the street, murmuring, "Now, it does my heart good to hear you say so, for I see you have a discerning eye. I had had qualms, I will admit it. Perhaps the yellow was too bold? The black too severe? But that it draws such praise from you—I am content."

Shaking his head, Mr. Hostro's companion fell in with Selector, and thus they each followed their leader down the street.

CMS WAS AT .90, CPS at .82. Val Con adjusted the stops on the 'chora as his fingers found an intriguing weave of sound, and the numbers in his head faded away.

Shrouded in the music, he did not hear the scant sound she made entering the room, nor did body-sense warn him of her nearness. The *thud* of disk to padded 'chora top was unexpectedly loud.

Trained reflexes stilled his startled reaction as his eyes snapped first to her face, then to the disk, and back to her face.

"Hello, Miri."

"What is it?" she demanded, voice harsh, finger pointing.

He dropped his eyes obediently and considered the bright design, hands folded in his lap as he sought the proper words, the correct inflection. *It is heritage*, he thought. *It is home.*

"It is a House Badge." He lifted his eyes again to hers, keeping his voice gentle and smooth. "The sign indicates Clan Erob, which is a House that chooses to seat itself elsewhere than upon Liad. They are respected Traders." He moved his shoulders. "It is what I know."

"There's writing on the back of it," Miri told him, her voice less harsh, but still carrying that edge he mistrusted.

He picked up the disk, flipped it in long fingers, and sighed.

"It is a genealogy. The last entry is incomplete. it reads: 'Miri Tiazan, born in the year named Amrasam.'" He let the badge fall gently back to the padding and looked up at her. "That would be approximately sixty-five Standards ago."

"Tayzin," she muttered, giving the name a Terran inflection. "Katalina Tayzin—my mother. Miri Tayzin—grandmother, I guess. Mom might've named me for my grandmother—she never said. Just that her mother'd died in 1358, back during the Fevers, when the fatcats . . ." She let her voice drift off, shaking her head.

"Didn't tell me a lot of stuff, looks like. When I told her I'd joined up with Liz's Merc unit, she gave me that thing there. Told me it'd belonged to her mother, and she'd be happy knowin' it was off Surebleak—and me, too." Her eyes sharpened suddenly.

"You knew," she said, and it was surety, not accusation.

He nodded. "I knew as well as I could, for whatever difference it might make. I was surprised to find that you did not know, and that you thought yourself so Terran." He offered her a smile. "Look at you. Everyone knows Liadens are short, small compared with other humans; that the heartbeat is a fraction off, the blood count a trifle different. . . ."

She shrugged, and the smile she returned him was real. "Mutated within acceptable limits. Says so in my papers."

"Exactly my point," he murmured. "Because it makes no real difference. No reasonable difference. I have it that we are all the same seed: Terran, Liaden, Yxtrang."

"Yxtrang, too?" She was onto the other point before he could nod. "You have that officially?"

He ran a finger over the smooth enamel work of Erob's badge. "My father did. He had access to the best of the genetics data, and to—other—information. In fact, he gave the information to the Terran Party."

"He *what?*" She was staring at him. "The Terran Party? What'd they do, laugh at him?"

He moved his shoulders against the sudden tension. "They tried to assassinate him."

Air hissed between her teeth, not quite a whistle. "They would, you know. Especially if they thought it was true. But you said—they tried."

He glanced down, took up the disk, and turned it over in his hands. "They tried . . . He was walking with my mother—his lifemate, you understand, not a contract-wife. She saw the man pull the gun—and she stepped in front, pushing my father aside." He turned the badge over and over in his hands, light running liquid over the many colors. "She was hit instead. They'd used a fragging pellet. She had no chance at all."

"So," she said after a long moment, "you do have a vendetta against Terrans."

His brows twitched together in a frown. "No, I don't." He flipped the badge lightly to the padding. "What good would a vendetta against Terrans do? Because one man with a gun did as he was ordered? Perhaps—probably— he thought he was protecting his family, his Clan, his planet, all of them, from some horrible destiny. I would think that the death of one man would be a cheap price to end such a threat, then and there."

He flexed his arms and leaned back. "A vendetta? Anne Davis, who took me as her own, raised me as her own—she was Terran, though my uncle, her lifemate, was Liaden." He glanced up, half-smiling. "You and I could be partners were you full Terran; there is nothing between our people that makes us natural enemies. No. No vendetta."

He picked up Erob's badge and offered it to her.

"I think," he said slowly as she took the disk from his hand, "that there is little purpose to thinking things like 'the Liadens,' 'the Clutch,' 'the humans,' or even 'the Yxtrang.' I think the best way to think—and talk—is in particulars: 'Val Con,' 'Miri,' 'Edger.' If you need to think bigger because some things take more people, it might be wise to think 'Erob,' 'Korval,' 'Middle River'—a group small enough that you can still name the individuals; a group small enough that you can, in time, know the individuals, the parts of the Clan. Where is the threat in 'Handler,' 'Edger,' 'Terrence'?"

She stood holding the Clan sign loosely, puzzlement shadowing her gray eyes.

"You didn't learn that in spy school," she told him flatly.

He looked down and began to stroke the keys of the 'chora.

"No," he said, very softly. "I don't think I did."

She clicked open her pouch and dropped the Erob-link within, her eyes on the top of his head as he sat bent over the keyboard once more.

"So how come you're a spy and not a Scout?"

The Loop flared and he was up, hands flat on the keyboard, primed to stop the deadly danger of her; he saw disbelief flash across her face even as her body dropped into a crouch, ready to take his attack, a trained opponent, growing deadlier by the instant—

"Miri." His voice cracked and he swallowed air; he raised a hand to push the hair from his forehead and exercised will to banish the Loop from consciousness. . . . "Miri, please. I would—like—to tell you the truth. It is my *intention* to tell you the truth."

He saw her make the effort, saw the fighting tension drain out of shoulders and legs as she straightened and grinned shakily.

"But I shouldn't push my luck, right?"

"Something very like," he agreed, pushing the hair on his forehead up again. It fell back immediately.

"You really do need a haircut."

The adrenal rush had left him drained, a little shaky,

but curiously at ease. He flashed a quick grin. "I find that suggestion hard to take seriously from someone whose own hair falls well below her waist."

"I like it long."

"And you a soldier!"

"Yeah, but, you see, my commander told me never to cut it. Just following orders!"

He laughed and found within himself an urge to talk, to explain—to justify.

"Orders can be difficult, can they not?" he said, sitting down again before the 'chora. "I came to this world because there was a man who was a great danger to many, many people of different sizes and shapes. A man who thought anyone whose heartbeat and blood failed to match his own was a geek—worthless—and who killed and tortured the hopeless.

"I was *ordered* here, but having seen the man act, I believe that *I* did what was proper. The reason I was ordered here, I think, is that a vendetta claim would have been sufficient to stop an investigation of my further motives, had something gone awry." He paused, then went on more slowly.

"After all, spy or Scout, I am a volunteer, am I not? I have already agreed to go first, to make the universe safe. A Scout or a spy—it is the same thing. I am an agent of change in either case. Expendable—too useful a tool not to use.

"Sometimes," he continued softly, "tools are programmed to protect themselves. This 'chora, for example, can be moved about within the hyatt with no difficulty. Yet, if we attempted to move it off the grounds, it would start howling, or perhaps it would simply not function at all." He looked at her carefully. "The 'chora may not even know what it will do when the boundary is crossed—some circuits are beyond its access. Tools are like that, sometimes."

Miri nodded warily. "But *people*—" she began and chopped off her words as the door cycled to admit Handler and Sheather.

"It has been arranged," Handler told them, "that we shall all six dine in the so-called *Grotto* located belowstairs in this establishment. There is said to be music, which our elder brother will find pleasing, and there is also dancing, which we thought might be pleasing to our human friends. And," he said, voice dropping to what Miri thought must be intended as a whisper, "the form of the Grotto may be pleasing to all of us, since it is a likeness of a cavern system found elsewhere on this planet. We have bespoken the table for eight of the clock, and we hope that there will be sufficient time before the celebration for you to refresh yourselves, adorn yourselves, and be ready. We would not wish the event to begin with unseemly haste."

The humans exchanged a glance, and Val Con bowed.

"We thank you for your thoughtfulness. Six hours is more than adequate for our preparations. We shall be ready in the fullness of time."

"That is very well, then," Handler said. "If you will excuse us, we shall take our leave so that we may make analyses and also prepare for the evening. It does bode to be a time of some discussion."

The humans bowed their thanks and acknowledgements, Miri attempting to copy Val Con's fluid style and finding it much harder than it looked. The Clutch adjourned to their own quarters.

Miri sighed. "Well, I don't know how much adornment I'll be doing, though the refreshment part don't sound too bad. Maybe I can order a fancy new shirt out of the valet." She was talking to herself, not expecting an answer; Val Con's reply made her jump.

"You can't go like that, you know," he told her seriously. "Not into the most exclusive resort on the planet."

"Yeah, well, I can't go in any of the clothes the valet's peddling, either! Have you looked at the prices on those things? I could mount an invasion of Terra for the price of a pair of shoes. I'm here to pick up my money, remember? It's gotten so I gotta water my kynak so I can have a second drink. I sure can't go into debt to finance something I'll wear once in my life!"

Val Con tipped his head, brows bent together in puzzlement. "You would be very conspicuous in what you are wearing now," he said simply. "And Edger has said that the expense of the trip is his, since he counts a debt owed me, and because he had not thought to come to Econsey to research the local need for knives. Even if he wished not to extend his cognizance to you, I might pay—"

"No." She frowned stormily. "That ain't the way I do things. I can just stay in my room, beg off that it's a holy day or something."

"Now that would be an insult, after Handler went to the trouble and thought of arranging a place where we can all eat and enjoy." He paused, seemingly studying the air.

"It would be best not to wear a gun." As he spoke, he opened his pouch and brought out a slender polished stick, something like a Drumetian math-stick.

"Perhaps you could wear your hair to accommodate this." With a flick of the wrist, the stick separated, becoming the handle of a thin, deadly-looking blade, smoothly sharp along the curved edge, wickedly serrated along the other.

Another wrist-flick and the slender dirk was merely a polished stick: knife to ornament. He reversed it and held it out.

Miri hesitated. "I ain't a knife expert—just about know how to use a survival blade."

"If anyone gets close enough to grab you," he said, all reason, "pull it out, flip it open, stick it in, and run. It is not likely you will be pursued." He extended it further. "Simplicity itself, and a precaution only."

She looked from the knife to his face; when she finally accepted the thing, she took it gingerly, as if she much preferred not to.

"I," she announced, "am being bullied."

"Undoubtedly."

"Lazenia spandok," she said, rudely.

His eyebrows shot up. "You speak Liaden?"

"Well enough to swear and pidgin my way through a battle plan. And if ever anybody was a managing bastard, you are. In spades." She turned toward her room, experimentally flipping the hidden blade out and in.

Behind her, he murmured something in Liaden. She whirled, glad the blade was closed.

"That ain't funny, spacer!" The Trade words crackled

with outrage. "I ain't a young lady and I don't need you to tell me to clean up my talk!"

"Forgive me." He bowed contrition and dared a question. "Where are you going?"

"To refresh and adorn myself. I've only got about five hours or so, after I decide what shoes to wear."

And she was gone, leaving him to wonder at the sudden bite of bereavement and at the impulse that had led him to address her in the intimate mode, reserved for kin. Or for lovers.

✧ CHAPTER SEVEN ✧

THE DOOR CLOSED with a sigh that echoed her own, and she spun, flipping the stickknife onto the desk.

Nasty little toy, she thought, wrinkling her nose as her hand dropped to the grip of the gun on her leg. Just as deadly, surely, but somehow—cleaner? More straightforward? Less personal, maybe?

She shifted slightly, then caught sight of herself in the bed mirror and stuck her tongue out.

Miri Robertson, Girl Philosopher, she thought wryly.

Ilania frrogudon . . . The echo of Tough Guy's murmuring voice contradicted her and she froze, biting her lower lip.

Liaden was an old language, far, far older than the motley collection of dialects that passed for a Terran language, and divided into two forms: High and Low. High Liaden was used for dealing with most outsiders, such as coworkers, strangers, nodding acquaintances, and shopkeepers. Kin were addressed in Low Liaden—longtime friends, children . . . But *never* a person considered expendable.

Yet at least twice he'd begun the motions that would have killed her, automatically, efficiently. She might have brushed her death a dozen times with him already; it had taken her time to realize what the mask of inoffensive politeness he sometimes wore was meant to conceal.

His other face—the one with the quirking eyebrows and luminous grins—was the face of a man who loved to laugh and who called heart-music effortlessly from the complex keyboard of the 'chora. It was the face of a man who was good to know: a friend.

A partner.

She moved to the bed and lay back slowly, imposing relaxation on trained muscles.

"A Scout ain't a spy," she informed the ceiling solemnly. "And people ain't tools."

She closed her eyes. Scouts, she thought. Scouts are the nearest there is to heroes. . . . And he'd said *First-in* Scout. The best of the best: pilot, explorer, linguist, cultural analyst, xenologist—brilliant, adaptable, endlessly resourceful. The future of a world hung on his word alone: Would it be colonized? Opened to trade? Quarantined?

Miri opened her eyes. "Scouts are for holding things together," she clarified for the ceiling. "Spies are for taking things apart."

And that babble he'd given her about tools!

She rolled over, burying her head in the basket of her crossed arms, and relived the moments just passed, when she'd known he was coming across the 'chora at her.

Gods, he's fast! she marveled. Suzuki and Jase would give a year of battle bonuses to have that speed for the old unit, never minding the brain that directed it.

Never mind the brain, indeed. She wondered why he'd checked himself those times she'd seen her death in his eyes. She wondered why he'd trusted her with that deadly little blade, why he'd spoken to her . . . And she wondered, very briefly, if he truly were crazy.

It seemed likely.

The thing to do with crazy people is get lots of room between you and them, she said to herself.

She rolled to her knees in the center of the great bed, bracing her body for the leap to the floor. Time to flit, Robertson. You ain't smart enough to figure this one out.

"Leave!" she shouted a moment later, when she'd moved no further. Damn Murph and the money. Damn the Juntavas and their stupid vendetta. Damn especially a sentence spoken in a language that might have been her grandmother's but never had been hers.

Yes, and then? Damn the man who had twice—no, *four* times—saved her life?

You're a fool, Robertson, she told herself savagely. You're crazier than he is.

"Yeah, well, it's a job," she said aloud, shoulders sagging slightly. "Keeps me busy."

She kicked into a somersault, snapping straight to her feet as the roll flipped her over the edge of the bed. On her way to the bathroom, she paused at the desk and picked up the little wooden stick. So easy to hide . . . She thought of Surebleak and the one or a dozen times in her childhood when such an instrument would have been welcome protection. Memory flashed a face she hadn't seen in years and her hand twitched—the blade was out, silent and ready.

"Aah, what the hell," she muttered and closed the knife, carrying it with her into the bath.

Sometime later, bathed, robed, and damp-haired, she called up the valet's catalog again. She frowned at the first selection, trying to place what was different, and nearly laughed aloud in mingled outrage and amusement.

No price was displayed.

All right, she thought, beginning the scan. If that's how he wants it. I hope I bankrupt him.

It took her longer to realize that she was trying to figure out which clothes might please him, which clothes might make him receptive to an offer to share that immense bed with her this evening.

"Pretty, ain't he?" she asked her reflection sympathetically, then sighed. Pretty and dangerous and fast and smart and crazy as the six of diamonds. She cursed herself silently, wondering why she hadn't recognized the emotion before. Lust. Not just simple lust, of the passing-glance variety, but lust of the classic Lost Week on Moravia kind.

Looking around her—and back at the clothes in the valet's tank—she wondered if he might be interested in a Lost Week sometime. Then she cursed herself some more. Since when did she have a week to lose?

CONNOR PHILLIPS'S service record, reluctantly provided by *Salene,* included a holo, which was duly copied and sent around to cops, firefighters, and disaster crews present at the "fire" at the Mixla Arms.

Sergeant McCulloh stepped forward immediately. "Yeah," she told Pete, "I seen him. Redhead kid, him, an' four turtles all left together." She corrugated her forehead in an effort to aid memory. "Said his name was something-or-nother-yos-something. Geek name. Dunno hers. 'Nother geek. Talkin' Trade with the turtles—something about all traveling together for a couple days. . . ." She shrugged broad shoulders. "I'm real sorry, Mr. Smith. Coulda kept the whole bunch right then, if I'd known."

"That's all right, Sergeant," the Chief of Police said, forestalling Pete's frustrated growl. "Now, did you overhear anything that might have indicated where they were going?"

The sergeant shook her massive head. "Nossir. Only that they should all go together."

"Well," the chief said, "that's quite a bit of help, actually. Four turtles and two humans traveling together? They'll be easy to spot." He smiled at his subordinate. "That will be all, Sergeant. Thank you for coming forward with that information. You've been very helpful."

"Yessir. Thank you, sir. Thank *you*, Mr. Smith." The sergeant whirled on her heel and marched out of the room, shutting the door crisply behind her.

"Great," Pete swore. "All we got to do, I guess, is put out an all-points on four turtles and two geeks and wait till we get a report."

"Actually," the chief said, leaning back in his chair, "that's close. We send out a picture and a note to report any combination of turtle and human. Instructions to observe and report to Mixla Headquarters. Under no circumstances are they to be taken."

"What!" Pete stopped in mid-pace, staring at the other man.

The chief shook his head. "Think about it. The boy's inventive—got himself a nice little diversion there: limited property damage, no risk to life—and if he's linked to the O'Grady incident, like you think, he's probably a tad dangerous." He propped his foot up on the desk top.

"Turtles occupy a very ticklish diplomatic niche. We can't afford to make them mad. And they will be mad, if they count the boy as a friend and some poor joke of a cop comes to arrest him." He shook his head. "The girl's an unknown, but it's a good idea to assume she's as dangerous as the boy—and the turtles are her friends, too."

Pete blinked thoughtfully. "So we wait till they're spotted and nailed, then hit 'em with everything we got so fast the turtles got no time to yell 'ho!' We can say 'sorry' later."

The chief nodded. "Exactly."

"FLAWED BLADES." Edger was saying when Miri entered the room in the early evening. "And only flawed blades, my brothers! All that we have now—warehoused, do you recall, Sheather? Nearest the river?—and all that thrice-accursed cavern can spawn! Who could have imagined such a thing?"

"What use can any being have for flawed knives?" Handler asked, squinting his eyes in puzzlement.

"Ah, they are to be given to certain special individuals in the organization of this Justin Hostro. These individuals are entrusted with tasks having much to do with the honor and integrity of the organization. It is Justin Hostro's thought that a blade used for such a purpose need be used for that purpose alone and never for any other. More, it should be a weapon of impeccable crafting, that it not fail during the task itself.

"These knives fit the criteria Justin Hostro has set down most admirably, is it not so, brother?" This last was directed to Selector, who inclined his head.

"It is, indeed, as if the Cavern of Flawed Blades were created and discovered only for this bargain we have struck with Justin Hostro."

Val Con, perched on the arm of a chair set a little apart from the circle of Clutch members, grinned at the undercurrent of venom in that comment and glanced up as Miri's door sighed open.

She was dressed in a dark blue gown that sheathed her like a second skin in some places, and flowed loose and elegant, like a fall of midnight waters, in others. On the right side, her hair was arranged in a complex knot through which was thrust a slender, gleaming stick; the rest of the copper mass was allowed to fall free. Her throat was bare, as was one arm; her hands were innocent of rings.

He stood as she approached Edger, and faded back toward his own room as she made her bow.

"Yes, my youngest of sisters," the *T'carais* boomed, recognizing her immediately. "That color becomes you—it sets off the flame of your hair. A wise choice, indeed."

Miri bowed her thanks. "I wanted to thank you for the chance to have this dress. It's the prettiest thing I've ever worn."

"The artistry of you is thanks enough. You and my

so-beautiful young brother—where has he gone?" The big head swiveled.

"Here." Val Con smiled, coming silently back into the room. "I had forgotten something."

He was beautiful, Miri saw. The dark leathers were gone, replaced by a wide-sleeved white shirt, banded tight at the wrists, lacy ruffles half-concealing slender hands. There was lace at his throat, and his trousers were dark burgundy, made of some soft material that cried out to be stroked. A green drop hung in his right ear, and a gold and green ring was on his left hand. The dark hair gleamed silken in the room's buttery light.

He bowed to her and offered the box he carried. "I am sorry to have offended you."

"It's okay." She took the box and cautiously lifted the lid.

Inside shone a necklace of silver net, holding a single stone of faceted blue, and a silver ring in the shape of an improbable serpent, clutching its jaws tight around a stone of matching blue.

She stood very, very still, then took a deep breath and forced herself to meet his eyes.

"Thank you. I—" She shook her head and tried again. *"Palesci modassa."* That was the formal phrase of thanksgiving.

Val Con smiled. "You're welcome," he replied, since it seemed safer to stay with Terran. He touched the necklace lightly with a forefinger. "Shall I?"

Her mouth quirked toward a grin. "Sure, why not?"

First she slid the ring onto her left hand, then raised both hands to hold her hair off her neck.

He slid the necklace around her throat with a skill that hinted at past experience, then gently took her hair from her hands, arranging its cascade down her back. Miri bit down on a sudden surge of excitement and managed to keep her face expressionless as he came to her side and bowed to Edger.

"I think that we are prepared to celebrate, elder brother," Val Con said. "Does it please you to walk with us?"

✦ CHAPTER EIGHT ✦

CHARLIE NARANSHEK slipped his service piece into the sleeve pocket of his dress tunic. He always carried it there, though his employers at the Grotto had supplied him with a large and very ornate weapon, with instructions to wear it prominently. It was a matter of feelings. Charlie felt better on his shift as bouncer when he knew that his daytime gun was at hand. He got the heebie-jeebies whenever he thought about having to draw and aim the pretty piece he wore on his belt.

Feelings, Charlie thought, slamming the locker door, were important. Clues to the inner man. It was smart to pay attention to one's feelings, to act with them.

He raised his hand as he passed the desk. "Night, Pat."

"Hey, Charlie?" She waved him over, spinning the screen on its lazy Susan so he could see the bright amber letters. "Take a look at this, willya? Something you might run into down on the second job."

He frowned at the letters: Be On The Lookout. . . .

"Four turtles and two humans? Are they crazy?"

Pat shrugged. "Who knows? Don't you think the

turtles would eat the Grotto up? That fancy no-grav dance floor?" She wiggled her shoulders in a uniformed parody of a dance that may have been in fashion on some steamy jungle world where spears and canoes were still considered pretty radical stuff.

Charlie grunted. "Sure. But it's not no-grav; it's *low*-grav." He shook his head at the screen. "'Observe, but do not contact. Report whereabouts to Headquarters, Mixla City . . . continue observation . . . Considered armed and dangerous'?"

He looked at Pat, who grimaced and touched her keypad. Physical descriptions of the two human members of the party scrolled into place.

"'Male, brown hair, green eyes, slender build, approximately five-five, age eighteen to twenty-five. Female, red hair, gray eyes, slender build, approximately five-two, age eighteen to twenty-five.'" He straightened, pushing the screen back where it belonged. "This is armed and dangerous? Ain't neither one of 'em big enough to pick up a gun, much less use it. The turtles now—one of them could hurt you, if he stepped on you."

Pat laughed and flipped her hand at him. "Get out of here, you damn moonlighter. I don't know what I expected from somebody who can't live on a cop's salary."

He grinned, moving toward the door. "See you later, Pat. Try not to let one of them kids take over the station while I'm gone, okay?"

"Yah—just don't go dancin' with no turtles, old man."

The door slid closed on her laughter and Charlie sprinted for the nearest taxi stand. He'd have to step on it now, or he'd be late.

✧✧✧

HANDLER had outdone himself. Not only was the Clutch party seated within an exclusive alcove with excellent sight of the musicians and the famous dance floor, as well as two of the six bars, but he had further arranged—since the Clutch, after all, were visiting human space—that the four nonhumans should eat their meal using Terran utensils.

One by one Edger extracted his set from the sheathing napkin, turning each fork, knife, and spoon this way and that, subjecting it to saucer-eyed scrutiny.

"What think you, brothers?" he asked the table at large, extending a spoon. "Is this also a knife? It has an edge, of sorts. . . ."

Handler pulled one of his spoons free and tried the balance in one large hand. "It is true that it *could* be a knife, elder brother, and it is not beyond our skill to encourage such a shape. But this other—" He proffered a dessert fork. "*Three* points? Six edges, I fear me."

"A trifle!" Edger asserted. "Think if we but bring the problem to—" Here sense was lost in a sonorous rumbling that Miri realized must be Clutch-talk.

She leaned to her partner. "Are they serious, or what?"

"Hm?" He started slightly and turned to her, his full sleeve brushing her bare arm. "Of course they're serious. Middle River Clan produces the finest knives in Edger's society. Which is the same as saying that they produce the finest knives anywhere yet discovered."

"What does that mean—the finest? Does it mean pretty or useful or indestructible?"

He grinned and refilled their glasses. "Yes. Middle

River knives are crystal, delicately crafted, superbly handled, exquisitely sheathed—things of beauty, without doubt. Also useful, since a knife is, after all, a tool. Edger and his Clan encourage as many blades as there are uses for blades, from screwdrivers to grace knives." He sipped wine. "Indestructible? Edger is very careful to say that a Middle River blade *will* shatter, under conditions that he likes to call 'traumatic.' These being the total destruction of the building or vehicle the knife resides within, while the knife is so resident. . . ."

She laughed. "But *spoons?*"

He removed one of the many folded in his napkin. Flipping the lace away from his hand in absentminded grace, he held the utensil out for her inspection and ran a finger around the edge. "There is symmetry, you see. And purpose. Utility. A certain pleasing quality, indeed, to the form." He shrugged and lay the spoon aside. "Who can tell? Perhaps soon—within, let us say, the late middle life of your grandchildren—Middle River spoons may be the very rage among the wealthy and influential."

"Indeed," Edger boomed, "such was my thought, young brother! If these be things that are used daily, why then should they be wrought of soft metal, that so quickly wears out? Why not, indeed, of crystal from our Clan's encouragement, so that they may be used for hundreds and hundreds of your Standard Years?"

Miri laughed again, raising her glass. "No reason at all! Humans are just shortsighted, I guess."

"We do not blame you for it," Handler said quickly, "for it is true that you cannot help the shortness of your lives. But it does seem wasteful and somewhat chauvinistic to condemn your works to obsolescence only because you, yourselves—" He floundered, the end of his sentence in sight and no graceful exit apparent, but Edger rescued him noisily.

"Not so, brother, for ephemera is an art form. Indeed, it may be art at its highest form—I have yet to conceive an opinion and have heard no others. Have we not all seen the works of this, our younger brother, employing the mediums of sound, of movement pattern, and reflected light? Done, gone, changing as it goes. Art, brothers. And who is to say that . . ." Perceiving that Edger was in the throes of his passion yet again, his Clan members composed themselves to listen.

The remaining two members of the party exchanged glances, grins, and a sip of wine.

CHARLIE CAME THROUGH the East door of the Grotto exactly on time and hardly out of breath, waving at his day-shift counterpart.

"Hey, George! What's the news, man? All quiet in underground Econsey?"

"Pretty quiet," allowed the other, a thin, dark man who'd been thrown off the force for hitting a kid and killing him. "There's a party over in the South quarter might bear some extra attention. Group of genuine Clutch-type turtles and a couple humans."

"Say what?" Charlie stared, then quickly forced himself to blink.

"Turtles," George repeated patiently. "Four of 'em. Two humans: male and female. Young. No problems— just a little noisy. But that's turtles for you—can't hold a conversation without cracking the walls next door. I just like to keep an eye on 'em. Not that we get that many 'phobes in here."

Charlie nodded. "Yeah, but you never know. I'll check in on 'em every so often. What about the kids?"

"Pretty couple. He's dark. She's a redhead. Not orange," he elaborated surprisingly. "Kind of a reddish brown."

"Auburn."

"Yeah, auburn. Little thing. Seem to be having a good time—all six of 'em. Million laughs." He shrugged and shuffled a step toward the bar.

"Well, good," Charlie said, taking his hint. "I hope they enjoy their stay in beautiful Econsey." He raised a hand. "See you 'round, buddy."

"Take it easy." George was already waving at Macy behind the bar to set up his first drink.

CHARLIE'S BEAT was the East and South quarters, with one eye tipped to the low-grav dance floor at the center of things. Janees Dalton patrolled West and North, one of her eyes also on the floor, and two floaters circulated, their eyes on everything.

East was quiet. Charlie intercepted a bill dispute before it got noisy and passed it to the nearest floor manager; he escorted an early drunk to the nearest exit and put her in a cab; he nodded hello to a couple of regulars and moved across to South.

Good mob tonight, he thought, flicking a glance to the dance floor and another to twin bars marking the gateway from East to South. He spotted one of the floaters, Mark Swenger, and waved him over.

"How's it goin'?"

"Not too bad." Mark grinned. A nice kid, he worked the Grotto nights and went to school days, aiming to be a lawyer. Charlie hoped that wouldn't happen—law was a bad way to lose a friend.

"What about the turtle party?" he asked. "Still running?"

"Oh, yeah. It looks like they'll be there for the next year." Mark shook his head. "Man, you would not believe the beer and wine that table's going through! They might *have* to stay a year."

Charlie tipped his head. "Disorderly?"

"Naw, just having a good time. A little loud, but I think turtles just *are,* since they're so big and everything. It's wild, though, to walk past and hear the big one booming out in Terran to the girl, and the next littlest one booming just a little less loud to the boy in Trade, and the other two going to town in something I don't think anybody can speak!" He laughed.

"Real cosmopolitan, huh?" Charlie was grinning, too.

"Real circus," Mark corrected. "But not obnoxious. Kind of heartwarming, actually. They don't seem to have a care to care about." He scanned the crowd and lifted a hand. "I'd better be drifting like the tides, man."

Charlie nodded, moving off in the other direction. "See you later, kid."

South was starting to fill up, though there weren't many people on the dance floor. Early yet for dancing, Charlie thought; the band was barely warm. He saw an opening in the mob around the hors d'oeuvre table and slipped through, working his way back to the far wall.

And there they were. Four turtles, looming and booming. Two humans: She, pale-skinned and tiny, the blue of her dress feeding the flame of her hair; he, dark and in no way large, casual in the fine white shirt, as if these were the clothes he always wore. Charlie saw him lean close to speak into her ear. She laughed and raised her glass to drink.

Armed and dangerous? Charlie thought. Fat chance. He flicked his glance to the floor, then checked out the bars, the snack table, and the main entrance to the Quarter as he drifted back to the wall. It struck him that the boy sat where he could take advantage of that same view and he wondered if it were by design. He snorted and shook his head. Old man, you been a cop too long.

An acquaintance hailed him from a center table and he stopped to chat a minute; he looked up in time to see the boy leaving the turtles' alcove. Charlie nodded to his friend, promised to call soon, and moved away, frowning at the redhaired girl, and at the empty chair beside her.

He did one more quick scan of the area—dance floor, bars, exit, hors d'oeuvre table—and nodded, satisfied. Then he headed for the turtles' alcove. It was time for his break.

MIRI LEANED BACK in her chair, occasionally sipping from the glass in her hand as she let the low, soothing rumble of the Clutch's native tongue roll over her. The evening had taken on a dreamlike quality which was not, she thought, entirely due to the wine.

There was no reason for it not to seem that way—all the well-known fairy-tale elements were there. Herself in a lovely dress, a necklace around her throat, and a ring upon her finger, each worth more than she could hope to earn in a year of superlative bonuses—gifts from a companion who was himself beautiful, charming, and entertaining.

And bats.

She banished the thought with a sip of wine and heard, beneath the thunder of the Clutch's conversation, the sound of approaching footsteps. Alarm jangled faintly—her partner walked without sound, and these steps did not belong to their waiter. She set the glass aside and turned.

A tall, wiry man, dark brown and cheerful, grinned and bowed, hand over heart. "My name's Charlie Naranshek," he said, straightening. "I saw you sitting here and I wondered if you'd like to dance?"

She eyed him, noting the ornate gun on the fancy belt, and the glint of silver thread in his dress tunic, then looked back at his face. He was still grinning, dark eyes sparkling. She grinned back.

"Sure," she said. "Why not?"

He helped her up and gave her his arm to the dance floor. "Be careful now," he cautioned. "This thing can be a little tricky till you get the hang of it—'bout six-tenths normal gravity."

She slanted her eyes at him, grinning. "I think I'll be okay."

Charlie hung onto her as they crossed fields, alert for any sign of unbalance—and made a derisive comment to himself when she made the adjustment to the reduced weight without the slightest falter.

"Been in space some?" he asked as they took over a few square inches and began to sway with the music.

She laughed, spinning. "Naw. Just on an awful lot of dance floors."

"Really?" he asked when they next came together. "But not on Lufkit. This here's the one, the only, the *exclusive* low-grav dance floor on the whole ball of mud."

She waved her hand at the table where the four turtles still boomed. "Crew like that, you figure we're gonna be doing some space."

Charlie grinned, refusing to be slapped down, and took her arm for the next move of the dance. "They could just be friends from out-of-town, couldn't they? And you and your—husband?—just showing them a good time?"

"Brother." She tipped her head. "Did you wait for him to leave?"

"Well, sure I did," he said. "Not that I don't think you're pretty enough to fight a duel over, understand—"

She laughed and spun away from him, obedient to the laws of the dance.

VAL CON RE-ENTERED by the South door and passed the two bars and the hors d'oeuvre table, not hurrying, but not dallying. The alcove was hidden by an eddy of people. As he broke through the crowd he heard the notes of Edger's voice, and then the table was suddenly in sight.

He froze, stomach clenching, then took an automatic breath and surveyed the room calmly, ice-cold sober. He caught a glimmer of blue in the pattern of the dance, saw a small pale hand join with a larger brown one, and moved deliberately over to the edge of the floor to wait.

THE DANCE BROUGHT them together again.

"You never did tell me your name," Charlie said.

"Roberta." She accepted his hand for a full spin and bowed as she returned. "My brother's Danny. If you want the names of the rest of the bunch, we'd better go someplace where we can sit down, 'cause it'll take awhile."

"That's okay." He frowned, noticing her start. "What's wrong?"

"Nothing." She threw a grin at him. "Nearly lost my footing."

"What! And you an old spacehand!"

She grinned again and whirled away for the last figure, again catching sight of her partner where he stood at the edge of the floor, watching the dance with a sort of detached, polite interest.

She completed her swing, dipped, and came up, swearing at herself for having yielded to the wine and the music and the dreaming. Her hand met Charlie's for the final time and the music stopped.

She smiled and began to move off the floor. "Thanks. It was fun."

"Hey! What about another one?" He was at her shoulder, reaching for her arm.

She eluded the touch without seeming to do it consciously, and set her steps straight for the still figure at the edge of the dance floor. "Sorry, Charlie, but my brother's waiting for me." She flung him another grin, hoping he would miss the tightness underneath it—hoping he would go away.

He stayed at her shoulder. "Well, there's no reason for your brother to want your head, is there? Besides, I think I owe him an apology for stealing his sister when he wasn't looking."

Hell, Miri thought. And there was the end of the dance floor and the man with the cold, closed face—

Teeth gritted, she faked a stumble, locking her hands around his wrists. He did not sway when her weight pushed into him; she held tighter, creasing the fine lace cuffs, and forced a breathless little laugh.

"Here's my brother now, so we can both apologize," she said to Charlie, giving the wrists she gripped a small shake before releasing them.

"Danny, this is Charlie Naranshek," she said, squeezing brightness into her voice around the lump of dread in her throat. "He asked me to dance while you were gone and I said yes. I'm sorry. I should've known you'd worry." She tipped her head, slanting gray eyes at his cold green ones.

Charlie added his voice to this, frowning slightly at the boy before him. Pretty, and that was a fact. But there was more warmth to be had from the eardrop or the faceted ring-jewel than from the eyes that rested on his. He moved his shoulders, grinning.

"I'm really sorry, Mr.—? But I saw your sister sitting there looking so pretty and so lonesome and all. I thought we could maybe have some fun. Do a little dancing. Talk. You know." He smiled again. "I understand how you could he a little upset. Man can't be too careful of his sister these days, and I know that to be a fact. But there really isn't any harm in me and I never meant to get her in trouble with you."

One eyebrow had slipped slightly out of alignment and the eyes themselves seemed somewhat thawed. "My sister is certainly capable of taking care of herself, sir, and I very much doubt that she is afraid of my displeasure." He offered a smile that went a lot farther toward melting his expression.

"If she's been feeding you stories of my temper, I'm afraid I will have to assure you that my bark is considerably worse than my bite."

This was much better, Charlie thought. "Well, that's fine. I'd have been real sorry to make trouble between a brother and sister." He turned to the girl. "So what's say we give it another round?"

She laughed and shook her head. "Sorry, Charlie. I think we've left our friends alone long enough. Be a shame to offend them."

Charlie's eyes flicked to the table where the four turtles sat, silent now, saucer eyes turned toward—the dance floor? Or the three of them? Charlie didn't know, though his stomach seemed to think it did.

Carefully, he made his bows—a low one to her, hand over heart, a slighter one to him, hands folded at belt level—and received theirs in return. He watched until they were back at their table before turning again to his duties as bouncer and peacemaker, his feelings in disarray.

VAL CON WAITED until they were both seated and the talk of Clutch began its sonorous weaving around them once more. He poured wine for the two of them and tasted his, playing for more time as he struggled to smooth out the unaccustomed emotion—anger, he told himself in vague consternation. He caught a glimmer of the Loop. CPS was at .79.

Taking up her own glass, Miri watched the side of his face. It was no longer the face she associated with lies and death, but neither was it the face of her charming companion of the early evening. Calling herself a fool did not improve matters, so she leaned back in her chair, sipped wine and waited for the storm to break.

Finally, he took a deep breath. "Miri."

"Yo."

"You must understand," he said slowly, watching the eddy and flow of people in the South quarter, rather than her face, "that I am a highly trained individual. This means that I react quickly to situations I perceive as dangerous. Given your present circumstance, to go while I am not in the room and dance with a man who carries two guns is—"

"*One* gun," she corrected. "You're seeing double."

"*Two* guns." There was very nearly a snap in the usually even voice. "Do not blame me because you are blind."

She sucked air in through her teeth, searched out and found Charlie in the crowd by the near bar, talking to a fat woman, and stared at him, considering.

"One gun," she repeated. "In the belt."

"Second gun," he instructed, still snapping. "Sleeve pocket, right-hand side. Also the belt itself is a weapon, in that it contains a device by which he may call for aid."

It was there—now she could see the flat outline of a

pellet gun in the pocket of his right sleeve. It would be a more serviceable weapon, she thought absently, than the pretty toy in his belt. She picked up her glass and tossed back the rest of her wine, heaving a huge sigh.

"I apologize," she said as he refilled her glass. "And I'll arrange to get my eyes checked in the morning."

THERE WERE TO BE fireworks over the ocean at midnight.

When the meaning of this announcement had been made clear to him by his youngest brother, the musician, there was nothing for it but that Edger must attend. Here was yet another manifestation of what he was pleased to name the Art Ephemeral. Only think of something made but that it may unmake!

Selector and Sheather had no interest in this display of art and made known their joint desire to walk about the city and see what wonders unfolded. This decided, they took their leave of the rest of the party, who each had another glass of whatever it was they were drinking, to pass the time until midnight.

"Would you bear me company tomorrow morning, brother?" Val Con asked Handler. "I've an errand to run, and your assistance would be valuable to me."

Handler inclined his head. "I am at the service of my brother's brother."

"An errand, young brother?" Edger asked. "Of an artistic nature, perhaps?"

Val Con laughed. "Hardly. It only seems to me that Miri and I will soon require transportation and I wish to arrange for it before the moment is upon us."

"My brother is wise. But know that our ship, which is at dock at the so-named Station Prime in orbit about this planet, is at your command, should you have need." He paused, his large, luminous eyes on the small form of his brother. "You are an honored member of the Clan, Val Con yos'Phelium Scout. Do not forget."

Val Con froze in the act of placing his glass on the table, then completed the action slowly. "You are too generous. I am made glad by your goodness and thank you. But I do not think we will need to commandeer your ship, Edger."

"Nonetheless," the *T'carais* said, quaffing beer, "remember that it is yours at the speaking of a word, should the need arise."

"I will remember," his brother promised softly.

"It is sufficient," Edger announced. "Now then, who accompanies me to this fireworks display?"

"I shall, elder brother," Handler offered, finishing off his beer in a swallow.

Miri smothered a yawn. "I'm sorry, Edger, but I'm so tired I'm afraid I'd go to sleep in the middle and fall into the ocean."

"Ah. But that would not happen," Edger told her, "for your brothers would surround and protect you. If you are very tired, however, it would be wisdom to return to your room and sleep. That is, unless you long to see this wonder?"

"Fireworks? I seen fireworks before. Guess I can miss this batch."

"Have you so, indeed? We will have to compare observations upon the morrow, if you would honor me?"

He heaved his bulk to a standing position, extending an arm to steady Handler, who appeared to have drunk one beer too many.

Miri stifled another yawn and grinned up at the hugeness of him. "Sure, we'll talk fireworks tomorrow. Why not?"

"It is well. Young brother, what will you?"

Val Con stood to help Miri ease back her chair and winced imperceptibly when she ignored the arm he offered. "I will go with Miri back to the rooms, I think," he told Edger. "I am tired, also."

"We will look forward to seeing you upon the morrow, then. Sleep deeply. Dream well."

Miri watched as Edger and Handler wove their majestic way across the crowded floor. That they did not bump into and seriously maim some innocent merrymaker, she noted, was not so much due to the elegance of their progress as it was to the vigilance of those same merrymakers. She grinned at her companion.

"Drunk as judges, as they say in my hometown."

"Why judges?" he wondered, allowing her to precede him around the table.

"Where I come from, Tough Guy, the only people dumb enough to be judges are drunks."

They threaded a less spectacular route through the bright swirls of people, arriving at the South door at the same time Charlie Naranshek came through the gateway of the two bars, on the second leg of his round.

"Aw, now, Roberta, you're not going to leave without one more dance, are you?"

Her brother, walking at her shoulder, spun quickly

and neatly, his eyes locking with Charlie's. She turned more slowly, grinned, and shook her head.

"Charlie, I'm beat! Exhausted. Done in." She waved a tiny hand at the noisy crowd. "Whyn't you go find yourself a live one?"

"Am I gonna see you again?" he asked, putting as much schmaltz as he could manage into the question.

She laughed and took her brother's arm, turning him with her toward the door. "If you look hard. Take care of yourself, Charlie."

"You do the same, Roberta," he told the empty doorway, and turned back to finish his beat.

✦ CHAPTER NINE ✦

A COFFEE POT and a tea pot, with attendant pitchers, bowls, spoons, and cups, had been set out with a plate of biscuits on the table by the two softest chairs in the common room. Miri laughed when she saw them and moved in that direction.

"Whoever said there ain't guardian angels is a filthy liar," she said, pouring herself a cup of coffee. "Want some?"

He nodded. "Tea, please, though."

"Coffee ain't good enough for you?" she demanded, switching pots and juggling cups.

"I don't really like coffee," he said, taking the chair with the best view of the door. He accepted his cup with a smile.

"You, my man, are a maniac." She sank into the chair opposite, sighing deeply. "How much did we *drink*?"

He regarded his tea doubtfully, judged it too hot to drink, and set the cup on the table. "Three bottles between us."

"Three! No wonder I'm acting like a lackwit knownothing. Oh, my aching head tomorrow—or is it tomorrow, now?"

"In a few minutes." He sharpened his gaze upon her face, picking out the tight muscles around her eyes, the smile held in place by will, not pleasure. . . .

As if she felt the intensity of his study, she moved her head sharply, tossing her hair behind a bare shoulder. "You and me gotta talk."

"All right," he said amiably. "You start."

The full mouth flickered into a grin, then straightened. "I ain't going to Liad, Tough Guy. Straight dope. No lies. I like who I am. I like how I look. I don't *want* to be somebody else." She took a sip of coffee, made a face as she burned her tongue, and set the cup on the table.

"I know that probably sounds crazy to somebody's got three or four identities going at once—but, hell, I'm just a dumb hired gun. And that's what I want to stay. So thanks, but no thanks, for the generous offer. I appreciate it, but I can't approve it."

He sat at ease, eyes on her face, hands loosely draped over the arms of the chair, ankles crossed before him.

After a time, she leaned forward. "Ain't you gonna take your turn?" she asked softly.

He lifted a brow. "I was waiting for the rest of it."

"You were," she said, without any particular inflection. She sighed. "Okay, then, the rest of it is this: I'm grateful for your help—which has been substantial and timely. I know I would've been a deader if you hadn't come along. I owe you a life, and I can't pay except to give you yours by splitting. Now.

"So, tomorrow I'll get my cash from Murph and then I'll walk out, easy and slow, with nobody the wiser. I don't need a car, so you can let poor Handler off the hook. And

I *sure* don't need a spaceship, so Edger can relax." She picked up her cup, took a less scalding swallow, and continued.

"I think that—with your help—the Juntavas is off the trail for the time being. I should be able to get off-world before they know I'm missing. I can handle it from here, okay? I've played singles odds my whole life long and I've managed to make it this far. . . ."

In the chair across from her, he had closed his eyes. As she let her voice drift to silence his lashes flicked up and he sighed.

"Miri, if you follow your plan as outlined, your chance of getting off-world is less than two percent. One chance in fifty. Your chance of being alive this time tomorrow is perhaps point three: thirty percent—three chances in ten. Your chance of being alive the day after falls by a factor of ten."

"So you say!" she started, anger rising.

"So *I* say!" he overrode with a snap. "And *I* say because *I* know! Did I tell you I was highly trained? Specially trained? One of the benefits is the ability to calculate—to render odds, if you will—based on known factors and subconsciously and unconsciously noted details, extrapolating on an immense amount of data I have noted. If I say you will likely be dead tomorrow evening if you leave without my aid, believe it, for it is *so*."

"Why the *hell* should I?"

He closed his eyes and took a very deep breath. "You should believe it," he said, and each word was distinct, as if he were following a ritual, "because I have said it and it is true. Since you seem to demand it, I will swear it." His eyes snapped open, captured and held hers. *"On the Honor of Clan Korval, I, Second Speaker, Attest This Truth."*

That was a stopper. Liadens rarely mentioned the honor of their Clan: it was a sacred thing. To swear on the honor of the Clan said they meant business, down-and-dirty, one-hundred-percent-business, no matter what.

And the eyes that held hers—they were angry, even bitter; they were bright with frustration, but they told no lie. She flinched, the weight of his meaning falling onto her all at once. He *truly believes* you're gonna be dead tomorrow if you leave this menagerie, Robertson.

"Okay, you said it, and you believe it," she said, making a bid for some thinking time. "You'll understand if I find it a little hard to believe. I never met anyone who could foresee the future." It was scarcely an apology, nor did it appease him.

"I do not foresee the future. I merely take available data and calculate percentages." His voice was steel-edged and cold. "You are not a 'dumb hired gun,' I think, and I am puzzled by your insistence on behaving like one."

The crack of laughter escaped before she could stop it.

"Count score for Tough Guy," she directed some invisible umpire, then grew serious again. "You mind if I play with your odds-maker for a couple minutes? Just to satisfy myself? I might not be dumb, but I sure am stubborn."

He picked up his cup and settled back in the chair. "Very well. You may."

"What are the chances of Edger turning us in?"

"None whatsoever," he said immediately. "To be as exact as the calculations go, it is more likely that *I* would turn us in than Edger would—the answer closely approximates zero."

"Yeah?" she said, brows rising. "That's good to know. Edger's easy to be fond of, the big ox." After a short pause, she asked, "What were the chances I could've killed you, the first time we were together?"

He sipped tea, watching the numbers appear on the scoreboard behind his eyes, then tried to relay the data dispassionately.

"If you had tried while I was unconscious, on the order of point ninety-nine: approaching surety. After I regained consciousness, before you returned my gun, and assuming that your own survival was a goal: perhaps point one five—fifteen chances in one hundred. Assuming your own survival was *not* a prime consideration, the odds would have approached point three—nearly one third chance of success."

He paused, sipped more tea, looked at the figures his head developed for him, and continued the analysis.

"Once you returned my weapon to me, your chance of success dropped to something close to point zero three, if you wished me dead, no matter what. Three percent, by the way, is a significantly higher chance than most soldiers would have against me, but you have speed, as well as excellent sense of location and hearing. Also, I do not believe that you would underestimate me because of my size, as other opponents have done."

He might have gone on—the figures *did* interest him. He found that her chance of surviving the first Juntavas attack had been as high as twenty percent, had he not shown up. The chance of her living through the second wave was much lower.

"Wait," she said, interrupting these discoveries. "That means you *let* me hold you. Why?"

"I did not wish to kill you. You were not a threat to my mission, nor to myself, nor to any of the projects I have been trained—"

"I'm obliged," she said, cutting him off. She poured coffee and settled back carefully, cup cradled in her fingers, her gray eyes on his face. "What odds that Charlie guy could have killed me down on the dance floor?"

He sighed, closed his eyes, and added several conscious variables to the equations.

"Discounting Edger and his kin, who are more aware than many people credit, and recalling that the weapon is new to you, but that you are a skilled soldier and he a mere policeman or security guard . . . During the time I was not in the room there was a point four chance of him wounding you, a point three chance of your being severely wounded or incapacitated, and a point two—or twenty percent— chance that an attack would have succeeded. All of these are first attacks with a handgun. With the Clutch present, he would have had no opportunity to follow up."

He opened his eyes, drank tea, and closed his eyes again, concentrating. It had been a long time since he'd done full odds this way.

"Once I re-entered the room his chance of wounding you dropped to about one chance in twenty—perhaps four point nine percent."

"Think a lot of yourself, doncha?" She frowned and

leaned forward a bit in the chair. "But, Tough Guy, what're the odds he *would* have?"

He moved his shoulders, unaccountably irritated. "Insufficient data. I don't know who he is or why he asked you to dance. He was armed with a hidden weapon, and although he is not a young man he is in good shape, has quick reflexes, and excellent eye use: a trained guard of *some* kind. That does not make him a murderer, it is true. But, in your precarious position, adding anything to the odds for the other side is very foolish."

"But," she insisted, "he *could* have asked me to dance because he thought I was cute and he wanted to dance."

Val Con nodded and poured himself some tea.

"You don't think so," she said. "Why not?"

"Something . . . a hunch, you'd call it."

"I see. And a hunch is different than that damn in-skull computer?"

He nodded again, pushing at his hair. "Hunches saved me a lot of times—perhaps my life—when I was a Scout: guesses, made with minimal information, or just feelings. The Loop is different—it takes a definite course of action or concern to trigger it. A hunch might simply make me uneasy of a certain cave, or wary of thin ice . . . It's not something I can see behind my eyes, plain and certain."

"Sure," she murmured. "It's obvious." She threw back the rest of her coffee as if it were kynak and sat the cup down on the table with a tiny *click.*

"Well, then," she began again. "Do you remember when we started our souls on the way to damnation by burning up that imported brandy?"

He nodded, smiling.

"How safe were we? The TP was all around, waiting for you. . . ." She was watching him very closely, Val Con saw; he was puzzled.

"Once we reached the lobby, there was virtually no chance that we would be recognized. Pete didn't know who he was looking for—a faceless voice on the comm? The last time we'd met in person I'd had a blond head, blue eyes, and glasses on my face. You and I could have walked across the lobby without danger, I believe. No one would have stopped us. In fact, they would have been happy to have us out so quickly."

"But you knew Edger and his gang were going to be there."

He laughed. "I had no idea that Edger was within light-years! That was coincidence, neither deducted nor felt. It is also why the Loop is not one-hundred-percent accurate: I could trip on a piece of plastic trash and break my neck."

"Well, that's a relief," she said, and he could see her relax. "I was starting to think you were superhuman, instead of just souped-up." Her mouth twisted. "Tough Guy?"

And what was *this,* he wondered, when things had been easing between them? "Yes."

"What are my chances—now—of killing, maiming, or just plain putting you out of commission on any average day? Do you have enough information to run that one?"

He did, of course: The equation hung, shining, behind his eyes. He willed it away.

"You have no reason to do any of those things. I have helped you and desire to continue helping you."

"I'm curious. If I had to," she persisted, eyes on his face. "Indulge me."

The equation would not be banished. It hung, glowing with a life of its own, in his inner eye. He combed the hair back from his face. "I do not *wish* to kill you, Miri."

"I appreciate the sentiment, but that ain't an answer."

He said nothing, but leaned over to place his cup gently upon the table, keeping his eyes away from hers.

"I want those numbers, spacer!" Her voice crackled with command.

He lifted an eyebrow, eyes flicking to her face, and began to tell her the facts that she needed to know before the figures were named, or acted upon.

"The data is very complex. You have much less chance now than before, I believe: I am too familiar with your balance, your walk, your eye movement, your inflections, and your strength for you to surprise me by very much. The fact that you have asked this question reduces your chances significantly. That you have seen me in action, know of the Loop, and are esteemed by me increases your chances—but not, I think, as much as they have been reduced." He drew a deep breath, let it out slowly, and continued, keeping his voice emotionless.

"So, the answer is that you would have, in a confrontational situation, approximately two chances in one hundred of killing me; three chances in one hundred of injuring me seriously. In a nonconfrontational situation your chances are much higher than before: I trust you and might err.

"On the other hand, your chance of *surviving* an attack on me by more than five minutes is significantly lower now

.han before—it would be a somewhat emotional event for both of us—and if it occurred anywhere within the ken of the Clutch it is likely that you would die over a period of days, were you to survive the immediate assault."

She sat very still, hunched forward in the chair. Her eyes dropped away from his to study the pattern of the carpet, and she took a deep, deep breath.

He sat frozen, also, until he was certain of the emotion he had seen in her eyes. It was not something he had seen in her before, and that it should be there now sent a cold thrust of something unnamable through his chest and belly.

Moving with quick silence he came out of the chair and went to one knee before her, slanting his eyes upward to her face, extending a hand, yet not touching her.

"And now, you are afraid."

She winced at the remorse in his voice, shook her head, and sat up straighter.

"I asked for it, didn't I?" She looked at him for a long moment, noting the wrinkle of concern around his eyes and the grim line of his mouth.

He doesn't *know*, she thought suddenly. He doesn't understand what he's been saying. . . .

On impulse, she reached out and brushed the errant lock of hair from his eyes. "But," she said carefully, "I ain't afraid of *you.*"

She stood, then, suddenly aware of her finery, the ring on her hand, the gifts, the confusion, and her early-evening plan of waking with him in the morning.

She rounded the chair, heading for her room.

Val Con rose to his feet, watching her go.

At the door, she turned, then paused as she saw the expression on his face. She waited an extra heartbeat as she thought she perceived the veriest start of a move in her direction, a flicker of—but that quickly it was gone. His eyes were green and formal.

"Good-night, Val Con."

He bowed the bow between equals. "Good-night, Miri."

The door sighed shut behind her. A moment later, he heard the lock hum to life.

⊹ CHAPTER TEN ⊹

IT WAS COLD and she shivered in the depths of the old wool shirt. It was a good shirt, with hardly any holes in it, a gift from her father in a rare moment of concern for his only child—brought on, indeed, by an even rarer moment of actually noticing her. She was so little, so frail-looking. Hence the shirt, which she wore constantly, inside and out, over her other clothes, sleeves rolled up to her wrists, untucked tail flapping around her knees.

It was damp, too, along with the cold—typical for Surebleak's winter. It was, in fact, rather too cold for a twelve-year-old girl to be out and walking, no matter how fine a shirt she possessed.

The wind yanked her hair and she pulled the shirt's collar up, tucking her pigtails inside. She unrolled the sleeves a little bit and pulled her hands inside. The wind blew some more and she laughed, pretending to be warm.

It was a good day, she thought, turning down Tyson Alley. She'd spent it running errands for Old Man Wilkins and had an entire quarter-bit in her pocket for wages. Her mother had the cough again, and the money would buy tea to soothe her throat.

The hand fell onto her shoulder out of nowhere, spinning her to the right. The blow to the side of her face sent her reeling into a splintering wall, dazed.

"Well, now, here's a nice tidbit, Daphne, ain't it? The buyers'll give us a sum for this one, won't they?" It was a man's voice, thick with dreamsmoke.

Miri shook her head, trying to clear it. Two figures wove before her sight—the man towering over her, his hand completely encircling the arm he held her by. His beard had once been yellow, but long neglect and an addiction to the 'smoke had turned it blackish and matted. He was grinning emptily. A gun hung on the right side of his worn belt.

"Scrawny as it is?" The woman stepped beside her mate, dressed like him in greasy leathers, but with a ragged blanket around her shoulders, serving as a cloak. "Besides, the buyers want 'em ready to use now, not in five Standards." She turned away. "Give it a couple slaps to scramble its memory and let's get out of this damn wind."

"Want to use 'em now? We can use this one now, Daphne. Yes, yes, we can—Look!"

He moved his other hand to pull at her fine shirt, tearing buttons and cloth. He yanked it down over her arms and flung it into the frozen mud against the wall. "Look, Daphne," he repeated, reaching out to tear at her second shirt.

Miri dove, grabbing for the gun in the shabby holster. His hand swooped for her neck, but missed, grabbing a pigtail instead. She screamed, twisting around like a snake, burying her teeth in the filthy leather behind his knee.

He yelled in shock and loosed his grip on her hair. She dove for the gun again, pulling it free with one hand as he swung in a swipe that bowled her sideways, bruising her ribs against the wall. He roared, and she saw the foot coming toward her; she swung with the butt of the gun and rolled, fumbling with the safety.

She heard another roar somewhere above her as she came to her knees and raised the gun, both hands locked around the grip.

"You goddamn brat! I'll brain—"

Miri pulled the trigger.

He staggered, eyes widening. She fired again, and the left side of his face was mush. He began to topple, and she scrambled out of the way, coming to her feet to spin, bringing the gun up and pointing it at Daphne, who was standing at the far wall, gaping, hands spread before her.

"Take it easy, kid," the woman started. Her voice was not steady.

Miri pulled the trigger. Again. And again.

The woman jerked with the first shot. The second slammed her against the wall. She was already sliding down with the third, and Miri thought she might have missed her mark.

Slowly, she let the gun fall to the mud. Gritting her teeth, she knelt at the man's side, avoiding as much of the blood as she could, and opened his pouch, snatching at the few plastic coins loose in the bottom.

The woman's pouch had more money in it. Miri took

it all, cramming it into the pocket of her trousers with the quarter-bit she'd earned that day.

She went back for the shirt, but when she bent to retrieve it, she began to shake. She started up, staring at the two corpses, her stomach churning. Gagging, she leaned over and threw up, then braced herself against the wall and shook some more.

Suddenly she heard excited voices, no doubt drawn by the gunfire, though in this part of town it was hardly a sound to wonder at.

Pushing away from the wall, Miri ran.

SHE WOKE, sweat-drenched and shaking.

Gods, but it had been a long time since that particular bogeyman had come back to haunt her. She forced herself to lie still in the wide, soft bed and breathe deeply until the shaking stopped. Then she rolled gently to the floor and padded across to the walldesk.

The clock told her it was morning. Latish morning. Arms crossed tightly over slight breasts, Miri went into the bathroom and turned on the cold water in the shower.

A VOICE cried out and woke him. He lay still, listening to the echo of the sound.

It had been his voice. The word: "Daria!"

Daria? A name, certainly. He lay quietly in the vast softness of the bed, eyes closed, waiting for his memory to provide the rest of it.

It was a time in coming. He dreamed so seldom, and he'd had to learn so *many* names. . . .

Daria dea'Luziam.

He weighed it in his mind, brows drawn together over closed eyes. But nothing else surfaced.

Irritated, he rolled sideways, snapping to his feet the instant he opened his eyes, and strode to the bathing area to splash cold water on his face.

Too much wine and too little sleep, he thought, rubbing dry with a towel. Much too little sleep. He caught sight of his reflection in the mirror above the sink and frowned into the face frowning there.

Daria?

Her image arose, finally, before his mind's eye: A slender woman his own height, dusky hair short and curling, eyes a vivid sapphire, laughing. Older than he, though not by so much.

The face in the mirror tightened and the frowning eyes widened slightly.

One year older, to the very day—she'd been eighteen to his seventeen. It was forbidden that those of the graduating class take lovers from the junior classes, but there had been ways, and they had found them. They had made plans. She would pass her Solo final testing—and spend the year before he passed his gaining Single Scout experience. Upon his graduation they would become a team. Such things were not unknown. And who better? She was at the head of her class, as he was at the head of his.

On the day she had departed for the Solo, she had kissed him, laughing, promising a triumphant return on their birthday, half-a-year distant.

But she had not returned on their birthday, and a search of the sector to which she had been sent eventually yielded a few random shards of metal and plastics which were thought to once have been components of a Scout ship.

Val Con shook his head sharply; he leaned close to the glass and looked into the depths of his own eyes.

You loved her! he accused himself. And you scarcely recall her name?

The eyes in the mirror returned his gaze, lucent and green.

After a time, he turned away and went to ask the valet for his clothes.

✦ CHAPTER ELEVEN ✦

IT FELT GOOD to be back in leathers, Miri reflected, yanking the scarf tight around her arm. She stood for a long moment, looking at the jumble of items on the counter before her: a polished stick, a blue and silver necklace, and a ring in the shape of a snake.

Hesitantly, she plucked up the necklace, folded it, and put it with the other treasures hidden in her pouch. The ring she slid back onto her left hand, smiling slightly, then she carried the stick with her into the bedroom.

She was nearly to the door when she caught sight of the wrongness and spun, knife flicking open, body ready to fight. When she saw that it was only a tray, holding a coffee pot, a cup, and a covered plate, reposing peacefully on the desk, she relaxed somewhat.

She frowned at herself, shaking her head, eyes moving from breakfast tray to door.

Locked. She had locked the door last might, and the telltale on the jamb informed her that it was locked right now.

Room service does not come into locked rooms.

Knife held ready, she approached the tray and looked cautiously down at its contents.

A curl of coffee-scented steam rose from the spout of the pot, and a breakfast of egg, roll, and broiled meat lay beneath the cover.

The note had been wedged between pot and cup.

She picked it up between thumb and forefinger—a single sheet of pearly hotel paper, folded in half, with her name written across it in a bold black backslant.

Frowning, she unfolded it, flipping the knife closed absently and thrusting it through her belt.

"Miri," the strong black characters read. "I have gone with Handler to procure a car and anticipate returning during the midafternoon. I will then accompany you on your visit to Murph and we will be on our way this evening. Enjoy your breakfast." At the bottom of the page marched several angular letters from another alphabet, spelling out what might have been his name.

Miri began to swear. She started in Liaden, which seemed appropriate to the occasion, switched to Terran, Aus-dialect, and moved methodically through Yarkish, Russ, Chinest, and Spanol. She flung the crumpled note to the tray, then shook her head and splashed coffee into the cup.

She drank while she paced, fuming; when she finished the cup, she clattered it back into its saucer. "Damn him to hell," she muttered, which left something to be desired as the climax to what had gone before. Turning her back on the cooling breakfast, she stamped to the door.

Edger and Sheather were standing near the 'chora, chatting loudly in their own tongue. Upon seeing her, Edger cut off his comment and raised a hand.

"My youngest of sisters! Good morning to you. I trust you slept well and profitably?"

"Well," she told him, smiling, "I slept. And you?"

"It is not yet time for us to sleep," Edger said. "Though it must be near, for I grow a bit yawnsome. Perhaps next month we will sleep for a space."

Miri blinked. "Oh." There was a movement to her right, and she turned to see Sheather shuffling forward, head bent at an uncomfortable-looking slant. He offered her something with his left hand.

She took it, wondering. It seemed to be a leather envelope of some kind, long and very thin, black like her leathers, but of a wonderful softness.

"For the blade you wore last evening," Sheather mumbled in his shy way. "It is my understanding that blades of that manufacture are metal, which is a substance much prone to rusting and edge-damage. It is important to protect it from such trauma. I regret that I was unable to offer you this last evening, but the youngest of my brother's brothers did not admit us to his thoughts.

"Please do not think us lacking in courtesy," he continued, "or suppose that we lament our brother's choice. It only sometimes comes about that the hastiness of human action leaves us at a loss." He bowed his head even lower, in what Miri suddenly understood as an effort to make himself shorter than she. "We wish you great joy and long, warm days."

She felt a sting in her eyes, touched, though parts of

this speech were somewhat confusing. "Thank you, Sheather. I'm—grateful. You and your brothers are very kind and I can't imagine you lacking in courtesy."

"Thank *you,*" Sheather replied, "and know that we look upon the flame of your being with awe and much affection." He straightened finally and backed away, nearly knocking over the omnichora.

Miri pulled the stick-knife from her belt. It slid easily into the soft sheath, which she hung on her left side, wondering as she did so if it was proper to cross-draw a knife.

"My sister?" Edger said. She turned to him with a smile. "My brother?"

He inclined his head. "It would honor me, were you to bear me company to the place of Justin Hostro's business. We are to collect our portion in advance this day, which is why I go hence. I would have you accompany me because it is clear that you are an accurate judge of humans, where it is very possible that I may not be.

"My brother, whom you call Handler, has raised the question of purpose for these flawed knives Justin Hostro would purchase. He quite properly asks what being deliberately orders flawed tools, stating that he will have none but? My brother is concerned by this behavior and feels that perhaps Justin Hostro is a thief, who will seek to cheat us of our purchase price."

Miri eyed him. "You want *me* to tell *you* whether this guy's a crook?"

"That," Edger replied, "is the essence."

She shrugged. "Do my best."

"It is sufficient. Let us go."

✧✧✧

CHARLIE NARANSHEK was not happy. He had expended a quantity of energy and lost quite a bit of sleep convincing himself that he did not have to report sighting the Kid and Turtle Gang by reason of the fact that be had not been on duty when the sighting occurred.

It was, after all, one of the silliest things he'd ever heard of. Turtles weren't desperate characters, just slow and funny. And the kids were just that—kids. A little bill-and-coo for brother and sister, maybe, but that wasn't the kind of thing the local force covered. Especially with a couple like this, who were from off-world.

Armed and dangerous. Sure. Somebody at Mixla 'quarters was having their little joke.

Having thus battered his conscience into submission, Charlie fell asleep, to be awakened moments later by his alarm. He stumbled through the morning routine, got to the station in time to pick up his partner and their cruiser and eased on down to the merchant's quarter to start the daily round.

As they turned the corner from Econsey into Surf, passing a snack bar and an amusement center, his partner suddenly sat up. "Hey, look at that!" he cried, pointing.

Charlie looked—and swore.

For there was a turtle coming out of the office of Honest Al's Rental Cars, with Al himself at his side. And trailing a few steps behind, in dark leathers and shirt, gun holstered efficiently on the right side of the belt, was brother Danny.

Still swearing, Charlie punched up the comm and called in the report.

✦✧✦

MIRI TOOK A DEEP BREATH of salty air and grinned up at Edger. "Nice day."

The *T'carais* paused to cast an eye skyward and test the air in a mighty inhalation. "I believe you may be right," he conceded. "The sky is bright and the air is fine, though not so fine as the air at home. But that is expected, and one would be churlish to deny other planets their days of prettiness, simply because they are not home."

She laughed and stretched her legs to more or less match his stride. "It might be a good idea," she commented, "to tell Mr. Hostro I'm your aide. If he's a fatcat, he'll figure that to mean 'bodyguard' and you'll gain some points."

"A good plan," Edger decided. "For it has come to my attention that it is profitable to proclaim one's consequence loudly when there is money involved."

Miri grinned and then wrinkled her nose as her elbow bumped the unaccustomed protuberance on her belt. "Edger?"

"Yes, my sister?"

"Edger, I ain't trying to be rude, but I think I better ask, 'cause I'm confused. Maybe I should've asked Sheather, but he's so shy. . . ."

"It is true," Edger said, "that my brother Sheather does not put himself forward as much as is perhaps desirable as one who would stride galaxies, but he is a thoughtful and meticulous individual, who seeks always to do what is proper." He looked down at her with luminous eyes. "Does our gift not please you?"

"Oh, no, it pleases me very much! But see—I don't know why I'm getting a gift at all and I'd hate for there to be a misunderstanding between us. 'Specially when it's so easy to open my big mouth and ask a question and hear what you got to say."

"My sister is wise," Edger announced as they rounded a corner and nearly bowled over two bejeweled ladies walking hand-in-hand in the opposite direction.

"Know then," he continued, not at all discomfited by the ensuing scramble, "that we have made you a gift to demonstrate our joy for and concurrence with our brother's choice of lifemate."

Miri blinked. "Which brother is that?"

"The youngest of my many, he whom you call Tough Guy."

"Right." She considered it. "Edger, did Tough Guy tell you he was going to—ah—marry me?"

"Alas, he did not, which I do not feel is like him. But I am persuaded that the matter slipped his mind, for he has no doubt been preoccupied with his art, planning, perhaps, his next composition." They rounded another corner, this time without incident.

"We were only made aware last evening, when it was seen he had given you the knife-within-a-stick, which he carried when first he came to us," he continued. "And then also was I assured that he had meant no insult by failing to speak, since he had chosen first to wed in our manner, with the gift of a blade. His own people, I believe, exchange gemstones or jewelry, which he gave later, in our presence."

"Hmmm. Is it okay for a person to take a lifemate

without telling *anybody* they were going to? Even the person they were going to marry?"

Edger considered it. "I have heard of such things among humans," he said after a time. "But I am certain that my brother would not behave in such a manner, for he is kind and would wish to make certain his attention was not repugnant."

She stopped, staring up at the bulk of him. Edger stopped as well, creating an effective block to traffic. People detoured around them.

"He's *what?*" She heard her voice crack and swallowed.

"My brother's heart is gentle," Edger said, his big voice surprisingly quiet. "He would hurt no being, nor thing, that was not his sworn enemy. Nor would he willingly cause distress. I have seen him to weep with one whose mate lay slain and comfort in his arms a babe nearly larger than himself. It is not possible that he would wed you without your knowledge and goodwill."

There was a long silence during which Miri kept her eyes closed and concentrated on breathing. Crazy, crazy, a voice in her head repeated. Crazy as the six of diamonds.

Edger's voice rumbled over her head and she opened her eyes to look up at him.

"And have you not found him so?"

She extended a hand and captured two of his three fingers. "I guess I don't know him that good," she said seriously and shook her head slightly, as if to clear it. "Thanks, Edger. I'm glad we could talk."

He inclined his massive head, allowing his fingers to remain within her grasp. "I, also," he said.

✦✦✦

"THAT'S OUR BOY!" Pete yelled, slapping the chief's shoulder.

The other man nodded and cut back into the net. "That appears to be him, Officer. Do not, repeat, *do not* approach the suspect. He is highly dangerous. We will be sending specialists from Headquarters. I want you to keep track of him, if it's possible without showing or risking yourselves. And find out where that turtle's staying. It's possible the girl's waiting there."

"Yes, sir," Charlie said, struggling manfully to keep his fume under wraps. "When do you think your specialists will be here, sir?"

"Three hours, at the outside," the chief said. "I'll get on the net to your Station commander and set up the timetable. You keep track of that boy. What'd you say they were doing?"

"They appear to be renting a car, sir. It might take 'em awhile, though, if they're looking for something the turtle can fit in, too."

"Right. Over—ah, Officer?"

"Sir?"

The chief considered Charlie's face rather more carefully than Charlie wished he would. "Just don't let them get in the car and drive away, Officer, okay? We want to clean this up fast, before the boy hurts somebody else." The chief leaned closer to the screen. "Just so you know—Charlie, isn't it?"

"Yes, sir." Charlie restrained himself from hitting the cutoff toggle and gave the chief his best wide-eyed wonder look.

"Well, Charlie, I know you're thinking that this boy doesn't look like much. Shows how deceptive looks can be. He's responsible for the deaths of five people in a robbery in Mixla City. Lined 'em up and shot 'em—just like that." He snapped his fingers. One of 'em was a little girl—eight years old, Charlie."

Charlie made appropriate noises, which wasn't really necessary, since his partner was making enough for both of them.

"So be careful, but keep a line on him. Remember that he's a Liaden—don't have to tell you how slippery *that* bunch is, do I?" The chief nodded at the screen. "Carry on, officers." He touched the disconnect.

Pete whistled in admiration. "Wish I'd thought of that."

The chief grinned, leaned forward, and punched the line for Econsey 'quarters. "Pretty good, wasn't it? A little atrocity goes a long way, Peter." He frowned at the busy signal from the board, cleared the number, and tried again.

"Better get your guys ready. Fifteen of the best ought to do it. I'll add twenty Mixla cops and twenty from Econsey." The line was still busy and he punched the disconnect. "Have 'em here in an hour. Can do?"

"Can do."

THE THIRD CAR had possibilities. The little guy was leaning over the engine; the slender hand hooked around the edge of the fender was all that kept him from tumbling headfirst into the workings. With the other hand he tested connections, checked fluid levels, and poked at the various brain-boxes. This went on for some time, while Honest Al and Handler waited, Al trying not to wring his hands.

Finally he was through, having ascertained whatever it was he had been trying to ascertain. He slid off the fender and rubbed the palms of both hands down leathered thighs.

"The engine is sound," he said, speaking over Al's head to the turtle, "and of a strength sufficient to our purpose."

"Oh, yes," Honest Al broke in eagerly. "It's one of the earlier models, when there was a demand for speed *and* size. It's not as new as the other two vehicles we discussed, but certainly a very fine piece of equipment."

The little man smiled at him. "Age does not matter in this case. Utility does. You see the size of the *T'caraisiana'ab*. The others of the Mission are built on comparable proportions." He nodded at the car. "I think that this vehicle might serve the Mission well. However, there are one or two other requirements."

"Certainly, certainly," Honest Al said, beaming. "This car was at the top of its line. Royalty, she was."

The little man smiled again and waved a hand, indicating the interior. "One concern—I believe the seats are adjustable?"

"Why, of course."

"Of course," the customer echoed. "But are they individually adjustable, I wonder?" He pulled open a door.

"The case is this," he murmured. "While most of the Mission are rather—large and will require sufficient space in which to ride, there are others of the Interface Team who are somewhat smaller. One such as myself, for instance," he said, smiling at Al, "would be hard put to drive this vehicle, were all the seats adjusted to accommodate the prime members of the Mission."

"There is this control here." Al demonstrated, varying the heights of each of the six individual seats, as well as moving them back and forth.

"Ah," the little man said in admiring accents. "That is excellent."

"And, of course, there is a private comm, plus an auxiliary band, whereby you may monitor weather reports, stock market closings. . . ." He twisted the dial as he spoke, demonstrating, while his customer murmured appreciatively.

"There is also, in this model, an environmental control—here—if their excellencies prefer, perhaps, a richer oxygen mix? More humidity? And this control polarizes the windows, if they find our light uncomfortable."

"Royalty, indeed," the little man said.

"And here," Al said, tapping a small dial set by itself in the far corner of the board, "is the emitter, which we will set to emit the proper code for the status of your Mission. In this way the police need only direct a reading beam at your vehicle to discover that you are persons of importance and should not be impeded."

"Wonderful," the other said, smiling. "I am certain that this vehicle precisely suits our need." He stepped back, frowned suddenly, and stood gazing at the mint-green exterior while Al's stomach sought refuge in his shoes.

"I am not sure that this color is as pleasing as it might be."

Honest Al's stomach returned to its original location. "How foolish of me!" He motioned to the little man, who attended him once again at the control board. "This device here—we manipulate it so. Now look."

The customer did as he was bid and, upon discovering that the exterior was now a brilliant yellow, grinned like a boy.

"Do you find that color pleasing?" Al asked hopefully.

"Let me speak with the *T'caraisiana'ab*." He moved away to where that person still stood gazing absently at the vehicle under discussion.

"We are almost decided, brother," Val Con said, switching to a liquid mix of Clutch and Liaden, "and I thank you for your kindness in accompanying me. Would you now care to watch the exterior of the vehicle and tell me when it has achieved a color that gives you pleasure?"

Handler rested his large eyes on the small form of his now-youngest brother. "I to choose the color?" he cried, gladdened. "It is you who are kind, brother, and I who am honored. I shall, indeed, watch and call out to you when the shade pleases me."

The little man came back to the car, throwing a smile to Al as he passed, and sat in the driver's chair. He manipulated the proper device.

The exterior of the car faded from bright yellow to gold to amber to bronze to tan to brown to sienna to—

A big voice boomed in a tongue Al did not understand, startling him out of his stupor. The vehicle before him was of a hue known to antiquarians as "fire-engine red."

The little man climbed out of the driver's chair and beheld what he had wrought, eyes narrowed slightly, as if he were staring into too bright a light. His gaze caught Al's and he shrugged.

"Ah, well. We will rent this car," he said, coming to Al's side and taking his arm. "The Mission is to be on-world for one local year. Let us pay you now for two years' rent, so that you have security on your investment. Is that satisfactory?"

Honest Al blinked, letting himself be gently guided back to his office. "Oh, yes," he managed. "Very satisfactory."

"Good. I am right in assuming that you will be able to adjust the emitting device now, so that we may drive the vehicle away?"

Al nodded, bereft of words.

"Excellent," the little man said amiably. "Now, about your fee. Would you prefer Terran bits or Liaden cantra?"

JUSTIN HOSTRO HAD a nice operation, Miri thought. His office was nearly as classy as Sire Baldwin's, though the taste in wall art and knickknacks was different. More cosmopolitan, she thought. Baldwin had been a devotee of the Art Terran, primarily, though an original Belansium had hung in his library.

There were *two* Belansiums in Justin Hostro's inner office, each depicting a planet seen from space. The quality that made each a treasure was the evocation of the feeling of actually being in space, with this world hanging before you, filling the big window on the obdeck.

Miri moved her attention from the paintings to Justin Hostro, seated comfortably behind his rubbed steel desk.

"This is the sum we have agreed upon. Please count it

and be certain that we have not misunderstood each other," he was saying.

Edger complied with this request, opening the pouch he was offered and removing the clear plastic rolls of coins. Liaden money, Miri saw, keeping control of her face. A bloody *fortune* in Liaden money. And this was just the fifty percent up front. For knives guaranteed to break.

Edger split the rolls into piles of seven each and brushed each pile back into the carrying pouch. He inclined his head. "The sum is correct in that it is the first half of the total agreed upon."

"Good." Mr. Hostro smiled and slid a sheet of printout from the folder before him. "This is the list of locations for the first shipments. I desire that three hundred go to each site, for a total first shipment of 3,000 blades. To aid you, the document lists each location by its Trade designation and by the local name." He passed the sheet to Edger, who took it carefully and scanned it.

"This shall be done," he said, folding the sheet and placing it in the pouch with the money, "within the next year Standard, as we discussed. The first shipment is required at the first location within three months Standard, is that correct?"

"That is correct," said the man behind the desk.

"Then," Edger said, rising and inclining his head, "we understand each other very well."

Mr. Hostro stood also, bowing his royalty-to-royalty bow. "I am pleased that it is so. It is rare to find camaraderie in business dealings. May we deal long and profitably together."

"May we so indeed," Edger replied. "It is very pleasurable, doing business with you. I hope in the future we shall deal as well." He began his turn and Miri, in her role as aide, moved to the door, going through first to check the hallway. Edger came after, and the door closed behind them.

Justin Hostro sat down behind his desk, the tiniest of lines between his fine brows. "Matthew."

His aide approached the desk. "Yes, Mr. Hostro?"

"That woman, Matthew. I feel that I have seen her face before. Perhaps in our files?" He made a steeple of his impeccable fingers. "Yes. In our files. Recently. Find out who she is, please."

"At once, Mr. Hostro." The aide removed himself to the file station in the corner of the room and began the search.

THE MANUAL WAS OLD and hard to read. Al squinted at the screen, trying to make out the index. White letters wavered on a flickering gray background, defeating his eyes. He sighed and looked apologetically at the little man, glad that the turtle had remained outside.

"Perhaps I'd better call the Registration Office. My eyes aren't as young as they used to be."

The little man was all concern. "Trouble, sir? Here, let me see if I can make it out. Of course: 'Diplomatic Uses, Y'" He manipulated the advance. "I'll have it in just a moment, if you would care to write it down."

Honest Al scrabbled under the counter and came up with a piece of torn pink cardboard and an age-old stylus.

"Here it is," his customer said. "Much easier than

bothering the Registration Office, don't you think? The code we need is: DY3-9736-X-7588-T."

"DY3," Al read back, "9736-X-7588-T."

"Correct."

"Well, that's fine. I'll just go out and program the emitter and you're on your way. Another five minutes, sir." He paused and made as much of a bow as his paunch would allow. "Thank you, sir, for your help."

The little man smiled. "It was no trouble," he murmured, turning off the manual. He waited until Al was safely outside before he spun the wheel back.

"EDGER, I'm gonna leave you here, if that's okay. Got some business to take care of."

"It is permitted," Edger replied. "When will you return to us?"

Miri shrugged. "In a little while, I think. Nothing complicated, but it's gotta be taken care of."

"I understand. Go and resolve your business, young sister. I look forward to the time when we shall see each other again."

She grinned, shaking her head, and moved off across the street. She turned around once to wave, but Edger wasn't looking.

THE BRIGHT RED CAR pulled against the curb half a block ahead and discharged its passenger.

Charlie pulled off to the side and likewise discharged his partner, reminding him that his only job was to keep the turtle in sight and stay out of sight himself. Then it was time for Charlie to be after the red car again.

The driver of the car did not seem to be aware that he was being followed. He drove safely and within the speed limit to a self-service lot in the seedy edge of town backing onto the hyatts. He chose a parking space facing the exit and got out to deposit the proper number of bits in the box.

Charlie pulled the cruiser across the nose of the red car and popped out. By the time he got around to the front, the driver of the other car was leaning against the door, arms crossed over his chest, waiting.

Charlie approached unhurriedly, nodding. "Danny."

"Officer Naranshek," the boy returned with distant politeness. Charlie shook his head and sighed.

"Thought it might interest you to know," he said, "that the cops have an All-Point out on you and your sister. Calling you armed and dangerous." He glanced at his wrist. "In about two hours the big boys from Mixla 'quarters'll be here to round the two of you up."

Danny nodded. "Thank you. I appreciate your concern."

"Yeah, well, you can stop appreciating it," Charlie growled, "cause it ain't for you, it's for your sister,"

"I know," came the even reply. "But I am grateful, nonetheless."

"Are you?" He took a breath. Ah, what the hell. "Mixla Chief says you shot five people there, one of 'em a baby girl."

Both eyebrows rose. "Lies. But I thank you for that information, as well."

"I *know* he's lying," Charlie said irritably. "But the point is, nobody else will. Human nature just naturally wants to expect the worst. More fun hunting lions than is pussycats."

The boy smiled faintly, unfolded his arms, and moved away from the car. "You'd best leave. It would be very dangerous, I think, if you were seen talking to me. Thank you again." He walked around the back of the car, heading across the lot toward the hyatts.

Charlie got in his car and backed it around. As he pulled out of the lot he looked in the mirror and was in time to see the boy vault to the top of the fence and drop to the walk on the other side, sure as a cat.

"MR. HOSTRO?"

"Yes, Matthew?"

"If you would step over here a moment, sir, I believe I have the woman's file."

Justin Hostro slid back from his desk and walked leisurely to the file station to lean over his aide's shoulder.

"Yes, I believe so. Excellent likeness, don't you think, Matthew? Miri Robertson." He laid his hand lightly on the other man's shoulder. "Fax me a copy of the file, please. I feel I should review the case before deciding upon our course of action."

✦ CHAPTER TWELVE ✦

THE YOUNG MAN in the alcove had never been happier in his life. Being endowed with a poetic cast of mind, he found that the conceit pleased him and set out to expand upon it as he sat next to the potted melekki tree, waiting for his beloved to appear.

Yes, life was a fine thing: pleasant slow days easing one by one into passionate nights filled with lovemaking, wine, and talk. Sylvia was a beautiful woman, loving, gentle, and giving. She was also quite wealthy—but that was hardly to be thought of. His feelings were such that they transcended mere finance.

There was a rustle from the back entrance to the alcove, and the young man smiled. The delightful creature was trying to sneak up on him! He eased out of his chair and turned to meet her.

The leaves shielding the back entrance parted and she stepped quietly through, right hand near her gun. "Hey, Murph. What's new?"

The smile fled, and his eyes made a fair attempt to leave their sockets. "*Sarge?*"

Both brows rose and were hidden by her bangs. "You weren't expecting me? I'm sure I wrote." She tipped her head, gray eyes thoughtful. "You look good," she said cordially. "Prosperous. No worries, either, huh? Sitting with your back to the door."

"There's more than one door," he told her, trying to ignore the sick feeling in his stomach. "Besides, I heard you coming."

She came another couple of paces into the alcove, and the look on her face was one he knew of old. He tightened his gut, determined to take his chewing-out like a trooper.

"You heard me coming, you stupid groundhog," she said, dividing her attention between his face and the portion of the lobby she could see over his shoulder, "because I let you hear me coming! And if I wasn't feeling softhearted today, you wouldn't be around to jaw off any of your damn guff right now." She pointed to the chair he had so lately quit. "Sit."

He sat.

She hauled another chair around to where she could keep tabs on the lobby, Murph, and the back entrance, then eased down and laid her hand alongside the gun. Leaning back, she considered him silently until he began to sweat.

"Look, Sarge," he began, thankful that his voice did not crack. "I've been meaning to make that bank transfer. . . ."

"Yeah?" she said interestedly. "Well, I'm glad to know you had such good intentions. Shows you had upbringing." She absentmindedly caressed the butt of her gun with one

finger. "Also shows you're a thief, my man, 'cause I st.
ain't got my money."

"I can explain—"

She held up a hand. "Is it *very* rude to point out that
explanations buy no kynak?"

He licked his lips. "I'll make the transfer."

"Hey, you don't have to do that," she said reasonably.
"Now I'm here, you can just give it to me in cash."

"*Cash?*" This time his voice did crack.

"Cash."

"Sarge, I don't have that much cash on me." He was
beginning to feel desperate, as well as trapped.

"No? Too bad. How much *do* you have on you?"

"About four hundred fifty bits." It was useless to lie to
her; he had learned that lesson well. "Most of it's in the
room."

There was a short silence. "Okay," she said. "I'll take
the four-fifty in cash and the rest in trade." She held out
a tiny hand, palm up. "Earrings."

"*What?* Sarge, look, come with me to the room, I'll
give you the cash I've got and call in the transfer for the
balance, okay?"

She sighed deeply, regretfully. He swallowed hard.

"Angus," she said earnestly, "don't push your luck."
She motioned with the outstretched hand. "Earrings.
Now."

He slowly slid the hoops out of his ears and laid them
gently in her palm. She closed her fingers around them,
her gray eyes moving down his person. Murph made a
convulsive movement with his hand, trying to hide the
ring in the clench of his fist.

Her eyes caught on the movement; she nodded and extended her hand. "Ring."

"Dammit, Sarge—" he started.

She raised her eyes to his.

He gulped and began again, more quietly. "Look, not the ring, okay? It was a gift from my—from Sylvia." She did not look impressed. "Look, it's my troth ring—more sentimental value than pawn value."

The outheld hand did not waver. "Here's the deal, Angus: I get the ring; you get to live long enough to enjoy the girl. Give."

Tears standing in his eyes, he pulled it from his finger and laid it in her palm.

Her brows rose at the weight of it. "Platinum set with ponget and sapphire? Some sentiment." The ring vanished the way of the ear hoops as she continued her inventory of his person.

"Let's see. . . ."

THE CLOCK IN THE LOBBY indicated that it was somewhat later than mid-afternoon. Val Con summoned a lift, rode to the third floor, and entered the common room by the hall door, braced for a blast of bad temper.

His brothers were seated in a loose ring in the center of the room, the sonorous phrases of their native tongue striking him with the force of thunder overhead as he closed the door.

Edger raised a hand to acknowledge his presence, but did not otherwise interrupt the flow of his speech. The low table to one side of the group supported heroic amounts of fruit and beer, as well as a new wheel of cheese and an unopened bottle of wine.

Miri was not in the common area. The door to her bedroom was closed.

He felt a slight prickle at the back of his scalp and wandered over to the door. Unlocked. He crossed the threshold cautiously.

The bed had been made and the room was professionally tidy, devoid of Miri. Likewise the bathroom. He left the room rapidly and made a whirlwind search of the rest of the suite, though he was already certain she was not within. The prickle at the back of his head had become full alarm.

Back in the common room, he approached the grouped Clutch and stood before Edger to make the obeisance that indicated he had urgent need to speak.

Edger responded with a flutter of the hand that told his brother that he would be heard next. There was nothing for it but to bow thanks and move away.

Choosing a piece of fruit and a chunk of crumbly golden cheese, Val Con hoisted himself to the edge of a higher table on the outskirts of the group and settled to wait his turn with what patience he could recruit, feet swinging above the floor.

SYLVIA SMILED at the young man and inclined her head as she passed by. She knew she was in her best looks, and knew that the costume she wore enhanced those looks. No assembly-line dresses out of the valet for her! This dress had been custom-made by an artist, and every line proclaimed it.

She paused to scan the lobby for the tall, athletic form of her betrothed, very nearly missing him in the alcove of greenery in which he sat. Smiling, she started across to him, then, seeing that he was not alone, she paused in the shelter of a pillar to study the situation.

His companion was a tiny woman, dressed in what seemed to be well-used leather clothing of the sort worn by laborers on space vessels or mercenary soldiers. Her hair was red, braided and wrapped around her head like a gaudy copper crown.

Angus had been a mercenary, Sylvia remembered; it had been a brief episode during his late adolescence. He had mentioned no friends from that period of his life, but perhaps this small person was such a one? Sylvia made as if to continue on her way, determined to be gracious to her fiancé's uncouth acquaintance.

Angus pulled the chain from around his neck and handed it to the small woman, who dropped it into her pouch.

Sylvia froze.

Angus was being *robbed!*

Outrage rose in Sylvia's breast. *No one* robbed her or hers. It was not done. Obviously, this small person badly desired a lesson in etiquette.

She stayed a moment longer, committing every detail of the woman's attire and person to memory, then turned on her heel and marched to the bank of public comms on the far side of the lobby.

She reversed the charges, since she never carried change, and punched in the code for her father's private office line.

His aide answered the summons immediate[...] inclining his head slightly as he recognized her.

"Hello, Matthew," she said, always gracious. "Please let me speak to my father instantly. It is quite important."

"Of course, Ms. Hostro."

"OK, Intaglia, take your group down to the entertainment level—I want the exits and the lift bank watched.

"Kornblatt, get this lobby cordoned off—I want somebody on the central comm station and somebody else on central power.

"Smith, you and me and this bunch here are gonna watch the lobby lift bank. Remember, now, all of you! These are highly dangerous individuals. We would prefer to have them alive, but shoot to kill if you have to. Stations!"

"WELL, YOUNGER BROTHER, I am pleased you have returned. This my brother has been describing your artistry in obtaining a vehicle, making it yet seem that you had not obtained it. Genius. You are an artist such as the worlds have not before known."

"You are very kind," the object of this praise murmured, brushing cheese crumbs from his fingers. He leaned forward. "Edger. Where is Miri?"

The *T'carais* took a moment to consider it. "I do not know, brother. She spoke of business to be resolved. Other than this . . ." He moved his massive head from side to side.

"We walked together earlier in the day," he said, "and spoke of things of importance to us. She was very prised to find that she had been wedded to you, my brother."

Val Con froze, and the look of naked shock on his face would have surely earned a crow of laughter from Miri, had she been present. He took a deep breath. "So she might be," he agreed, though his voice was not perfectly even.

Sheather glanced up from his contemplation of the carpet on which he sat. "We wished only to increase joy when it seemed, last night, that you had knife-wed our sister. True, you had not said to us that you would do this thing, but we know humans to be hasty, and our eldest brother would have it that you could very well be so absentminded as to not inform your brothers, were you planning another of your compositions. Did we do ill, brother?"

He wet his lips, odds running in his head. "Yes," he said, "I am afraid that you have done ill."

"It sorrows me," Sheather said. "May we inquire how we have done so?"

There was a longish pause, during which Val Con banished the tickertape of calculations running before his inner eye. He sighed.

"It is very complicated, brother. Most of the ill would have been done when you hailed her as my mate. She fears me and this will have made her more afraid. It may, however, be mended."

"She *fears* you, brother?" This was Handler, but Val Con had turned back to the eldest of them all.

"Edger, please tell me when Miri left you and exactly what she said."

Edger blinked his huge eyes. "It was three of the cloc.
when I entered the lobby of this hyatt, the youngest of my
sisters having left me at the door but a breath earlier. Her
words are in answer to my query of when she might return
to us. She said: 'In a little while, I think. Nothing
complicated, but it's gotta be taken care of.' Thus did we
part company."

He let the breath he had been holding go: The odds
were slim that she would lie to Edger. He closed his eyes
and rubbed his forehead. "All right. But it is now five of
the clock and she is not returned."

"It means only that her business has taken longer than
she had anticipated," Edger rumbled.

Val Con opened his eyes. "So I hope, as well." He slid
from the table and bowed deeply.

"Speak," Edger commanded.

"I would that you forgive my hastiness, brother. It is
not thus that I would behave." He held his hands out,
palms up. "Events unforeseen have entered the situation
and it may mean that your ship, indeed, will be required
to serve us. Is all in readiness? If the need is upon us,
could we embark and depart this very night?"

"He Who Watches has been told to expect you, alone;
with the youngest of my sisters; or my sister, alone. All is
in readiness for you. There is food in plenty and of a kind
nourishing to humans. There are books in many
languages, as well as several kinds of musical
instruments."

"You are kind. It saddens me that I must ask further."

"Speak," Edger commanded once more, large eyes
glowing on his young brother's face.

"I go now to seek out the youngest of your sisters. Should it befall that she returns here while I am gone, pray tell her all that has transpired between us at this meeting and ask that she bide until six of the clock. Have I not returned by this time, she must go to the parking lot at Pence Street and Celeste and look for the red car. This vehicle she may enter by encoding '615' in the lock. She must change the color from red immediately and go to the nearest shuttle port. She must stop for nothing. Once on station, she must seek out your ship and depart." He bit his lip and closed his inner eye on the equation that denied it. "Say that I have computed the odds and that they are not good. But say also that she is a person with luck and, if she is wily and careful, all will be well."

"I will say these things to my sister," Edger promised. "Shall I say also that this last you do not believe?"

Val Con drew a breath. "Brother, I pray you will not. It is a matter of human definition—truth of another order."

"I understand, and all will be done as you have instructed. The name of our ship is—but you are in haste. Remember only that it is at Dock 327, Level F."

"Brother, I cannot say how the greatness of your heart makes glad my own." He bowed to Edger, then to the rest of the silent Clutch. "Gather much wisdom, oh, my brothers, and use what you have gathered well."

"A long life to you, young brother, and much joy in it," Edger replied, releasing him.

Val Con moved, not running, but quickly, the door opening and shutting like a conjuring trick—then he was gone.

Edger turned back to his kin, motioning that Selector should pour him a beaker of beer. "Our brother," he said, taking a draft, "is a very great artist."

JUSTIN HOSTRO NODDED. "Yes, I see. A happy circumstance, Sylvia, though I am sure it is very sad that she has chosen to rob your friend. . . ." He let his voice fade out as he glanced down at his desk and shifted papers. His daughter, used to his ways, held her tongue and waited with what grace she could muster.

He looked up again, smiling faintly. "Sylvia, my dear, I shall be sending a group of my associates to your hyatt to escort this lady to my office. In the meantime, please do me the favor of keeping her—available."

Her perfect brows twitched together. "Available, Daddy?"

He moved a hand, banishing details. "Available. Buy her a drink, invite her to your room, seduce her—but keep her in that hyatt for twenty minutes more. Then you may let her go. Understand?"

"Yes, Daddy."

He smiled. "Good. You and your friend are still planning to dine with me this evening, are you not?"

"Of course," she said, surprised.

He nodded. "Till then, my dear . . . Oh, and Sylvia—"

She paused with her hand on the disconnect. "Yes, Daddy?"

"Do be careful, dear. The lady in question has rather an—uncertain—temper, I fear. You don't want to make her angry with you." He smiled again and cut the connection.

Sighing, Sylvia left the booth and started back across the lobby.

VAL CON SUMMONED a lift, thinking hard. She would have gone across the street to Murph's hyatt, of course. To wait? Or had she arranged to meet him? The lift's door *swished* open and he entered, directing it to the lobby.

When the lift stopped, bell *dinging*, the door slid away and he took two steps out.

"There he is!" yelled a voice that had become all too familiar.

Val Con froze, his gaze flicking over the crowd of carefully placed individuals. Too many had guns. Far too many were pointing them at him. Directly before him stood Peter Smith.

In the charged silence, he heard the safety click off on Pete's gun.

He kicked, spinning as his foot connected with Pete's hand, diving back toward the open lift. A pellet whined past his shoulder as he hit the floor and rolled the rest of the distance. Another got through the doors before he had ordered them closed and slapped the 'rise' button.

At the fifteenth floor, he stopped, wedged the door open with a Terran half-bit, ran to the summons box, and demanded more lifts.

Three came immediately—one discharging a middle-aged couple who walked hand-in-hand down the hall, never seeing the slight young man who slid behind them and wedged open the lift's door.

Four out of seven lifts accounted for and the odds

were nigh on to perfect that the three remaining were going to be bringing him lots of company in just a little while.

Well, then, what next? Into a room and out the window? He grimaced. From the fifteenth floor, with people no doubt shooting from below? No need to calculate that one.

Down the service ramp? If there was one. He had not committed every detail of this building to memory, more the fool he. He'd allowed himself to believe that he was secure, protected from harm by Edger's reassuring bulk.

He shook his head. It would have to be back the way he'd come then, striking for the Grotto and its dozen or so exits.

He spun slowly on his heel, surveying the empty hallway. Surely there must be something to aid him? Memory stirred after a moment and he moved off to the right, down a short dead-end hallway.

The cleaning station was locked, but that was easily remedied; he made his choices quickly, ears cocked for the sound of an elevator arriving on the floor, wishing he had a partner with eyes on that lift bank.

Gathering up his collection of bottles and paper, he went back to the lifts, leaving the door to the station unlocked and swinging gently to and fro.

THEY WERE LEAVING the alcove as she came near, and she could see Angus's shoulders drooping in depression. The little woman kept up with his pace easily, silent in her leather boots.

Hidden by an ivy-covered pillar, Sylvia watched them

cross the lobby to the lift bank. When they claimed their car she followed and stood watching the floor indicator. Fourth floor—back to their rooms! The little bitch wasn't satisfied with taking what he had on him; she wanted more.

Shaking with rage, Sylvia summoned a lift.

VAL CON FROWNED at the telltale. For reasons best known to the police, the three elevators not currently with him were grounded—two at lobby level and one at the Grotto. He had a theory regarding this maneuver, but it bore checking out.

Wadding paper into a tight roll, he soaked it with alcohol and touched it with flame. It flickered and caught, smoking nicely.

Gingerly, he tossed it into the first of four elevators and unwedged the door.

MURPH SIGHED as the door to his room slid back. He sighed again, more deeply, as he went to the desk and inserted his finger in the lock. A drawer made a sudden dimple in the smooth plastic side, and Murph removed from it a money pouch, which he offered to the woman at his side.

She nodded at the desk. "Count it. I know you got the best intentions going, but your memory's rotten, my man."

He did as he was told, unsealing the pouch with a jerk and upending it over the desk. Bits rolled and clicked; one escaped to the floor.

Irritably, he bent and captured it, adding it to the first stack of ten.

There was a sound at the door.

Murph looked up as the panel slid back and his fiancée entered, lithe and elegant and high-colored in an evening dress picked out with gemstones. He was on his way to embrace her when he heard the unmistakable sound of a safety being thumbed off.

Sylvia froze, eyes wide, nostrils slightly distended.

Murph spun. "C'mon, Sarge, what d'ya think, she's got a bomb in her pocket?"

Eyes on the woman at the door, Miri shook her head. "Finish counting, Angus." She motioned slightly with the gun, indicating that Sylvia should close the door.

"Nice dress," she said, when this was done. "Me and Murph're just finishing up some business. Shouldn't be more'n a few minutes, now, and then I'll be gone and you two can comfort each other."

Sylvia swallowed, decided to ignore the gun, and turned her attention to her beloved, who was completing the last stack of coins.

"Four fifty-seven fifty," he said, straightening.

The woman with the gun spared a brief glance at the piled cash and nodded, eyes back on Sylvia. "Fine. Back in the pouch."

"Angus," Sylvia demanded in throbbing accents, "is this woman robbing you?"

"Robbing?" the woman in question repeated. "Not at all. Murph owes me money—his severance from the Mercs, plus interest, like we agreed when I made him the loan. He's been a little backward about paying, but I think we're all right and tight now, don't you, Murph?"

Angus held the refilled pouch out to her. "I still think

it'd be better if you let me call in the transfer, Sarge, rather than taking all that jewelry. You're not going to get half what it's worth—"

"But I'll get it *now*," she cut him off, sliding the moneybag into her pouch. "And I need it now! Hard cash—not a bank note I might not be able to collect on for awhile." She spared him a withering gray glance.

"I had money for you when you needed it, you miserable cashutas! I don't wanna hear any bellyaching about paying me what's owed when I need it." She moved her gun, infinitesimally. "Out of the way, honey."

Sylvia licked her lips and stayed put. "But, Sergeant— it *is* Sergeant, isn't it?—if it's cash you want, I have some with me, as well." She smiled her most winning smile.

"At least let me buy Angus's ring back."

✧ CHAPTER THIRTEEN ✧

A LIFT SENT upward should rise, not sink. Thus, the theory was confirmed.

Sighing gently, he entered the middle elevator, slid the knife from the neck sheath and began to work on the destination plate. It was a sinful use of the blade, but there was no help for it, and he worked with careful rapidity until he had loosened a corner of the metal plate. Sliding the knife away, he pulled a length of wire from within his vest and twisted one end into a hook.

Moments were squandered while the hook was caught and released by the workings behind the plate. Finally, the button that concerned him most drifted inward, obeying pressure from the wire in his hand. He nodded and carefully let the wire down to hang precariously in position.

Then, he went to prepare the remaining lifts.

RING, STYLUS, and pin were bought back for a total of eight hundred bits, bringing the cash received to the sum originally borrowed, give or take a hundred. Miri kept the necklace and the earhoops for the unpaid interest.

"See you 'round, Murph," she said, sealing her pouch and turning to go. She frowned at the woman before the door and motioned with the gun.

"OK. honey, business complete. Outta the way."

Sylvia wet her lips. "You know, Sergeant? I think I could probably borrow another two hundred—if you wanted your interest in cash, too? It would take just another couple minutes. I'd need to make a call to my—"

"Angus, your fiancée talks too much. I'm done and I'm leaving. She's in my way. You can move her or I can move her. Choose."

Murph started, then moved a step toward Sylvia. "Let the sergeant go now, love. She's finished here."

"But Angus. it would be no trouble. If she'll just wait here while I call Daddy for the loan—"

"No!" the little woman snapped. "I been here long enough, honey. Move, or I shoot you. You won't," she confided, "like that."

Murph had heard this threat before and knew it to be in earnest. Putting chivalry aside, he pushed forward, wrapped his arms about his beloved and lifted her out of the way. She pounded on his shoulder with ineffectual fists as the woman in leather dove past, slapping the door open.

ALL WAS IN readiness. He unwedged the doors in rapid succession and took careful grip on the wire sticking out of the control panel.

All right, Commander, he told himself, here's the plan: Bypass the lobby via homemade jury-rig in hand. Exit on the Grotto level and get over to Murph's hyatt, fast. Do not speak to strangers, especially policemen. Simplicity itself.

He shook his head as the bell *dinged* outside his lift.

Commander, old son, you're an optimist. He smiled wryly.

THEY JUST MISSED nailing her in the room. As it was, one saw her as she slid around the corner toward the service lift and set up a yell.

Miri ran. The luck was in: a cleanbot hauling a load of supplies and paper goods was just leaving the lift. She grabbed its head and threw her weight into a spin that sent it bumbling out of control and into the shins of the man in the lead; then she dove into the lift, slapped *down,* and leaned on it.

Down it went, obedient to unceasing imperative, and stopped with a bump that would have made her nervous, if she'd had time for luxuries.

She was out before she'd gauged her surroundings, and the lift was closed and rising before she thought to wedge the door.

Well, can't help that, she thought. Look for the other way out before the cheering section gets here.

The light was dim, but that was to be expected in a sub-basement stacked with boxes of cleaning supplies and gods-knew-what else. She was in the guts of the hyatt, the tenement within the palace. Miri took a deep breath of dank air. Almost made a body feel at home. Now, which way was out?

CHARLIE NARANSHEK SPUN on his heel at the watchpost, almost dislodging his partner of the evening, one of Mixla City's specialists.

"What the *hell?*"

The specialist glanced incuriously at the group of men entering the hyatt opposite. "Some more of our guys, maybe, making sure he don't break for across the street."

But Charlie had seen a face. "Wrongo, chum. Them's Juntavas."

"Yeah?" the specialist said, returning to his bored surveillance of the street. "Busy night."

THE DOOR was locked, a circumstance that reminded her of the punch line to a very dirty joke. Across the basement, she heard the whine of the lift, coming back down.

She considered the lock: a shaft of metal extruded from the door, sunk deep into the jamb. No fancy computer lock had been used to protect the paper goods. But it was effective, real effective.

The lift-whine was louder. Miri shifted her shoulders, elbow bumping on the obstruction of sheath and blade—

The knife was in her hand before she had fully formed the thought. Carefully, she wedged the tip where bar entered the wooden jamb, probing.

Across the cellar, the lift door opened.

THE LOBBY was filled with smoke; alarms began to scream and sprinklers to sprinkle. The racket reached the sharp ears of the Clutch, three floors up, and Edger so far forgot protocol as to cut short a question being posed by his brother Selector to rise and move, with haste, to the door.

"Come, my brothers! Did I not say he is great? Let us

see what he has wrought in this present." So saying, he was gone, vanished into the hall.

Handler, Selector, and Sheather followed, though Selector did tarry a moment to wonder, for Sheather's benefit, at the excitability of their kinsman.

"For you would suppose," he said, "that by the time one has his twelfth shell—and is, besides, the *T'carais* of so mighty a Clan as our own—one would have put aside such childish hastiness and behave as an adult."

They were in the hallway proper before Sheather had framed his reply.

"Perhaps," he offered diffidently, for he was very conscious of his status as a lowly Seventh Shell, "it is that our brother, himself, is an artist."

THEY HAD SPLIT into groups and were prowling the rows of stacked goods one by one. Miri bit her lip and continued working the blade. She almost had it. . . .

With a *click* too loud for oversensitive ears, the bar retracted into the door. Miri was through in the next instant and turning the key on the other side, firmly engaging the lock once more.

She took a deep breath and wrinkled her nose. The ramp she stood on smelled bad, though the 'bots probably didn't mind. And by rights, she shouldn't either, because the ramp led up and that was just what the doctor ordered.

So she'd head up, preferably to the Grotto level, where there was lots of access to outside. Once out, she'd find a comm and buzz Edger, who would no doubt tell her what Tough Guy had decided she should do next.

Which did raise an interesting point: What *was* she going to do next?

One thing at a time, Robertson. Don't get ahead of yourself.

The smell was getting less bad—or her nose had made an adjustment of heroic proportions—and she was hearing noises from above. Lots of noises. Well, maybe somebody was having a party. The more the merrier— and the easier for her to slip through and out, unnoticed.

The ramp curved and abruptly ended at a door. She worked the lock as quietly as possible and opened it a crack, peering through. The kitchen beyond was pristine, huge and empty; she slid through and eased the door shut.

The party in the next room was a doozy—both louder and not as loud as it had been from the ramp. She'd lost the vibration of feet on floor that she'd had from underneath, but there was something—

She froze and the sound came again. Party, indeed. *That* had been pellet whine, or her great-aunt Agnes had been hatched from an egg.

She made her way cautiously across the impeccable expanse of floor to the double chrome doors, eased one barely open, and peered out.

Men and women with guns—about thirty of them— deployed with more caution than tactics around the empty echo of the Grotto. Whatever it was they were after was holed up behind the eastern-most bar. And whatever—or whoever—it was could definitely shoot. Whenever one of the armed horde showed the slightest portion of body, that portion suddenly acquired a pellet-hole. Methodical.

Which could only mean that the prize in this tiger hunt was her partner.

Miri frowned, then grinned as another of the enemy was punctured—hole in the shooting arm, very pretty.

Odds look about even, she noted. Wouldn't lay a busted bit on either side. . . .

Her grin suddenly widened and she ducked back into the kitchen.

POLICEMEN, VAL CON THOUGHT, squeezing off another shot, had no sense of humor.

Or sense of futility, for that matter. Why in the name of all they might hold holy would they just sit out there, shooting and being shot at, taking loss after loss and inflicting no damage? Why didn't they just pack up and go home, call it a day, admit they'd been bested—any or all of the above? And soon. He was running out of pellets.

MIRI PROPPED the door at the top of the ramp securely open and a little time later did the same for the door into the cellar.

By the sounds, her pursuers were still beating the rows for her. She grinned and moved toward the nearest sound.

The man was peering into a carton that might have concealed her had it not been full of bottles of cleaner. Miri extended a hand and toppled a near bundle of brooms.

He whipped around, pulling his gun, and she was off, making a lot of noise as she ran.

The racket roused his buddies, who came racing to his

aid. Miri rounded the corner farthest from the ramp door on one wheel, skidded to a stop in the face of five of them, then whirled and was going back the way she'd come before they had time to understand that she'd been there.

For good measure, she fired a shot over her shoulder, parting the hair of the man in the lead, then she was moving flat out, streaking past another bunch of them, knocking one into three others like tenpins and twisting around the corner to the ramp door.

Roaring, they came after. She checked for a moment, glancing back to make sure that somebody twigged to the vanishing act.

A lean man with no hair whatsoever rounded the corner, gun leveled.

Miri dove through the door.

IT WAS NOT possible that he could win. He supposed he would take a formidable honor guard with him, but the thought brought no comfort. Nor did the equation that hung before his mind's eye. He gritted his teeth in a final effort to banish it: Suicide is an unacceptable solution.

The equation faded, to be replaced by another bearing a strong resemblance to the one he had denied in Edger's presence. Very soon now he would be dead. Miri might yet be alive, but the end for her was also quite near.

He leaned out from his cover and fired, striking his man cleanly in the eye. A pellet screamed by, chipping the plastic by his head as he huddled back into protection. Cracking his gun, he loaded the last of his ammunition and eased his position a little, glancing around the corner of the bar to gauge the next shot.

There was a banshee howl that raised the hairs on the back of his neck, and out of the kitchen burst an apparition in dark leathers and white shirt, brandishing a gun, a squad of armed men at her back.

"We're coming, Tough Guy!" the figure in the lead screamed, firing into the group at siege.

Confused, they returned fire as the rushing squad broke up and made for cover, returning fire on their own while their erstwhile leader dove sideways, rolling, taking advantage of the shelter offered by tables, chairs, and bar to work her way toward his position.

Val Con grinned and waited, occasionally adding shots of his own to the melee to distract his attackers from her movement.

She was at his side in a ridiculously short time. Sighing, she slumped against the inside wall of the bar, peering out at the fight through a filigreed screen.

"Hello, Miri."

She shook her head at him. "I don't know how you get into these fixes. Leave you alone for five minutes—"

"*I* get into fixes?" He waved at the floor. "What do you call *that?*"

She opened her eyes wide. "Hey, I'm your rescue, spacer. And I want you to know I wouldn't do this for just anybody."

He laughed and snapped off a shot at a woman crawling toward their hiding place. She collapsed and lay still.

Miri peered out from her end, added a few pellets to the general merrymaking, and ducked back. "Nice party."

"You might think so," he told her, "but I've been here for some time and it's getting a bit rough for my taste."

"Yeah?" She jerked her head toward the most accessible exit, half a block down the room. "Wanna leave?"

"If you don't mind." He cracked his gun, showing her the empty chamber. "Give me some pellets and I'll cover you."

THE CALL CAME over the emergency channel: All available units to the Grotto, immediately. The description, though terse, sounded more like pitched battle than the arrest of two half-sized bank robbers.

His partner was off at once, sliding his sidearm out as he ran. Charlie took two steps in that direction and stopped, near blinded by a flash of brilliance.

Spinning on his heel, he headed for the lot at Ponce and Celeste, moving at a dead run.

MIRI WENT OVER the fence while Val Con circled around to the front of the lot, checking the street.

She dropped silently from the top and moved quickly in the deepening dusk, using the few vehicles there were for cover, striking out in a diagonal and wondering what she would do if there were *two* red cars parked in the front row, facing out.

She left the shadow of the last car enroute and stepped out into the open.

There was only one car in the first row. Between her and it loomed a figure, too tall and much too blocky.

She froze, hand twitching toward her gun in reaction before she stilled it.

"Hi, Charlie."

"Hello, Roberta." His own gun was out, steady on her gut. "Where's your brother?"

"Bound to be around somewhere," she said lightly, keeping her eyes on his face, not on the gun. "He usually is."

"He wouldn't be down the Grotto, would he? Shooting cops with the rest of the Juntavas?" He was coldly sure of it, and the certainty kept his gun hand from shaking.

Can you shoot her—kill her—if you have to? he asked himself. He didn't know.

She was shaking her head. "We ain't Juntavas, Charlie."

"No? The cops go in to get you, the Juntavas goes in across the street and—boom! A war. Juntavas protects its own, but it ain't much on helping out strangers."

"It was an accident. And the explanation's complicated." She decided to push it. "Charlie, look, I'm in a hurry, okay? How 'bout I give you a call next time I'm in town, we have a drink and tell you all about it?"

No reaction. She hadn't really expected one, not with him in uniform and all, but it had seemed worth the try. Where the hell was Tough Guy?

"The story out of Mixla 'quarters," Charlie was saying, "is your brother's wanted for killing five people—eight-year-old kid was one of 'em." He watched her face closely, trying to gauge her acting ability.

She frowned and shook her head. "Not since I've known him. Not a baby." She took a breath. "Not to say he wouldn't. Just that he hasn't. I think."

Her gaze sharpened, locking on a movement in the dusk beyond his shoulder. Almost, she sighed.

"Charlie," she said, very quietly. "I like you, which is why I didn't draw on you and why I'm telling you this: There's a man behind you with a gun. He'll kill you, without an instant's hesitation or a moment's remorse, unless you drop that piece now."

He hesitated, weighing the chance of it being a lie, keeping the gun where it was.

She flung out both hands, her face revealing something that looked like fear in the uncertain light.

"C'mon, Charlie!"

He dropped the gun and kicked it to one side.

"That's fine," she said gently. "I'm real sorry, but you're gonna have a headache when you wake up."

The blow clipped him just above the left ear, hard enough to do the job. He carried her face with him into unconsciousness.

THE SLEEK BROWN car moved with sedate purpose through the streets of Econsey, toward the mainland and the shuttleport. The windows were opaqued so that the vulgar were denied a view of the vehicle's occupants. The emitter broadcast its message to all with the means to read it.

"Wasn't that just a bit harsh?" inquired the man in the seat next to the driver.

"Wasn't which?" she asked, slowing to a stop in obedience to a flashing signal.

"He will kill you, without an instant's hesitation or a moment's remorse. . . ." he quoted flatly.

She glanced at him. He was sitting straight in the comfortable seat, staring out the window. The tension in him puzzled her. She eased the car through the intersection as the light steadied and shrugged her shoulders.

"You have shown that tendency in the past," she said as mildly as possible.

Perhaps he snorted. Or perhaps he only let loose a breath that had been too long held, all at once, and with a vengeance.

"I'll try to rehabilitate myself," he said, and there was no inflection at all in his voice. After a moment, he slid down in the seat, moving his shoulders until he found comfort within the cushions, and closed his eyes. "Don't stop for anything," he told her. "And wake me when we get to the port."

It was her turn to snort, but he did not appear to hear; the rhythm of his breathing told her that he was asleep.

Irritably, she yanked on the wheel, snapping the car from left to right. He rolled bonelessly with the jerk, his breathing unaltered.

"I guess you'll want tea and crumpets when we get there," she muttered. She smoothed the car through another curve and onto the main highway.

THE BEST PLACE for a roadblock was on the Econsey side of the last bridge to the mainland, and that was exactly where they'd set it up. Miri sighed and let the car slow fractionally.

"Hey, sleeping beauty."

He eased to a sitting position, in no hurry about it.

"Roadblock," she told him, stating the obvious.

"Maintain your speed."

She slanted a glance at his face. He didn't *look* crazy.

But, then, he never did. Well, what the hell. She kept the car on course and steady.

The roadblock loomed closer, lights flashing, and she could make out the expressions on the faces of the people lining the roadway before them.

Then something very strange happened. The 'block began to move clear of the road and the guard fell back, holstering their pieces or bringing them to rest.

Miri took a deep breath, meticulously keeping the pace.

The roadblock lumbered clear a bare moment before impact. Miri let her breath out in rationed units as the brown car continued its stately progress across the bridge and onto the mainland.

"Tough Guy?"

"Yes?" He was settling back into the seat, no doubt arranging himself for another nap.

"Why'd they do that?"

"Possibly they judged an interplanetary incident too high a price to pay for stopping and searching the Yxtrang ambassador's private vehicle." He yawned.

"Oh." She was silent for a short time, digesting his words. "I don't want to pry into your private life or anything, but you didn't by any chance *steal* this car from the Yxtrang, did you?"

"To the best of my knowledge, the Yxtrang delegation for this sector is presently on Omenski."

"Good place for them," she agreed. "Hope they fall in love with the place and never leave." She made a left-hand turn into a wide thoroughfare and then the tower light from the shuttleport was directly before them.

"Sorry I'm so dense," she said, "but I didn't have a nap. What made the cops think we were the Yxtrang ambassador?"

"The emitter says we are." He shook his head and sat up straighter in his seat. "I'm afraid I must have read the wrong code out of the manual at the rental office. It was really very hard to read—grainy and flickering. One of the connectors loose, I should think."

She looked at him. "You wouldn't have had anything to do with that, I guess."

He turned to face her, eyes wide. "How could I have?"

"Never mind, I don't think I really want to know."

The port was less than a half-block distant now and she was beginning to feel loose for the first time since she and Murph had started their negotiations.

We just might pull it—

"Oh, *damn.*" She swung the car—easily, easily—into a side street, moved to the end, and turned into a wider avenue, heading away from the tower light.

"Did you see what I thought I saw?"

He nodded. "Yes. Checking people as they go in. I'm afraid neither of us can pass for Yxtrang at any distance."

"Funny, the things you live to regret." She took a breath. "Now what?"

There was a pause, which she was inclined to think was bad news.

"Let's get a bit closer to the port and leave the car. If we can mix with a group going through, we might have a chance to confuse things and get by."

She laughed and made a left; shortly thereafter a right turn headed them back to the port.

"No plan, but, sister, do we got guts!" She pulled to the curb and killed the power, grinning. "Okay, let's go crash the gate."

✧ CHAPTER FOURTEEN ✧

THE SITUATION LOOKED even worse from the street than it had from the car. Even granting the two of them awesome powers of mayhem and confusion, Miri was ninety-five percent certain that they wouldn't be able to fade through the checkpoint. She didn't bother to ask her companion for the official figures.

Nor did he offer them, just stood at her shoulder in the pool of shadow they'd chosen as their observation point and silently watched the procedure.

After a time, she felt him shift next to her. "Let us get a drink."

She turned her head, but it was impossible to see his face in the inkblot they occupied. "Sounds like the most useful thing we can do," she agreed. "Maybe two or three. Then we can come back and try to bull on through. Won't hurt so much when we get perforated."

She heard the shadow of his laugh as he moved out onto the sidewalk. "No faith, Miri."

"None," she said, catching up. "My folks weren't real religious, either. Are we really gonna take a kynak break with the cops *and* the Juntavas within eight seconds in every direction?"

He turned down a slender alleyway at the far end of which multicolored neons promised cheap warmth and noise.

"Why not?" he asked.

Or, she translated, do you have a better idea?

She didn't, so she followed.

THE THIRD BAR was noisiest, full nearly to overflowing with men and women in leathers and other work clothes. It was the perfect place for them to hide, though there seemed barely enough room to accommodate two more bodies, no matter how small.

Val Con hesitated at the door, weighing the scene, while Miri stood at his shoulder, watching the crowd absently. She stiffened suddenly and he snapped his eyes to her face, looking for a clue to the trouble.

She was grinning and leaning a bit forward, eyes squinted against the smoke. In a moment, she turned to him, grin undiminished.

"Tough Guy, you're a genius. Let's go." She started forward.

He dropped his hand, gently encircling her wrist. "Tell me."

"Part of that mob in there's the Gyrfalks—my old unit." There was no missing the excitement in her voice. She jerked her wrist and he let it go. *"C'mon,* Tough Guy."

He followed, afraid of losing her in the press of bodies and the eddying smoke as she pushed and wove her way through, moving with the stride of a person with a goal in sight.

What the goal was, Val Con couldn't tell. He was satisfied to keep her in sight, and re-established himself at her left shoulder when she caught up against a temporary body-jam.

The jam sorted itself out and she moved on, he maintaining his position as they broke out into the center of the room.

There it was less crowded, though a goodly portion of available floor space was taken up by the biggest Terran that Val Con had ever seen: Eight feet tall if he was an inch, shoulders wider than Edger's shell, chest and ribcage said his planet of origin had been just a tad light on oxygen, and there was not an ounce of fat on him. His shoulder-length blond hair was tied back with a black cord. His full beard was curled and very likely perfumed. He was drinking something brownish from a liter pitcher, an arm draped possessively across the shoulders of a slender dark woman who would have dwarfed any man but this one.

Miri strode straight up to the blonde godling, Val Con just behind her; she stopped with legs braced and hands on hips, head craned upward.

The godling finished the contents of the pitcher and extended a long arm to deposit it on the bar. His lapis gaze fell upon the face of the woman before him.

"*Redhead!* By the highest, iciest, most diamond of the Magnetas! By the deepest hellhole of Stimata Five! By—"

Words failed him and he reached down, encircled

Miri's waist with his huge hands, and threw her upward as if she were a doll; he caught her and gave her a kiss that might have drowned someone less alert.

She captured his ponytail, yanking on it and smacking the side of his head with the flat of her hand.

"Jason! Put me *down,* you overgrown bumblebear!" She swatted him again and Val Con winced with the force of the blow. *"Put me—"*

"Down," Jason finished, placing her with the utmost gentleness atop the bar. "Of course, my darlin'. Down it is, and nicely, too. Ah, it's a sight for a man's heart to see you, my small—but there's something amiss! *Barkeep!* A kynak for the Sergeant, on the double! Or will you have a triple, my love?"

"A single," Miri said, collapsing crosslegged to the bar and waving a hand at Val Con. "And one for my partner, too."

Jason's eyes lit on the little man in dark leathers, noting the gun belted for a crossdraw from the right, but seeing no other hardware. The stranger was slender, though with a certain whippiness about him that said he'd do well for himself, hand-to-hand. A fighter, and no nonsense. The sort of person one would want at Redhead's back.

He shifted his attention to the beardless golden face, encountering eyes as warm and cuddlesome as shards of green glass: Jealous, then. Not the best trait possible, since partners were not always lovers, but who cared, if it kept him sharp?

"Partner, is it?" he drawled, turning back to Redhead. "Bit exotic for your taste, I'd have thought. . . ." No reason not to hone the little man a shade finer. He looked around. *"Barkeeper!* Ah, here we are, my love. . . ."

The barman shoved a glass into Miri's hand and held the other out to Val Con, who looked into the dark depths and dared a sip. He was not quite able to control the shudder that ran through him.

Miri laughed. "Like this—" she told him, knocking back a quarter of hers. "Don't *taste* it, for pellet's sake! It'll kill you."

"It may, in any case." He tipped a brow, half-smiling. "How well does it burn?"

She laughed again, then turned where she sat, holding both hands out to the woman who approached.

Small by Terran standards and built along the lines of a bulldog, her very short hair a glossy, unrelieved black, her blue eyes set at a slant in a rosy-cheeked, plain face, she looked efficient and practical. She took Miri's hands, leaned forward, and kissed her gently on the mouth.

Miri returned the kiss with evident pleasure and kept one of woman's hands captive as she turned back. "Tough Guy, this is Suzuki. She's my friend and Senior Commander of the Gyrfalks." She waved a casual hand at the blond godling. "That's Jase."

"Oh, cruel, my small," the godling cried. "Heartless, heartless. When I think of the nights I spent sleepless without you—"

"Without me *what,* you noshconner—on guard?" She turned back to the woman. "Why do you put up with him?"

Suzuki appeared to give it some thought. "I believe," she said finally, in a voice that should have been too soft to carry through the surrounding din, "that it is because of the beard. The care he takes of it! The hours spent grooming and perfuming it! Even in the heat of battle have I seen him fondle it. Yes." She nodded. "I do think it's the beard. Though, of course," she added, as one being completely impartial, "the snoring is nice, too. Do you remember, Redhead, when we were on that frontier—Sintathic?—and we needed to set no guards at night, because the animals were so frightened of Jason's snores?"

There was laughter from the group that had gathered around them and Jason dropped his massive head into his hands and moaned in mock agony.

More laughter from those around and Val Con allowed himself to relax infinitesimally, putting aside also the desire to set a knife into the godling, for the principle of the thing. He acknowledged a liking for Suzuki: It would be an honor, indeed, to serve in a troop of her command.

He shifted position to the left of the bar, put down the glassful of horrible stuff—and became aware of someone standing much too close, trapping him next to the counter. He turned the slight amount he was allowed and frowned at her.

She grinned: a mid-sized Terran; large, the way a lifter of weights is large; a gun on each hip and the hilt of a survival blade showing at the top of the right boot; breasts straining taut the cord that laced her shirt. Her grin broadened and she extended a blunt hand to stroke his arm from shoulder to elbow.

"A pretty toy, Sergeant," she said over his head. "We fight for him, yes?"

Miri laughed, snapping off another quarter of her drink. "We fight for him, no. Go away, Polesta."

"Come, Sergeant, you know me. It will be fair, this fight—a thing for the songs, eh, no matter which may take the prize. Would you pass the chance of a meeting between two such as we?"

"With pleasure. Where's your partner? You're drunk."

Sensing an opening, Val Con shifted balance cautiously, but, drunk or not, Polesta was alert and blocked the escape route with a casual hip.

"The Sergeant will not fight me?" she demanded. There was a strong feel of ritual about the question. Val Con tensed, anticipating Miri's answer.

"Now you've got it!" she said admiringly. Then, dropping her voice and putting a snarl in it, she said, "Get out of here, Polesta. I don't fight drunks and I don't fight crazies, so you're safe on two counts."

"The famous Sergeant will not fight," Polesta announced to the room, which had grown much too quiet. "So, I take my prize by forfeit."

He dove, trying to get around to the right of her, lower than her normal reach—and was blocked for an instant by a pair of leathered legs. He felt her fingers knot in the hair at the nape of his neck to jerk him back, throat exposed.

Unbalanced, he didn't struggle; he got one leg where it belonged and braced himself for the twist—

She brought her mouth to his and kissed him—harshly, thoroughly, with lots of tongue and amid roars of laughter from the gathered onlookers.

He kicked and twisted, not giving a blazing blue

damn if it broke his neck, but the move for some reason surprised her and she lost her grip.

He landed on his feet next to the bar, back stiff, eyes glacial. His face had lost color, Miri noted, and every line of him expressed outrage. Not the polite killer here, but a man in a towering fury. She rolled to her feet silently on the bar, ready to back his play.

Deliberately, he turned his back on Polesta and took up his glass from the bar. He turned back and took a swig of kynak. He rinsed his mouth.

Then he spat.

Turning away again, he gently replaced the glass on the bar.

Huge laughter burst from the crowd as Polesta's face went red as a Teledyne sunset. "No one insults me so!" she cried, and swung.

He dodged, making use of the space that had suddenly opened around them to get far enough away from her to have room to move.

She swung again, and he grabbed her arm as it rocketed past, twisting his body *so,* inspiring Polesta to the heights. At the last moment he clenched himself to take the sting out of the maneuver, and let her go.

She hit the floor six feet away with a sound like an infant earthquake. Val Con took a deep breath as a man separated himself from the now-silent crowd and went to the inert warrior. After some cajoling, including a few brisk slaps to the face, Polesta was gotten to a sitting position, though she still seemed rather groggy.

Val Con drifted back to the bar, people slipping out of his way, and settled his back against the solid plastic at

Miri's right hand, ignoring Jason's gape. He felt drained—almost exhausted—and wondered briefly why this should be so. The throw had used very little of his own strength, trading as it did on his opponent's momentum.

Miri shifted at his side, and he looked up at her face.

"Pulled your punch." It was a statement, not a question.

"*You* wanted me to rehabilitate myself," he reminded her, hearing the snap in his voice. He held out a hand. "Give me some of that stuff."

She gave him her glass, and he drank what was left, properly. He drew a hard breath and let it explode out of him.

"Awful, ain't it?" she said, taking back the empty and handing it to Jase, who raised his eyebrows. She jerked her head slightly; he assumed a martyred look and went in search of the bartender.

The crowd had split into other patterns now. Across the room, Polesta's partner had managed to get her to her feet. Suddenly, she pushed away from him and started purposefully, if unsteadily, toward the bar.

"Where is he? Run away, eh? Thinks it's done, does he? I'll—"

Her partner jumped in front of her, hands on her shoulders, heels braced. She shook like a mastiff and he held on; he continued to hold on even when she raised her fist—and lowered it.

"Well?" she yelled at him. "I'm insulted. And I should take it, eh? Be meek. Be mild."

The man shook her, though she did not appear to feel it. "Polesta, the Sergeant was right. You're drunk. You made a mistake. He showed you it was a mistake. It's all over, okay? No harm done." He glanced over his shoulder, catching the green gaze of the man at Redhead's right.

"A mistake," he repeated, urgently.

"A mistake," Val Con agreed gently. "No harm done."

Some of the dreadful tension left the man; he returned his attention to Polesta, pushing at her shoulders. "Come on. Let's get some coffee and something to eat. We're due to move in another hour. You'll lose your kit again if you don't sober up some before then. . . ." Talking so, he led her away to claim a table near the back of the room.

Val Con took the glass Miri put in his hand and finished off half in a swallow.

"I think you're right," he said.

"About which?" she asked, noting with approval that his face once more had the proper depth of color and that his shoulders had loosened up a little.

He put the half-empty glass on the bar and twisted his head to grin up at her. "I need a haircut."

She grinned back. "Maybe. Might grow it a little longer, instead, and tie it up with a ribbon, like Jase."

"No, thank you," he began, but then the subject of this conversation was with them and he cut off what he'd been about to say.

"What say we all grub together," Jason boomed "We got a little over an hour before we shuttle out—"

Miri reached up and captured an ear. "Before you what?"

"Shuttle out. Did you think we were going to stay on Lufkit, my small? No wars here—Now, darlin', don't twist it off, I'm attached to it. Part of a matched set, as they say."

She released him and slid to the floor. "Where's Suzuki?"

"It's what I've been telling you, love. You and your partner have been invited by Senior Commander Rialto and Junior Commander Carmody to dine with them in the admittedly limited elegance of the back dining room of this establishment, there to talk over old times and weep into our kynak."

"Tough Guy—"

He was at her shoulder. "Let us, by all means," he murmured, "dine with Suzuki and Jason."

IT'S POSSIBLE, Val Con thought, leaning back in an unsteady plastic chair and sipping carefully from a steaming mug, that the only reason people drink kynak is because even coffee tastes good afterward.

He set the mug back on the table and sighed very gently. Across from him, Suzuki smiled.

"I have not yet thanked you for saving Polesta's life," she said in her soft voice.

His brows twitched together. "Saving her life?"

"That kill has four moves, does it not?" She didn't wait for his nod. "All who watched saw that you executed but three—and so Polesta lives. I am thankful for that because she is one of the unit's strongest fighters—a berserker. It is unfortunate that the traits that make her so valuable in action cause her to be such a trial when we have been inactive." She paused to drink coffee.

"I admire the skill with which you were able to subdue

her," she continued. "I would not have thought it possible, short of killing, which is why I believe Redhead would not fight."

Miri snorted. "That waste of time? Best thing anybody could do would be put her away. She's bats, Suzuki."

"Valuable, nonetheless. As you well know. I did not say you would come out the loser in such an encounter, my friend, but that you would not take from me what you know I consider essential to the unit." She laid a hand on Miri's arm. "You chose your partner wisely."

Miri laughed and picked up her mug, forestalling the need for an answer.

"Besides," Jason commented, "Polesta's probably so mad now she'll take on the other side all by herself when we hit Lytaxin. Give the rest of us a paid vacation." He shook his head at the little man, both admiring and envious. "My lad, you are *fast.*"

"Best remember it," Val Con returned, retrieving his mug and finishing off the contents.

Jason laughed and turned away. "So, then, Redhead, what about signing back on, taking that promotion we offered you? Lytaxin'll be a job o'work—I won't lie to you, my small—and we'll be in sore need of you. I don't doubt you've found civilian life a trial—and travel's expensive when the client's not paying." He held out a large hand. "What about it, Redhead? A lieutenant's badge and the chance to get shot at first? You'll not turn it down?"

Miri looked at Suzuki, who nodded. "We would welcome you back. You know that. We cannot offer your partner what he has not earned, but he is a skilled fighter and we would be happy to add him to the roster. There is no reason why he should not be at your shoulder."

No, Val Con thought, the equation flaring like iced lightning. No, it's a bad solution, Miri!

She touched Jason's and Suzuki's fingers lightly. "Ask me later," she told them. "I'm glad you want me back." She tipped her head. "Favor?"

Suzuki nodded. "If it is within our power."

Miri glanced at her partner; he was wearing his no-expression expression, and her stomach tightened a little as she turned back to Suzuki.

"We need to get to Prime without publicizing it," she said. "Port's got some kind of damn check going. We can't pass it—you can ask why, but it's a long story." She paused, waiting for the question.

Suzuki drank coffee. "You want us to sneak you through the checkpoint and onto Prime?"

"Yeah."

The Senior Commander of the Gyrfalks shrugged. "I see no reason why it cannot be done," she said, looking at her Junior.

Jason grinned hugely and leaned precariously back in his chair to stretch. "Piece o'cake."

"See to it, then." She glanced back at her friend. "Other favors?"

"No—yeah. Can the Treasury afford to buy some jewelry? I need cash, not geegaws."

Suzuki's eyes dropped to touch the snake-shaped ring and rose again, quizzically. Miri laughed.

"Other jewelry. Everybody's entitled to *one* geegaw."

"Well, let's go find Ghost and see what she says."

Suzuki pushed away from the table and laid her hand on Jason's shoulder in passing. "Want to start getting everyone together? It's time."

"Nag, nag," he muttered, coming to his feet. "I'll just take Tough Guy with me, shall I? Have him ride up with Yancey's bunch."

Val Con rose slowly. "Miri."

"Yo."

He hesitated, then shrugged irritably. "Dock 327," he told her. "Level F. Meet me there, fifteen minutes after we hit."

She turned away, taking Suzuki's arm. "Sure," she said.

"HOW LONG," Daugherty demanded, "is this going to go on?"

"Until they tell us to stop?" Carlack hazarded.

"Which could be in the next twenty years. Or maybe not."

Daugherty had been on duty since early morning, just ten minutes short of finishing her shift when the order had come through: All Personnel to Man Port Access Yards Until the Present Emergency Has Been Resolved. She had cause to be bitter, Carlack thought, but none at all to be dramatic.

"The Chief of Police thinks they'll have 'em before the night's out. They're desperate criminals, I heard on the band. Every cop on-world's looking for 'em, so they've gotta try and get off. The Chief was real sure they'd try it as soon as they could."

Daugherty said something uncomplimentary regarding the Chief of Police's personal habits. She added, after a moment's further consideration, a rider that hinted at a far more accurate knowledge of anatomy than of practical genetics.

Carlack sighed and considered sending down for more coffee and some sweet rolls.

"Oh, blessed Balthazar," Daugherty whispered, but it didn't sound like a prayer.

Carlack looked up. "What?"

"Mercenaries," she snapped, on her way to the door. "Hundreds and hundreds of mercenaries, coming in the wrong damn gate!"

SENIOR COMMANDER HIGDON was in a foul mood. This was not necessarily a bad thing; certainly, it was not unusual. A methodical man and a high stickler, he did not relish being delayed, nor did he allow the considerations of mere civilians to outweigh the obligations of the lowest soldier in his troop. He so informed the two models of civilianhood who had dared stop him as he entered the port gate at the head of his unit, demanding that all wait, line up, and show papers.

Commander Higdon did not approve of papers.

Daugherty gritted her teeth. "Police orders, Commander. No one to shuttle out without showing papers and being cleared. There are desperate criminals on the loose and the police think they'll try for the shuttle. Chances of catching them once they're on Prime go way down. If they manage to get on a spacer, they'll never be brought to justice."

"And a good thing that would be, too!" the Commander said with obvious relish. "Society is killing off all its good stock—its 'criminals'! Hunting them down and killing them off. We'll be a society of cows, if the police and the lawmakers have their way. Ought to hunt *them* down and nail their hides to the shed! To hell with all of 'em." That settled to his satisfaction, he turned to his Junior to relay the march order.

"Be that as it may," Daugherty pursued, "we've got our orders and we're going to do our job. How do we know you haven't got those crooks mixed in with your outfit, there?"

"I wish I might!" Higdon returned. "Can always use a good fighter. As for your orders—to hell with them, too. I've orders of my own, and a deadline to meet, and I'm afraid I have the means to convince you that my necessities are the more pressing." He raised his hand.

There was a large sound in the night—the sound, Daugherty realized suddenly, of many, many pellet guns being brought to ready.

She opened her mouth, not at all sure of what she was going to say—and was saved by the appearance of a smallish round-faced woman in standard leathers who marched up to the maniac at the head of the line.

"What in the name of all that's damned is the hold-up?" she demanded. "We've got a schedule to keep, Higdon."

"This civilian and I were just discussing that, Suzuki," he said. "She seems to think we're required—that each and every one of us is required—to show papers before boarding shuttle for Prime."

"What?" The woman turned to Daugherty, who wished briefly that she'd never been born. "We are expected. We have a private shuttle. We are short on time. We take our own chances. No more delays." She walked away.

Higdon raised his eyebrows at the two before him. The man, he saw, was decidedly pale. The woman was made of sterner stuff, but she was obviously well aware of her personal inadequacy in the face of an armed and at-ready unit of seasoned mercs.

She stepped aside, dragging the man with her. "Okay, Commander. But I'm required to inform you that we will report your infringement to the Chief of Police."

Higdon laughed and brought his hand down. Safeties were snapped on and firearms returned to holsters. In good time, the Junior gave the order to march.

Line upon line of them marched across the field to the private shuttle, entering the hatch in good formation. In a much shorter time than one might imagine, the last of the mercs had entered the hatch; the door was sealed and the shuttle lifted.

Daugherty, who had been on the line with the nearest police unit, reported this fact. The cop on the other end looked bored.

"It's not real likely the mercs are hiding 'em," she told Daugherty. "The Chief's got 'em figured as loners. I'll let him know they wouldn't stop for the check, but it probably ain't worth a fuss. They've had this lift scheduled for the last ten days. No surprises."

YANCEY, it turned out, was the slender brunette Jason had been with earlier in the evening. She grinned at Val Con, spoke a word of admiration for his skill, and handed him over to a man with bluish-black skin and a shock of bright orange hair.

"Tough Guy's your partner 'til we hit Prime, Winston. Don't let anybody break him."

He jerked a thumb at his charge. "Him? Better he makes sure nobody breaks me!"

Yancey laughed and went away, and Winston tapped Val Con on the arm. "C'mon, youngster. Gotta pick up my kit and get in line."

They did so, waiting in line rather longer than Val Con liked, though he spent a good deal of time craning his neck around tall Terrans, looking for a short, slender figure.

"Sonny," Winston told him finally, "you can leave off worryin' about Sergeant Redhead. First of all, she's the toughest somebody in this whole damn unit—that's counting Polesta. Second of all, Suzuki'd skin alive whoever let somethin' fatal happen to her; and then Jase'd stomp'em to a grease spot."

Val Con grinned. "I guess I'm wasting my time."

"Yours to waste, boy. It just does seem—uhp! Here we go."

They moved down the slender alley, out into the main thoroughfare, and down to the port—not so much marching as walking in rhythm, as a unit.

Short of the port gate, they stopped, and the sounds of an altercation came to them faintly. The sounds of weapons being armed was rather louder and Val Con felt himself draw taut. Where was Miri?

Winston dropped a light hand to his arm. "Just relax. It's only Higdon throwin' one of his tantrums. Man's got the rottenest temper this side of Yxtrang. Just ain't happy 'less he's feelin' mean. I don't know how he keeps his unit, and that's a fact—you gotta think about more'n bonuses and pillage-right when you sign on, *I* think. 'Course, there're lots of people around, an' every one of 'em's got their own idea 'bout what's right—" He paused, and the sound of safety catches being clicked back into place reached their ears.

"Now we'll get on."

They made their way through the gate, across the field, up the ramp, into the shuttle, and down a hall, where they had to find something to grab onto—standing room only.

Val Con stopped by a strap set too high in the wall and braced his legs. Shortly, the ship clanged as the hatch closed, the lights dimmed, and he heard the subsonic whine as the engine gyroscoped into full power.

"You okay, boy?" Winston asked.

"I'm fine."

The shuttle lifted.

✧ CHAPTER FIFTEEN ✧

PRIME STATION.

VAL CON moved with the rest of the troop through Docking Tunnel 6, Level E, and into the main corridor. He touched his companion's arm.

"I leave you here," he said. "Thank you for your care."

Winston grinned. "Son, I don't want Sergeant Redhead wastin' *me.*" He slapped the Liaden gently on the shoulder. "Be good now." He went on with the rest as Val Con dropped out of line and slid into DownTunnel Sirius, which accessed Levels F through L.

The DownTunnel was a slow, easy float, designed for tourists, not spacers. He drifted to F Level, snagged a loop, and rolled lazily into the corridor beyond. Docking Bay 327 was to the left and around the curve of the Station's wall; he set off at a light bound, savoring the slight reduction in gravity.

She was not at the entrance to the dock. He frowned, checking his inner clock. Seven minutes had passed since they'd hit.

Fair enough—he had told her fifteen.

Back against the corridor's inner wall, positioned so that he could watch the hall in both directions, as well as the entrance to Number 327, he settled in to wait.

According to Winston, the mercenaries were to rendezvous at Dock 698, halfway around the station on Level E. From there, they would board private transport and be en route to Lytaxin within twenty minutes of hitting Prime Station.

He frowned again, groping after some faint sense of importance attached to the planet's name. Lytaxin?

Footsteps sounded beyond the curve of the wall and he stiffened, hand flicking to gun. With a grating effort of will, he relaxed back against the wall and a moment later exchanged a casual nod with a woman in the uniform and utility belt of an electrician. The sound of her steps faded to nothing in the other direction, and he strained his ears to catch the slight clues of Miri's approach.

She wasn't coming. He was certain of it, though no numbers appeared to support the certainty. She'd thrown back in with Suzuki and the Gyrfalks: The mercs were her safety; she wouldn't believe the Juntavas would hunt her there.

Then he was running, streaking down the corridor, looking for an UpTunnel to Level E—and finally the numbers began, flickering and flashing like lightning before his mind's eye.

A mistake, Miri! he cried soundlessly. And the harm done only too clear.

He sighted an UpTunnel, grabbed the loop, and rolled inside, giving an extra kick to send himself rising faster;

he ignored the loop at E level, tucking and rolling, spacer-style, and running on the bounce.

Val Con ran, dock numbers flashing by and the equations flickering, flickering. At Dock 583 a load 'bot was jammed cross-corridor, while three humans yelled instructions at each other. He pulled more speed from somewhere, kicked, rose, slapped the top of the 'bot with both hands, flipped, and hit the corridor beyond, running. The shouts were meaningless sounds, far behind.

Sixteen minutes.

Access Tunnel 698 was empty, though he heard voices ahead. The mercs were still in the holding room, then.

He was three feet into the room before a cry went up, and two more before the first of them moved to block him. He sidestepped, twisting, then parried an arm that came from nowhere, slapped aside a knife—

Seventeen minutes and the numbers within danced maniacally before his mind's tired eye.

A gun appeared in a hand before him; he scooped it away, spinning, into the crowd of bodies. There were fewer bodies now—he could see his goal and forced himself to slow the pace at which he moved toward her.

A large obstacle dropped into his path; he dodged, only then recognizing the blockage as something called "Jason." His goal was half a yard ahead, watching him inscrutably. He called her name as heavy hands fell on him and his arms were twisted behind his back.

"Suzuki!" Eighteen minutes.

"I hear," she said in her soft voice. "What do you want?"

"I must speak to Miri. She is in great danger if she stays with the unit."

He was breathing deeply, Suzuki saw, but not painfully, as might a man who had been moving so quickly and doing so much. He stood within Jason's grip as if it were too small a thing to regard, as if he barely knew he was restrained. His eyes were a bright and lucid green.

She shrugged. "We are all of us here in great danger. It is the nature of our business."

"A different danger. A danger that threatens the entire troop. The Juntavas would make little, do you think, of killing several others with the person they wished to destroy? And even if they proved squeamish, how could you be sure that the next soldier you hire is not an assassin hired to kill Miri?" He leaned forward infinitesimally in Jase's hold. "You cannot protect her against the Juntavas, Suzuki. Not if you must ever sign on another soldier or share quarters with another unit."

"And *you* can protect her?"

"Perhaps."

An aide appeared at Suzuki's shoulder.

"Commander? I—there's been a delay. We leave within the hour, not immediately, as planned."

Suzuki nodded absently, eyes still on the man whom Jase held captive. Or did he? Was it not rather, she wondered, that he suffered Jason to hold him, that she might feel secure and so hear him speak?

"If she chooses not to hear you?" she asked him. "If she comes with the unit, which is her right and her privilege?"

"She dies within the Standard, even if she never sees action. I swear to you that it is true."

There was a long silence, during which blue eyes

measured green. He was insane, Redhead had said. Certainly he was to be feared. . . .

"Allow me to speak to Miri," he said, and the measured voice sounded only sane. "I beg you, Suzuki."

And he was not a man who begged, whatever else he was.

Suzuki drew a breath. "Let him go, Jason."

There was a fractional pause before she was obeyed. The little man took as much notice of his freedom as he had of his captivity.

Suzuki raised her voice. "Redhead!"

"Here." And she was at her commander's shoulder, gray eyes blazing on his face.

"Can't you tell when you've been ditched, you scruffy midget? I gotta spell it out for—"

"Redhead."

Miri chopped off in mid-curse, eyes snapping to Suzuki's face. "What?"

"Hear him. It may be that he is truly insane, as you have said. This does not mean that he lacks information or that he holds less than your best interest next to his heart."

"Providing he has one." Her eyes were back on his. "Talk."

"Stay with the Gyrfalks and die within the Standard. True and certain. On my Clan."

Her brows rose, but she said nothing.

He flung his hands out, palms upward. "Miri, please. Take the ship—alone, if you fear me. But you cannot stay with the Gyrfalks and live."

"Odds?"

"None," he told her, flatly. "Point nine-nine-nine guarantee that you will be dead within the Standard. The Juntavas has this reputation." He drew a deep breath. "Take the ship, Miri."

"Odds if I do. Alone." Her eyes were hard on his.

"Point six against five Standards' survival."

"If we take the ship together?"

"Even odds over five Standards."

A brief silence. "*Your* chance of survival, if I take the ship alone. Figure it for five, if you gotta."

He opened his mouth—then closed it, brows pulling tightly together.

"There are no odds over five Standards. Point eight against my surviving nine months."

Her eyes widened slightly. "And if you go with me?"

"Over five Standards, sixty per cent against survival." He shook his head. "Miri, take the ship."

"If I leave you, you'll die!" she yelled. "Didn't you *hear* yourself?"

"I heard."

"Then *why?*"

He moved his shoulders. "When a man is insane, does he require another reason?"

She sucked in a deep breath and released it, then stepped to Suzuki and hugged her, catching the kiss on her lips. As she strode past the tall man and the small one, her fist flashed out to strike the larger in his treelike arm.

"Take it easy, Jase."

Val Con stood, watching her go. At the door she turned around.

"Let's move it, Tough Guy. I ain't got all day!"

He followed her then, weaving his way through the silent mercs. At the door, he, too, turned.

"Jason!" His left hand flashed, throwing underhand.

Reflex extended Jase's arm; he snagged the spinning thing and swore.

"What is it?" Suzuki demanded, coming close.

He held it out. "My survival blade. Damn little sneak had it out o' my belt."

Suzuki lifted a shoulder. "Well, then, maybe she *does* have a chance."

"But she said he's crazy!"

"Isn't everyone?"

IT HAD PROVED impossible to check out the mercenaries. First of all, there were just too damn many of them. Second of all, none answered questions, no matter how delicately put, except maybe to snarl an obscenity or show a sudden gun or laserknife in a hand trained to use it.

The other avenues of questioning normally open to him were closed in this instance: Mercenaries took unkindly to the murder of any of their number, and it was hardly in Costello's best interest to allow a soldier he had questioned under "persuasion" to stay alive.

So, though he disliked it, he sent a terse report of his failure on an extremely tight beam to the surface of Lufkit. He added that Lytaxin was the destination of the troops, more to show that he had the best interests of the organization at heart than because he believed it possible that the boss did not already possess the information.

Odds were fairly certain that he had already alerted his contacts in Lytaxin's sector. It was just that he had had his heart set on stopping them before they'd gotten out of Lufkit's jurisdiction. A matter of pride. Bosses had a lot of pride.

Ah, well, Costello thought, there's just so much one man can do.

His board chattered to itself for the space of time it took the message to reach its counterpart on-world, and Costello extended a pudgy hand to cut the power. He stopped short, eyes disbelieving on the bright purple knob that had just lit: Stand By For Instructions Incoming. What the *hell?*

HE WHO WATCHES was in a dilemma. He had obeyed the commands of his *T'carais* and made ready the vessel for occupancy by humans, even to removing a container of beverage and another of foodstuffs from the nether hold and placing them where they could be easily seen, by the map table in the control room.

Certain things had been taken from their places and put into containers which were then moved to the storage facility attached to the docking area. The temperature of the water that flowed in the pools had been lowered to the normal blood temperature of humans, and the lighting had been adjusted so that their eyes might not take harm from journeying too long in dimness.

The temperature of the atmosphere within the vessel had been lowered—except, of course, in the Room of Growing Things—and the oxygen-nitrogen mix adjusted. All this had Watcher done, correctly and in great haste, as commanded by the T'carais, and now all was in readiness, waiting upon the arrival of the humans.

Wherein lay Watcher's dilemma.

Watcher loathed humans. They were soft. They were little. Their high voices squeaked across the ears like nails across a slateboard. They were forever rushing hither and yon, stopping neither for pleasantries nor protocol. It was no wonder, Watcher thought, that they died so soon after they were born. They were without cause or benefit to the universe, and Watcher regarded them—individually and as a species—with the fascinated horror of a man phobically afraid of spiders.

The *T'carais* had left further instructions, which Watcher was unable to fulfill until the advent of these humans. The instructions included demonstrating the drive and the ship's controls, as well as aiding in the setting of whatever course the humans deemed appropriate. He was also to instruct them in the proper way to activate the autopilot so that the ship would return in its time to Lufkit Prime Station and He Who Watches.

Well and good. It would not be easy to be in the close proximity to humans necessitated by the teaching of the controls, but he was confident that he could do it. Edger had further instructed—and there lay the horror at the core of the dilemma—that, should it be requested by these humans, He Who Watches was to accompany them wherever they wished to go and to serve them as he was sworn to serve the brother of his mother's sister, the *T'carais*.

The thought of a time to perhaps be computed in

months in the company of humans—even one human—caused Watcher to experience distinct feelings of illness, to the extent that he actually considered not opening the hatch when the summons let him know that they had, indeed, come. But steadying him was the thought of the punishment that would be his when it became known that he had refused the order of the *T'carais*.

Clenching his loathing to himself, Watcher went to open the door.

SHOULDER TO SHOULDER and silent, they walked Level E's long hallway.

At the DownTunnel, Miri stepped in first, floated down, and rolled out. Half a second later, Val Con also rolled into the corridor, using the loop and not hurrying. He landed on the bounce and tottered, catching himself not quite instantly.

She frowned, slanting a look at his face as they went on.

He looked bad, she decided. The skin was stretched tightly over his cheekbones, and his eyes looked as if they were too far back in his head; there were lines engraved around the generous mouth, and his shoulders slumped slightly.

"You okay?" It was the first either had spoken since leaving the mercs.

He spared her a sharp green glance. "I'm tired."

Very tired, he thought, forcing himself to keep her pace. Well, there was only a little farther to walk and a few moment's talk with Edger's watcher before he could rest—would rest. It was imperative that he rest . . . Shutting that thought away before the rhythm sapped the strength he had left, he lifted a hand to point.

"There."

"Let's go." She turned with him into the entrance tunnel. "What's this one's name?"

"He Who Watches, Edger called him."

"Watcher?" she wondered, brows knit.

Val Con shrugged. "It should do," he said. "I've never met him."

"Oh."

The hatch was before them, the summoner set dead center. Val Con reached up and pressed it, fighting the desire to lean forward and let the opaque crystal of the hatch hold him up.

Time passed. Miri reached past his shoulder and hit the summoner again. "What if he's asleep?" she muttered.

There seemed to be no reason to answer, for which he was grateful. Words were blurring in and out of focus, as if his mind were unable to deal with the process of converting sound to meaning.

The hatch began silently to rise.

When the opening was wide enough to accommodate them, they stepped through into the room beyond, where a Clutch person somewhat smaller than the smallest of Edger's entourage awaited them. He moved his hand on a control board set in the solid rock wall and the hatch slid down and sealed.

The Clutch person bowed—and Miri clamped her jaw on a gasp. No shell! she thought and then saw that she was wrong: a very small shell sat high like a knapsack between his shoulders. Maybe he was a kid.

Completing his bow, their host began to speak sonorously in what she recognized as Clutch speech. He had barely gotten into the first syllables of what could have been a first word when Val Con moved.

He bowed—not as deeply as he bowed to Edger, or even to Sheather, barely a heavy nod of head and shoulders—and cut across the other's speech.

"No doubt," he said in Trade, "the *T'carais* has informed you that we are in great haste. There is no time for the exchanging of names or other formalities. Please take us to the control room and show us what we must know."

Watcher froze, outrage warring with loathing in his soul. Regretfully, he put both aside. His *T'carais*, as the soft creature before him said, commanded. His was to endure and obey.

"As you will," he returned, dropping the jagged shards of the language called Trade from his tongue with what he hoped was seemly haste. "The control compartment is in this direction." He turned to lead the way, not looking back to see if they followed.

The control room was about the size of the Grotto, Miri thought, or maybe even bigger. It was hard to be certain because of the way the controls faced the large crystal suspended on the far wall. Star patterns were depicted within the crystal and Miri looked at it harder, giving herself a sharp mental shake.

Navigation tank, dummy, she told herself. Pay attention.

She pivoted slowly, taking in the rest of the area. A large table sat near the wall opposite the navigation tank, flanked with upholstered benches. Cubbyholes were cut into the wall to one side and in back—most were sealed, but a couple were open and empty—and two large cartons were pushed into the corner. Stenciled on the side of one was FRAGILE and on the other, THIS END UP.

The wall to her left was blank, though she thought a closer inspection would reveal more storage bins, and a wide shelf was built out from it at what might have been convenient sitting-height for Edger.

She frowned and continued her pivot. The room wasn't completely symmetrical; her mind kept trying to insist on the proportions she was most comfortable with, and the effort to really look at what she was seeing made her a little queasy. She tried to concentrate on the walls themselves, noting that they seemed to be made of seamless rock, rather than matched plate steel, and frowned harder.

From behind her she heard the rumble of Watcher's voice and the broken-edged sound that was Val Con's reply. She went quietly to the control board and leaned over her partner's shoulder.

"This is the recalibration device. When the ship is at rest you will remeasure and realign. Comfort requires it. If *this* has occurred, you must also recalibrate, utilizing this device—so."

Val Con nodded. "How often does the ship rest?"

"The ship rests four hours for every eight that it labors."

The man took a deep breath, forcing the air far down into his lungs and closing his eyes to better see the mental picture. The initial procedure was *thus*. To recheck, measure and align, one waited until the ship was at rest and made required adjustments *so*. The ship returned to labor when its rest was done, with adjustments or without them. He nodded and opened his eyes.

"Very good," he said, pushing aside that part of him that wondered what the sounds meant. "We must now set our course."

"Where is it that you wish to go?" Watcher inquired around the terror he felt. Only let it not be years!

"Volmer. Planet Designation V—8735—927—3 . . ."

Behind him, Miri shifted. "That's a Liaden planet! I told you, Tough Guy, I ain't going to *Liad* and I ain't going to any world *controlled* by Liad!"

From somewhere he brought forth a last shard of patience and lucidity and made it her gift. "It is a planet of the federated interests of Liad, Terra, and Clutch." His voice was nearly even. "From it we can depart to any of the fourteen prime points. I know that you will not go to Liad."

She wasn't convinced. "I don't like it, and I ain't—"

But his patience was gone and time was running out. "Be silent!"

She blinked—and shut up.

Watcher was pushing at the pastel crystal buttons, lighting and extinguishing them in a pattern that looked random to her nonpilot eyes. After a time, he stood away from the board.

"Your destination has been set," he said. "You will arrive in approximately three weeks, ship time. Of course, you will have to recalibrate your chronometers at journey's end. When you disembark, assuming you have no further need for this vessel, you will press this." He pointed to a large red disk set by itself on the right side of the board.

"You will have sufficient time after you have depressed the disk to exit the ship before the return journey begins." Was it possible that they would not ask, he wondered, hope beginning to stir.

Three weeks? Miri frowned, laboriously working out the sector designation in her head. No. He was translating the time units wrong somewhere. The trip shouldn't take more than two days. Oh, well, he was just a kid. As long as he had the destination coded right, they would be okay.

Val Con pushed himself away from the board and made the slight bow once again. "I thank you for your assistance. I—" He paused, his intention clear and glowing within his mind.

"I would that you say to my brother Edger," he began, forming each word in his head before speaking it, "that, should it come to his attention that I have lived—less long—than others of my kind, it would—please—me that he extend to this, his sister Miri, all honor and—and aid—that he would have made mine, had I—lived—to return to him, as I had promised." He paused to review this. It seemed to contain the germ of his desire.

"Say also to my brother," he continued, the words coming more and more slowly, "that I have been honored and enriched by his acquaintance and that my—love—goes with him in his endeavors." It was insufficient, he knew, but he could go no further. Edger would understand.

Watcher stared at the small, soft, swaying thing before

him. He almost understood why his T'carais so honored the creature. Then the red-furred one reached out its many-fingered hand to the one that had spoken; Watcher's stomach turned and the moment was gone.

"These things shall be said to my kinsman, the T'carais." He bowed. "I will signal you when I have reached the end of the tunnel. You will then press the disk that is blue, as you have been shown, and your journey will begin."

Val Con nodded, ignoring Miri's outstretched hand and forcing himself to stand unaided. "I must ask that you make considerable haste in gaining the end of the tunnel. We must be off within five Standard minutes."

Outrage again flared in Watcher, not quite overcoming relief. He would not have to serve these monsters, after all! He would only have to wait in the dim quiet of the corridor, with occasional forays out for food, until the ship returned to him. In the face of this reprieve, rudeness could be suffered.

"It shall be as you have said." He turned without further formality and left the control room.

A minute later, Miri heard the hatch slide up, then down. She looked at Val Con, who was swaying where he stood, his eyes on the blue disk.

"Boss, are you nuts? I don't need Edger's protection. You gave us even odds, remember?"

"Miri . . ." His voice faded off; he did not look at her.

She went to the nearest bench and sat. "Shut up," she finished for him. "Yes, sir."

A portion of the board lit and Val Con raised his hand, laid it over the blue disk, and pushed.

In the navigation tank, the stars went away.

"Already?" Miri demanded incredulously. "Maybe he meant three *hours.*"

COSTELLO ROLLED OUT of the DownTunnel and moved along F Level, not running, but pushing the walk.

Turtles, for Panth's sake! As if he hadn't had enough trouble trying to talk to mercenaries, now he had to go and try to talk to turtles. Ah, well, he got paid by the hour and it was overtime tonight, for sure. Maybe even hazardous duty pay.

A largish green person was exiting the tunnel to Number 327. Costello quickened his pace. The green person did things to the door controls and pressed the summons stud. Costello started to run.

"Hey, you!"

The turtle did not turn around. Rather, it laid its head against the tunnel door and stood very, very still, as might someone who breathes free air again after a time in captivity.

Costello arrived panting, and laid his hand on Watcher's arm. "Hey."

Watcher opened his eyes. When he saw the horrid, misshapen hand resting upon his arm, he jerked back and whirled to face the perpetrator of that outrage.

Costello held his hands out, fingers spread placatingly. "Hey, I'm sorry. No harm meant. It's just that I'm looking for some friends of mine. Thought you might have seen them." He paused, but the turtle only stared at his hands.

"Two kids," Costello said, picking up the thread of his story. "Boy about—oh, twenty, twenty-five; dark brown hair, green eyes, thin. Girl—pretty little girl—eighteen, or maybe twenty; red hair, gray eyes. Thought you might've seen them," he repeated.

Watcher made no reply.

Costello decided to play it tough. "Look, you," he snarled, moving closer and jabbing with his finger. "I know you're hiding something. It ain't gonna do you no good to play dumb, see? 'Cause there's ways of making guys like you talk. So you just tell me where them kids—"

Enough! Enough of outrage and sickness and terror and too many fingers on hands too small! Enough and too much!

Watcher struck.

And Costello screamed, pulling back a hand from which two fingers had been cleanly bitten away.

✧ CHAPTER SIXTEEN ✧

WALLS, MIRI THOUGHT, should be stable things. They should not, for instance, be fuzzy one minute and translucent the next. Nor should they be shot, from time to random time, with sudden neon-bright color.

Her hands shouldn't seem to go into the wall when she touched it, and her feet shouldn't look foggy. In fact, things in general shouldn't be that—indefinite. And why did she feel so good? She wasn't drunk!

Miri sighed, which felt very good.

The good news, as far as she could tell, was that they wouldn't be on the ship very long—not the way they'd been able to slip away from Prime without a head start, clearing Jump or anything.

Yeah, that was pretty good, just sliding—

She couldn't concentrate on the thought. The wall she'd been staring at ghosted momentarily, becoming largely green fog, and she thought she saw a diamond the size of a dozen landcars on the other side.

Absently, she ran a hand down her arm. She did it again. How soft her shirt was! She stroked her arm a third time, eyes slitted in pleasure.

Putting her hands on her thighs, she immediately discovered the tactile delight of supple old leather, well-kept and clean—and snapped to her feet, holding her hands away from her body. There was a pattern in the floor she hadn't noticed before: layers and layers of large prints—the prints of Clutch feet—one on top another, pressed into the hard rock floor.

She half-laughed, then frowned as the idea struck her. She was assuming the semipsychedelics were drive-effects. What if instead there was something wrong with—her? What if she was sick? Or crazy?

Well, crazy'll be company for Tough Guy, she thought philosophically. Worse fates could befall.

Still, her fear needed to be checked out. On impulse, she unwound her braid and pulled the length of hair over her shoulder where she could see it.

It was as she had feared. Her hair was foggy, each strand a little brighter and a little less definite than normal.

Flipping the braid behind her shoulder, she turned and strode out of the bookroom, heading for the control area and her partner. When an entire wall went bright gold as she passed by, she stuck her tongue out at it.

VAL CON GOT UP when the control board began to shift.

Well, not *shift* so much as—fade? There was a rainbow iridescence at the edge of things that made him acutely uncomfortable; he tried hard to determine where one of his fingernails actually ended.

That experiment was interesting. He could touch edge

of thumbnail to edge of thumbnail and *feel* it, except he'd swear he could feel it before they touched and after they were parted. Even more unsettling was that his thumbs and the fine hair that grew on the backs of his hands appeared to have a certain lack of substance.

Tired. He was very, very tired. He needed to rest.

But he hadn't been able to rest—and the so-called Survival Loop kept popping up, over and over, unbidden, each time giving him figures which seemed not to concern him, but still initiating bursts of energy as it insisted to that *this time* he might not get home.

Home? He closed his eyes, trying to picture the place, but the weird effects disrupted the efficiency of his memory's eye.

Shan? he thought, in something like desperation. Nova?

But the faces of his kin did not arise.

Edger? There was no difficulty recalling *that* person, down to the bone-rattling boom of his voice; and with it this memory brought attendant memories, of life with the Middle River Clan. . . .

Go home, he thought. Rest. Go home and be musician for the Clan . . . .

But there had been those equations when he'd played the 'chora—the Loop, showing him that the longer he played, the less chance he had of ultimate survival. And now these fadings and flashings, when things had been feeling so—unreal—in general. . . .

Seated at the map table, he took quick inventory. The effects observed were not akin to any poison he had been trained to recognize: they seemed to be nearly psychedelic, yet *actual*—which argued against an airborne spore or something of that nature.

It had to be an artifact of the drive—he hoped.

He massaged his wrist gently, astonished at the intense pleasure the action gave him, and closed his eyes.

CMS: .2.

Not so unusual. Except that he hadn't given the Loop a mission to calculate.

Music. Edger had said there were instruments on board. Gods, I could use a 'chora now! he thought.

The display in his head dropped the CMS to .1 instantly.

There was no sense to that, was there?

Was there?

Why should music endanger him? He needed to relax; he needed sleep, rest, a chance to let stretched reflexes loosen. He'd used the 'chora for that quite successfully in the past.

If there was space—and there had to be space on a ship this size—he might begin a session of *L'apeleka*.

He shook his head. Composure was needed to practice that Clutch discipline. He had taken time, between missions, to enter as far as the Fifth Door without a partner, and had never failed to feel more— alive.

I have to go home, he thought.

But no, that wasn't getting him anywhere. The flashes behind his eyes showed a new reading on the CPS, a figure he didn't want to admit to consciousness.

His thirty-day chance of personal survival was down to .09.

"The mind must be composed for proper utilization of the Survival Loops," he recalled.

If only he could relax! He was certain the figures would be higher.

One wall flashed brilliant gold, went to streaked yellow with orange specks, then turned red as the floor flowed green; and his hand looked even *less* distinct.

It was good that Miri was not there, he reflected.

He would find it impossible to deal patiently with her questions, her demands for attention—yet he was glad that had gotten her out of Juntavas territory, that she'd have a chance to get on with her life when they raised Volmer. Glad that he'd gone back for her.

And why had he? What was she but a deadly danger, growing more deadly all the time? The things she knew—the things that he, himself, had told her! The things she had seen—and she saw much, he was sure. She was a threat and a danger, to himself and to his mission—

"What mission, dammit!"

He was on his feet, glaring around at the chaotic walls. Deliberately, he took a breath and combed his fingers through his hair.

Relax, he told himself gently. Stop thinking so hard. This was Edger's ship; likely it would take a Battlewagon a week to break in, if there were trouble. He had security, safety—for the moment. For the next week or two. He was secure. He could relax.

Carefully, refusing to look at the flowing floor, he crossed to the opposite wall and sat on the wide upholstered shelf. He lay down after a moment and began to review the plans he'd had for helping Miri, wondering if that were the mission the Loop was figuring.

No, he reminded himself, you're at low energy. Training tells you to be at your best before attempting long-range planning. Relax.

Closing his eyes, he reached for the simple relaxation drill he'd learned as a Scout cadet, so long ago: Recall the colors of the rainbow, one-by-one, and assign each a special property. Relax the body somewhat, then the mind; relax the body more and the relaxed mind would relax still further. Using that as a beginning, one could go to sleep, set goals, or enter special states for study, review, or reflex-reaction control.

Relax. He began the ritual, lying quietly, hands loose at his sides. Visualize the color red. Red is the color of physical relaxation. . . .

It took concentration, with the other colors flashing in his head. Red. He held it before his mind's eye, using it to relax tight chest muscles; he felt the warmth of his blood, flowing; he eased tense neck muscles, then leg muscles—and moved on with the technique. He saw *through* the colors flickering behind his eyes, seeing only the color he desired as he went through the layers, relaxing physically, mentally, physically, mentally.

He felt as if he were floating, barely conscious of the comforting pressure of cloth and leather against his skin. Mentally, he approached the switch level, the depth of mind where he might assign his concentration to a project or merely go to sleep, if he chose that path.

His thought was focused on the color violet—the end of the rainbow. Behind the color another image began to form unbidden, undesired. He tried to suppress it, but it grew more vivid. He recognized the sequence; one of the training-review programs from The Lectures, the series of tortures and teachings that had graduated him from Scout to spy. Too late, he thought to break the rainbow's spell; found himself locked in, forced to watch: *There*. Before him: People dying. His targets. His *victims*.

That program rated the efficiency of kills; it was not supposed to impose itself after training.

But it was rating his last fight.

The man shot in the eye: That was rated highly efficient; the shoulders of a crawling man protect the heart and lungs, and a spine shot is unlikely.

The woman who had half-crouched: That was efficient, slightly off-center to the left in the chest. Even if not a death-shot, she would be out of action for the duration of the incident.

Now he was swept fully into the review: five, six, seven, ten, twelve—every shot he'd taken to save Miri, to save himself, all those people, dead yet recalled so vividly. Not many poor-risk shots, not many misses. Dead people. Blood on the floor, on the wall. The knife throw at the hidden assassin was rated circumstantially excellent: that man *and* the woman should have been shot.

No! That was Miri!

Relentlessly, the training-review went on, driving Val Con further and further into the dead past.

THE WALK to the control room convinced Miri of several things. One was that her shirt felt indecently

delicious against her: soft and comfortable and erotic all
at once.

Another was that the sheer size of Edger's ship hadn't
really hit her before. So far she'd passed a room that was
half swimming pool and half lawn, and another room that
was a gigantic sleeping compartment.

The third thing she'd become convinced of was that
the strange effects—the colors and the shifting fuzziness
of things—were *real.* They were nothing like the
hallucinogens she'd taken years ago, nor did they bear
any resemblance to the truly weird stuff that had
happened in her head that time she'd been poison-
speared in the leg.

Comfortable in her certainty, she stepped into the
control room—and stopped.

Val Con was not at the board.

She tried to ignore the strange colors of the floors and
walls, the odd rainbows snowing out of the crystal in the
center of the . . . it was hard to define things with all this
change going on. She scanned the room again.

There! He was lying on one of the long slab seats, but
he hardly looked restful. In fact, he looked poisoned,
somehow, transfixed—muscles all in stark relief, mouth
grimacing, eyes screwed shut.

Miri approached slowly and stood frowning over him.
His fists were clenched, she noted. He was breathing.

"Hey, Tough Guy!"

There was no response.

"Pay attention to me!" she tried, raising her voice.

Nothing.

She put her hand on his shoulder. "C'mon, Tough

Guy, this is important!" She shook the shoulder, lightly at first, then hard.

"Tough Guy! Let's *go!*" The command voice didn't work—and that was bad.

He was sweating, the renegade lock of hair plastered tight across his forehead, his face a muddy beige color.

Miri bit her lip and felt for the pulse in his wrist. It was strong and steady, but fast. That was all right for now, but it wouldn't stay that way if he didn't come out of it soon.

She yanked on his arm, pulling him into a sitting position, hoping to see a reaction. Any reaction.

Nothing.

"Val Con!" she cried, using her voice as a whip, making his name a command to return. "Val Con!"

He did not respond.

She swore, softly and with feeling, recognizing battle shock, otherwise known as hysterical paralysis. She'd seen enough of it to know the symptoms—and the cure.

Some people could be pulled out easily, by a familiar voice calling their name. Other people required more drastic measures. Pain, physical and immediate, worked best.

She hurled herself forward, shouting in his face. "*Val Con!*"

Nothing. Not so much as a stutter in the rapid rhythm of his breathing.

She stepped back, surveying the logistical problems. Several approaches seemed to guarantee certain death, assuming that this patient recovered with the quick completeness of the patients she'd treated in the past.

Probably he'd recover much, much faster.

In the end she decided for a kick to the shoulder, hoping the spin would have her out of range before he snapped out of it.

She tried calling his name and shaking him again, just in case the gods had had a change of heart, then took a deep breath and kicked out, spinning as she connected, moving to the left—

The impact hit her with the force of an enhanced bullwhip, smacking her and rocking her; her left arm was a dead thing, hanging useless in the socket. He was coming and she dodged; she knew he would grab her and as he threw her she began to roll, going with it, eating momentum with each revolution, trying to stay tucked with the arm that was dead—and slammed against the far wall, breath exploding out of her in a cry.

Far away, she heard a sound that might have been her name.

Tired, she thought carefully. He was tired. That was why she was still alive.

"Miri!"

She pried her eyes open and rolled awkwardly to sit against the wall, arm still numb. He was kneeling at her side, close enough to touch, and the muddy agony was gone from his face.

"I'm okay," she said, willing it to be so.

The horror eased from his face, but a tightness around the eyes remained. "Forgive me. . . ." He let his voice fade away, shaking his head.

She tried a grin, to which he responded not at all.

"Hey, everybody makes mistakes," she said. She eased

herself against the wall, gritting her teeth as sensation began to return to her arm, and laid her good hand on his sleeve. "How 'bout getting me a drink of water, friend?"

He rose and moved away. She leaned back and closed her eyes, trying to gauge from the quality of the pain whether or not her arm was broken.

Some obscure sense nudged her and she opened her eyes to find him kneeling beside her again, wordlessly offering a mug.

The water was cold, which felt luxuriously good on a raw throat. She set the empty mug on the floor at her side, and the grin she offered him this time was nearly real. "Thanks."

He did not reply; the horror was a shadow lurking far back in his eyes. "Miri, how can you be my friend?"

"Well," she allowed, shifting her shoulders, "it *is* more of a challenge some days than others."

But he was having no part of humor. She sighed and moved her arm, flexing the fingers. Not broken, then.

"You should have taken the ship without me," he told her.

"I don't waste my friends," she snapped. "And you were standing there, risking bloody mayhem because you figured me at less than a Standard and you had less—and didn't care!" She shook her head. "Tell me why you did that—why you saved my life this past three or thirteen times. No reason for *you* to be *my* friend!

"And I lied to you," she added, after a moment. "Tried to run out and leave you to die."

"You did not know. And it is reasonable that my life expectancy be shorter than yours. You go into battle, fight an enemy pointed at you as you are pointed at him, collect your fee, and move on. Should you meet an old adversary in a bar a Standard or ten or twenty hence, what would ensue?"

"Huh? I'd probably buy him a drink, and then he'd buy me one, and we'd be cryin' into our third about the good old days."

"Exactly. Were I in the same position, however, my old acquaintance would immediately renew hostilities. With every assignment, I add one or two such enemies. Sooner or later, my luck will be down, while the luck of a person I wronged in the past will be up, and I will die. As such things go, I am on the wrong side of the wager— three years is a long time for a spy to live."

"You're telling me you're waiting to be gunned down?" She eyed him in disbelief.

He shook his head. "No. I was chosen to be who— what—I am now because I am a survivor. I fight when there are no odds at all in my favor. I manage to stay alive, somehow, some way. It's a good trait in a Scout. Apparently it is essential in a spy." He tipped his head. "You still have not told me why you brought me with you, when you fear me, when you could have come alone."

"I told you: I don't waste my friends. Even a friend who's crazy, or who could kill me."

"No!" His reply was too sharp, too quick.

Miri raised her eyebrows. "No? Well, you're the oddsman." She laid her fingers lightly on his forehead. He flinched away and she shook her head. "I don't think they did you any favor, putting that thing in your head. No wonder you're crazy."

She shifted again, raising her arm above her head. She felt as good as new, except for an ache high in the shoulder and another that spoke of bruised ribs when she breathed deeply. "Help an old lady get up?"

He stood and bent, settled his hands about her waist, and lifted her easily to her feet.

Fighting dizzy nausea, she made a grab for his arms and dropped her head forward against his shoulder. He held her patiently, and she suddenly noted how good his hands felt on her, how soft his shirt was and how warm, with the warmth of the skin beneath.

She pushed away and he let her go, though he stayed at her side as she walked across the room to the table, which was getting bigger and smaller in a rhythm she could almost hear.

"I think we both better get some solid, old-fashioned sleep," she told him. "Sleeping rooms down that hall. I'll show you."

She turned, staggered, and would perhaps have fallen, except he was there, hand on her elbow. The instant she was steady he withdrew his support and she turned to look at him fully.

Horror still lurked in his eyes. She was suddenly struck with a fear that it would never leave them.

Reaching out, she tucked her arm through his, pretending not to feel the slight withdrawal. "Maybe we'll do better if we lean on each other, huh?"

He did not answer, though he let her hold onto him and thus force him along the hallway.

She glanced at his face. "Val Con yos'Phelium, Second Speaker for Clan Korval."

"Yes."

"Who's First Speaker?" she asked, firmly ignoring the kaleidoscopic hijinks the walls and floor were indulging in.

"My sister Nova."

"Yeah? What's Second Speaker do?"

He almost smiled. "What the First Speaker commands." There was a slight pause before he elaborated. "Second Speaker has no power, except if the First Speaker is unable to perform her duties. In that situation, the Second Speaker takes these upon himself until the First Speaker is again able or until another has been chosen."

"How do you choose a First Speaker?" Miri persisted. "By age? Nova's older than you?"

"Nova is younger, a bit. Shan is eldest. He had been First Speaker after—after Uncle Er Thom died. But he is a Trader, you see, so he trained Nova for the task and then refused Second, saying he would be off-world too often." His voice was almost back to normal. "Nova is best choice for First: she is on Liad most of the time and is a Rememberer, which is an aid when speaking for the Clan before the Clans."

"You ain't on Liad much, are you? How come you drew second slot?"

He actually smiled. "It gives Nova just cause to complain that I am so seldom at home."

She laughed and nodded at a shimmering doorway. "Here we go."

They entered and he allowed her to lead him to the bed, finally retrieving his arm as she sat, feet swinging high off the floor. He turned to go.

"Val Con."

One eyebrow tilted as he looked back; the horror was still there.

She waved at the bed. "You're beat too, remember? That's what started this whole thing. And this bed's big enough for all the Gyrfalks to sleep on and not be crowded." She grinned. "Your honor's safe with me."

He shadow-smiled, sighed, and came back. "All right."

Sitting on the edge of the bed, he stroked the coverlet and glanced at the woman who already lay curled, eyes closed.

"Miri?"

Her eyes flicked open. "Yeah?"

"Thank you for your care. I was—trapped—in my thoughts. . . ."

"No problem. Used to have to do it three-four times a year. Part of the joys of being a sergeant. Now go to sleep, okay? And turn off the light, if you can figure out how it works."

He laughed softly. "Yes, Sergeant," he murmured. He waved a slim hand over the flat plate set high in the wall above the bed. The light dimmed to two glowing bulbs, one red and one blue, miming alien moons.

He lay atop the coverlet, staring at them, afraid to close his eyes. . . .

"Go to sleep, kid," Miri grumped at him.

Obediently, Val Con closed his eyes.

And slept.

HE WOKE, unsure of what had called him back, and lay listening, eyes closed. Silence—no. The sound of someone breathing in sleep, nearby. His right arm was numb and appeared to be pinned.

He opened his eyes.

There was Miri, face drowned in sleep, head resting on his right arm, one hand beside her cheek, fingers clutching his sleeve.

He felt a surprising twist of something sharp in the center of his chest—painful, yet not painful. He clamped his teeth to contain the gasp and took several deep, slow breaths. The sensation became less sharp, though it remained, warm and cold together.

He had never seen her face at rest before; he noted the slim brows that curved above the lightly lashed eyes, and the spangle of freckles across her nose, spilling here and there onto her cheeks. Her full mouth was smiling faintly, as if what she dreamed pleased her.

Beautiful Miri, he thought and was surprised at the thought, even as he extended a hand to stroke her cheek.

Six hours before, he had tried to kill her.

He snatched his hand back, fist clenched, and flung his mind away, seeking that which had awakened him.

The ship has ceased its labor.

He shifted slightly. "Miri."

She stirred, lashes flickering, and tried to settle her head more firmly on his arm.

"Miri," he repeated. "Wake up."

The gray eyes flicked open, regarding him softly for the space of a heartbeat before they sharpened. "Why?"

"The ship has stopped, and I require the use of my arm."

She frowned, released his shirt, and twisted to a

sitting position with a cat's awkward grace. "Stopped? Are we there?"

"No," he said, trying to rub feeling back into his numb arm. "The ship rests after eight hours in drive, Watcher said. It is out of drive now, which means we have four hours in normal space to recalibrate and measure and make necessary adjustments." A needling sensation signaled the return of utility to his arm; he swung his feet over the edge of the bed and dropped lightly to the floor.

Miri surveyed the room. The psychedelic effects seemed to have stopped while they slept, and she thanked the gods for their favor. She slid across the bed and jumped down.

"Well, what're we waiting for? Are we going to the control room or ain't we?"

SHE STARED AT the navigation tank for several minutes before she walked over to the board and sat astride one of the benches, facing her partner.

"Val Con?"

He flicked a glance at her, then returned to the board. "Yes."

"Umm—I ain't a pilot or a navigator, so maybe I'm missing something, but—ain't that the same star pattern we were in when this tub went into drive?"

He sighed and straightened a little on the bench to ease his back. "No, not exactly. We are actually four light-years from Prime." He bent forward to check a dial and moved his eyes to her face again, half-smiling. "Or, put another way: We've just reached Terran short-Jump."

"What!" She stared at him, suddenly suspicious. "You're laughing at me."

He held up his hands. "No—or at *us.* Clutch ships are slow—rather like Clutch people. I don't remember how it is exactly that their drive works—one of those things people make you study but there isn't any real use for it. . . ." He pushed three knobs in sequence, glancing up at the tank. "But it does work on an entirely different principle than Terran or Liaden ships—Electron Substitution Drive. For whatever good a name may do."

"Like saying you understand how a Terran ship works because of the Congruency Flaw," she agreed, frowning absently at the tank. "Boss, it's gonna take us a hundred years to get out of the sector."

"Not quite. Three or three-and-a-half weeks to Volmer, assuming Watcher has coded the destination properly."

"What I said." She tipped her head. "You don't remember anything about how this drive works—just that it's different?"

"I do sometimes forget things," he murmured.

"Just don't seem like you, somehow." She stood. "I'm going to the bookroom. Unless there's something useful I can do here?"

His attention on the board, he shook his head. She left, shrugging and trying to ignore the flare of irritation she felt.

✦ CHAPTER SEVENTEEN ✦

IT HAD TAKEN some time to get things sorted out. Happily, the victim's fingers had been retrieved intact and there was an excellent chance that they would be successfully replaced. The incisions, the doctor told Mr. Ing over the comm, had been almost surgically precise.

That out of the way, it had taken rather longer than Ing had hoped, though no longer than he had expected, to coax information from the young Clutch person seated on the other side of his desk, seriously taxing the structural integrity of the sturdiest chair available on the Station. Finally, however, Ing had the short-form name of a kinsman.

The blur on his screen became the head and shoulders of another Clutch person. "Yes?" it inquired.

Ing inclined his head. "May I have the honor," he began in Trade, "to speak with he who is named in the short form Twelfth Shell Fifth Hatched Knife Clan of Middle River's Spring Spawn of Farmer Greentrees of The Spearmaker's Den, The Edger?"

The big eyes blinked. "You are, please?"

Extremely brief, for Clutch. Ing began to entertain hopes of putting it all neatly to bed in another three or four hours. "This person is called Xavier Ponstella Ing, Dayside Supervisor Prime Station Municipality of Lufkit."

The person on the screen inclined its head. "I shall inform the *T'carais*. Please do not sever the connection." The screen was abruptly empty of Clutch persons, displaying instead an abstract design in blue, green, and orange.

Ing glanced over the comm at his prisoner. "Perhaps," he tried, "it would be well for you to come here, where your kinsman will be able to see you and where you will be able to speak with each other more easily."

There was a pause long enough to let Ing wonder if his words had been understood. Then the youngling levered himself out of the chair and came around the table, shuffling, to stand behind Ing's shoulder.

On the screen the abstract was replaced with the countenance of yet another Clutch person. This one was old, Ing saw: his shell nearly covered his shoulders.

"I am he with whom you requested speech, Xavier Ponstella Ing. To save your time, it should be said immediately that, among humans, I have no objection to the name Edger," the big voice rumbled through the speakers, picking up some static. Ing adjusted the gain and bowed his head profoundly.

"This person is most often addressed as Ing," he said. "I'm afraid there has been an altercation on Prime between your kinsman, whom you left to watch your vessel, and a human." He paused, but Edger seemed willing to hear him out completely.

"I am not sure how it came about," he continued, "for the human was in shock from his injuries when aid arrived, and your kinsman appears to have less than a good command of the trading tongue. The short of it is that your kinsman seems to have bitten two fingers from the hand of a human person on this station. This is a criminal offense—it is called Assault and Battery—for which we have punishments. Since this incident involves your kinsman, however, I would not presume to punish him without your knowledge and consent." Ing hoped the old boy was a reasonable sort.

"This human person," Edger said. "What was the name?"

"Herbert Alan Costello," Ing said, wondering.

"Ah. And the condition of Herbert Alan Costello? It seems that I have heard it dangerous for humans to experience the state called 'shock.'"

The old gentleman was really concerned, Ing thought. He hadn't expected that, considering the kid's attitude.

"I have recently spoken with the doctor, who assures me that the fingers will be able to be replaced and that function should return, perhaps wholly, but certainly to the ninetieth percentage. It was most fortunate that we were able to recover the fingers in such excellent condition."

"Most fortunate, indeed," Edger agreed. "You spoke of punishment. It is the custom of our Clan to mete punishment to members of the Clan. It would shame me to have it said that I am so lacking in propriety that I allowed a kinsman of mine to be corrected by one of another Clan, no matter how shamefully he had behaved.

It would mean much to me, were you to honor this custom. I assure you that this person will be punished in full measure for his crime."

"It would also mean much to me," he went on, "if you would ascertain the sum of Herbert Alan Costello's medical expenses, as well as the cost of maintaining his household while he is unable to pursue his rightful occupation. I will pay this sum to Herbert Alan Costello, and also whatever blood-price is appropriate. I depend upon your advice in the matter, since I cannot presume to place a price on such damage to a human, who may not regenerate what he has lost. I would do everything that is proper, so that this disgrace does not mar the goodwill that exists between the Clutch and the Clans of Men."

Ing blinked. "You are very generous," he began.

Edger waved a large hand. "I am mortified that one of my Clan should have acted in such a manner. I repeat that he will not go unpunished. He is young and without experience, it is true, but there is no excuse for the lack of courtesy that you have brought to my attention. It is mine to rectify, and to hope that Herbert Alan Costello regains the full use of his hand."

Edger shifted his gaze upward and back, his large eyes hardening. Ing felt a moment's sympathy for the kid behind him.

"I am also ashamed," Edger said, speaking to Ing, though his eyes were on Watcher, "that you have somehow been led to believe that my kinsman does not speak Trade. His knowledge of that language is adequate. It is beyond my comprehension that he would not have spoken when addressed in that tongue and thereby made an accounting of himself to an Elder-in-Charge."

Ing would have sworn that Watcher cringed.

"Maybe," he offered, "your kinsman was also in shock of some kind. The condition does sometimes rob persons of language for a time, even the tongue they have spoken since birth." Hell, it was only a kid.

"You are kind," Edger said with awesome dignity. "I take note of your effort to soften the blow to our honor, but I am not persuaded that this was the case.

"Watcher!" he snapped, still in Trade. "You will come to me. You will come with whatever person or persons Xavier Ponstella Ing deems proper to send with you, so he might be assured that you will damage no other beings before you are under my eyes. You will come in whatever haste or deliberateness Elder Ing adjudges proper. Above all, you will speak when spoken to, and answer all questions honorably and in the best fullness that time allows. You will think upon the uses of courtesy among and between all peoples, and you will have an accounting of yourself and your actions to lay before me when you arrive. Have you understood all that I have said to you?"

"Yes, *T'carais*." Watcher's voice was barely audible.

"And will you obey?"

"Yes, *T'carais*," Watcher replied even more softly.

"I leave you then to the care of Elder Xavier Ponstella Ing, to remove you to me within his own customs and traditions. Goodbye." This last had apparently been meant for both. The screen went suddenly dark.

The kid looked decidedly shaken, Ing thought. "Okay, Watcher, why don't you have a seat while I arrange transportation? We'll have you on-world within the next day."

No matter what other punishment awaited him should he show further lack of courtesy, Watcher could not bring himself to thank Elder Ing for this consideration of him.

EDGER CERTAINLY HAD an amazing number of books, even granting that fewer than a third were written in a language that Miri could read. A brief search among those produced *The Young Person's Book of Space Drives,* by Professor Thos. Swift, and *A Beginner's Course in High Liaden,* by Anne Davis.

Anne Davis? The name was vaguely familiar. Miri scouted up a reader, curled up comfortably on the upholstered ledge that seemed to be the Clutch's answer to overstuffed chairs, and fed that tape in first.

"Anne Davis," the bio at the beginning told her, "was a Heidelberg Fellow and respected comparative linguist. Her work included compilations and cross-checks of the major Terran dialects, and is considered a touchstone of contemporary linguistic research. However, she is best known for her in-depth study of High Liaden, as well as the several grammars and self-paced study texts of this complex and beautiful language. A manuscript outlining the grammar and following the structural shifts of Low Liaden was left uncompleted at the time of her death. She is survived by three natural children: Shan, Nova, and Anthora yos'Galan; and a fosterchild: Val Con yos'Phelium."

Miri blinked, remembering his story of the aunt who had taught him to play the 'chora. Just your luck,

Robertson, she thought. Leave off wondering who he really is and up pops verification.

She rewound the book and set it aside for later study, then fed the other into the reader, arranging herself more comfortably against the ledge and manipulating the forward control.

"There are four kinds of space drives in use in the known Galaxy at the present time," Chapter One informed her cheerily. "The three best known are the Terran, or Congruency Flaw Drive; the Liaden, or Quark Retraction Drive; and the Clutch, or Electron Substitution Drive. The fourth kind of drive is that used by the Yxtrang, but no one has yet been able to discover exactly what kind of drive it is."

"Bloody guess not," she commented. Yxtrang never let a ship fall to capture, instead destroying full battle crews if necessary. A few ships had, nonetheless, been taken— mostly by the sneaky Liadens who, to be fair, had been trying longer. Those captured ships had destroyed themselves when entry was forced, taking the boarding parties with them. The best thing about Yxtrang ships was that there weren't many of them. The worst thing was that there were any at all.

"Terran and Liaden ships," the text continued, "make use of a mathematical probability called the Similarity Constant, which allows ships to cover great distances very quickly. Since Terran and Liaden mathematicians envision this concept in slightly different ways, the Congruency Flow and the Quark Retraction Drives are not exactly equal in terms of the time it takes vessels to cover a given distance.

"For instance, a Terran cargo ship might traverse 50 light-years within 50 seconds. The same journey might take a Liaden freighter 50 hours. This comparison, of course, is for ordinary purposes of calculation.

"It has been reported that Liadens possess some vessels at the one-and two-man size which, though not necessarily faster than Terran ships, are able to perform close-in maneuvers that allow them a head start on a vessel that must put several light-hours between itself and the nearest planetary body before commencing the Congruency maneuver."

Yeah, so Liaden Scout ships are fast and do tricks and you're jealous, Miri thought. What about Clutch ships?

"The Electron Substitution Drive utilized by the members of the Clutch takes advantage of the ability of an electron to appear in a new orbit before leaving its original orbit." Huh? "This means that Clutch ships move along in a series of physical 'burps' of about one light-day, always making sure that there is room for it where it is going before it leaves where it is."

Miri closed her eyes and scrubbed her hands vigorously over her face before reading that last bit one more time.

"This method of travel," the book continued, "is extremely efficient of energy as it utilizes the mass available around the ship to aid propulsion. It is this aspect of the drive that accounts for the Clutch's navigation through densely populated starfields, rather than attempting to avoid these, as do Terran and Liaden vessels. The Electron Substitution Drive is also much,

much slower than the other two drives we've discussed, but time is rarely of the essence to Clutch people. . . ."

Working with the forward, she scanned the rest of the book quickly, looking for reports of side-effects of the Clutch's goofy drive. She found nothing. Apparently humans didn't ride in Clutch ships. Which made sense, in a way: Why take three weeks when another ship can make the trip in two days?

She shook her head and leaned back. That was another problem with being so short-lived, she guessed. One had to risk one's life for a chance to live more. She wondered what the psychedelics were like for Edger.

Pushing the reader to one side, she stretched and fished in her pouch for a ration stick, then stopped with her fingers on the seal-rip. There's supposed to be real food somewhere on this tub, she thought. Tough Guy— Val Con—probably he knows where.

She rolled to her feet and headed leisurely for the control room.

IT TOOK A LITTLE over half an hour to line up a special shuttle and guard. Watcher would be escorted on the shuttle from Prime to Econsey Port, and in the truck that would bear him from there to the hyatt where his kin awaited him. He should, Ing told Watcher, be with Edger within the next planet day.

Watcher bowed his head, as was proper when addressing an Elder-in-Charge, and spoke as politely as he was able, though the tongue called Trade barely lent itself to courtesy. "Thank you for your care of me. I regret the inconvenience."

"Well, I regret it, too," Ing said frankly. "But it's done now, and you'll have to take your punishment. Just take what's coming to you and then shape up, okay? Nothing like this needs to ever happen again."

Watcher murmured that there was no doubt much in what Elder Ing said. Watcher would devote thought to his words.

Ing left it at that and showed the kid to a holding area where he would be guarded by a nervous security woman until the transport personnel showed up to claim him.

TAKING THE LEFT hand hallway from the library, rather than the right, Miri bypassed the swimming pool and came instead to a garden. Plants hung in pots, climbed trellises, and crept along the ground, surrounding artistic little clearings and comfortably shaped benchstones. It was a pleasant place, except that the light was a little dull and the temperature rather more sultry than Miri, bred on cold Surebleak, could like. Still, she lingered for a time, inspecting some purple and yellow flowers creeping along the floor, and studying a cheery red cluster of fruit on a trellis-climbing vine. She wondered idly if these were grapes and what sort of wine they'd make.

Eventually she moved out of the garden, going down a short corridor that intersected the hallway of the sleeping rooms, which in turn led very quickly to the control room.

Val Con was not in the control room. No reason why he should be, she allowed, with the facilities of a ship this size at his command. Still, she was irked and, spying the pile of—things—on the table, worried.

She approached the table cautiously and stood with her hands behind her back, frowning as she sorted the items by eye.

Well, there was his gun. And that was surely the throwing blade he'd shown her in the alley outside her hideout—how long ago? But *that* was only the cord from his shirt, and the flat metal rectangle looked for all the worlds like a creditcard, and *those* were his boots. . . .

He entered the room silently at her back and she turned on the instant, eyebrows up.

"What've you been doing to your face?" she asked. "It's all red."

He smiled and came over to the table. "Edger's soap is *sand*. I'm pleased to have skin left of any color."

She surveyed him without comment: hair damp, face slightly abraded, shirt unlaced, sleeves rolled up revealing more abrasion on his arms, and she wondered about the force he'd used with the soapsand. He was beltless and barefoot. She flicked her eyes to his face and discovered no trace of last night's horror. He returned her gaze calmly, his eyes a clear and bottomless green.

Breaking that gaze, she waved her hand at the pile on the table. "Cleaning house?"

"These are weapons, Miri. I want you to hide them, please."

"How come I get all the fun jobs? And why? And even if I do, boots ain't weapons, friend. Neither is a belt, except under certain exceptional conditions I'm willing to risk. Man shouldn't walk around with his shirt unlaced—ain't genteel. *And* you oughta keep the creditcard—never know when you're gonna need cash."

He picked up the black cord that had laced his shirt, slid it through his fingers, and allowed his hands to go through the proper motions.

"Garrote."

The creditcard he used to shave a curl of rock from the wall behind him. He offered her the shaving.

"Guillotine."

He flipped the belt to reveal the inside surface and its three distinct layers.

"Explosives, electronic picklock, sawblade."

He laid the belt down and pointed.

"The right boot has an explosive charge built into the heel, as well as a climbing spike that extrudes from the toe. The left has the climbing spike and a manual picklock in the heel."

He sat, abruptly drained, and waved a hand to include the jumble of wires, pins, and metal doodads.

"Whatever the moment demands. Push a pin behind an ear; drive a piece of wire into an eye—death. Or—"

"I get the picture," she interrupted and then stood for a long, silent time, surveying the pile. Something caught her eye and she pulled it to her.

A black sheath of the finest suede, enclosing and caressing the blade within. The handle was made of something that gleamed like polished obsidian, yet was warm to her touch.

Gently, she curled her hand around it and pulled the blade free.

It glittered in the light, catching and dispersing rays— a live thing, she would swear it, made all of green crystal and black.

With reverence she slid the blade back into its nest—the fit was not proper for her hand, and she knew that the knife had been made for one grip alone. Silently, she held it out to him.

His hand jumped forward, clenched, then dropped.

"Edger gave you this." It was not a question. "Let's keep it simple, kid: You kill me with the knife Edger gave you, and I won't argue that I didn't need killing." She pushed it at him. "*Take* it!"

Hesitantly, he obeyed, running his fingers over the handle in a caress.

Miri turned sharply, flinging her hands out. "And all the rest of it, too! Put it on, put it back, throw it out— *I don't care!* It don't make sense to hide 'em, so I won't." And she suddenly sat, breathing a bit too hard and hanging on tight to her temper.

"Miri, listen to me. I can kill you—"

She snorted. "Old news, spacer."

He shook his head. "I-can-kill-*you*. At any time. I—believe you may be right and that I am—walking on the knife's edge." He paused to even his breathing. He had to make her understand! "You might take your gun out to clean it, and I would react only to the gun—not the cleaning—and you would die. Last night, I very nearly did kill you—"

Her fist hit the table as she snapped to her feet "With your *hands*, you *cashutas*! You never went for *one* of those damn things, and it's my belief you won't!"

She sat as suddenly as she had stood, swallowing hard in a throat gone dry, eyes fixed on the shine and glitter that was a silver snake holding a blue gem fast in its jaws.

"I don't believe you'll kill me," she said. "I won't believe it."

He waited for her to look up, then spoke with utmost gentleness. "Miri, how many people have I killed since first we came together?"

She rounded her eyes. "Weren't *you* counting?" A sharp shake of the head followed. "Those were strangers. In self-defense. War conditions. And last night was a special case. You were out of your head—battle shock. I've seen it before. Knew you'd come out of it like a tiger fightin' a cyclone. My mistake was thinking I could get out of range in time. So we screwed up and we're alive to argue about it. Some people have all the luck."

"Miri—"

"No!" she yelled. Then she continued more calmly. "No. I don't wanna hear any more about it. The only way to convince me you'll kill me is to do it, *accazi*? I think you're the craziest person I ever met—and that's a compliment considering what you've managed to get done while quietly going bats. And I think the thing responsible, the thing that's making you so bats, is that damn—*estimator*—sitting in your head talking to itself.

"People ain't ciphers, and situations with people in 'em are by definition random, subject to chance, mischance, and happy circumstance. You can't calculate it." She rubbed her hands over her face and took a deep breath. "You derail that thing and you'll be sane as a stone; chuck this damn job and get one playin' the chora somewhere ritzy. . . ." She let her words trail off and rubbed at her face again.

He waited, watching her.

"Aah, I talk too much." She pushed to her feet, waving a hand at the pile between them. "Here's the deal: You point me in the direction of food and I'll make us something to eat, okay? And while I'm doing that, will you for Great Panth's sake get *rid* of this stuff?"

✦ CHAPTER EIGHTEEN ✦

VOLMER.

The price of obtaining that single word had been high, but orders had been to spare no expense. Upon being told what his money had bought, Justin Hostro nodded and issued more expensive orders yet.

A ship. Two dozen men of the first rank. Weapons. All to be assembled immediately and sent forthwith to Volmer.

Matthew bowed and saw that all was done as ordered.

IN THE END, he relaced his shirt, pulled on his boots and stood to wrap his belt around his waist. From the weapons pile he pulled back Clan knife, throwing knife, gun. Rediscovering in himself the strong distaste that he'd felt as an agent-in-training for the pins, doodads, and acid, he pushed those aside; he hesitated briefly before reclaiming the creditcard and wire.

Taking the pile of discarded junk to the far side of the room, he opened a compartment in the seemingly blank wall, piled everything inside, and shut the door. At the control board, he touched two knobs in sequence, nodding in satisfaction at the slight vibration that followed.

Miri glanced up from her labors with dinner as he returned to the table. "What'd you do?"

"Spaced it. I never liked them." He shrugged. "The first time I saw that little pillow filled with acid I nearly lost my last meal." He perched on the edge of the table, watching her.

She put the cover over the bowl that would eventually contain a mushroom soufflé, picked up two nearby mugs, and handed him one, waving at the bowl.

"Dinner takes about forty-five minutes to reconstitute. I hope you like mushroom soufflé a lot, 'cause that's all that's in that box. An' I hope the wine's okay, 'cause the other case is full of nothing but." She grinned. "Sorry 'bout the stemware—came with the kitchen."

"It looks fine to me." He sipped, one eyebrow lifting in appreciation.

"I was afraid it was gonna be real good," Miri said wistfully.

"It is good," he said, puzzled. "Taste it."

She sipped gingerly, then sighed. "Yeah. Trouble is, stuff like this tastes so fine you want to keep drinking it. Kind of ruins your mouth for *kynak*."

"Liz said you like fine things," he murmured.

"Liz *said*," Miri corrected sharply, "that I got no sense about beautiful things. That I think pretty can't hurt as bad as ugly. It's an old line." She glared at him.

He endured it, sipping.

After a moment, she shrugged. "Edger says *you're* gentle and good. So what?"

His face tightened with the unexpected bolt of pain. "Certain people have thought so. . . ."

"Yah." Her tone was disbelieving.

She did have some reason to doubt that, he thought. Who, indeed, might have thought such a thing?

"Edger," he began, suddenly needing to hear the names of those who loved him. "Shan, Nova, Anthora—"

"Relatives," she jibed.

"Daria—" Too late, he clamped his mouth on that name.

Miri raised her brows. "Daria? Who's that? Your first grade teacher?"

"We were lovers."

"And then she discovered your true nature."

He took a large swallow of wine and looked into the depths of the mug. "She died," he said clearly.

"Yeah? You kill her?"

He gasped, head snapping up, eyes sharp with outrage. His mouth twisted and he forced himself to take slow, deep breaths. "No," he told her. "I had not yet reached the place where I might slay what I love."

Slapping the mug to the table, he slid to his feet and walked out.

Miri stood for a long time, breathing—only breathing. When she was sure of herself again, she picked up the mug and went to find him.

HE WHO WATCHES was ushered into the presence of his *T'carais* by four human guards and roundly ignored while that exalted person offered them food and drink. They refused, politely enough, if briefly, saying that duty required them to return to port immediately they had relinquished Watcher to his kinsman's custody.

Thus they took their leave, and Edger at last turned his attention to the son of his sister's sister.

"Have you an accounting of your actions to lay before me?" he inquired in Trade.

"Kinsman," Watcher began in their own language.

"No." Edger waved a hand. "We shall speak in the tongue known as Trade, since you require practice in its use." He motioned permission to speak. "You may proceed with your accounting."

"Kinsman," repeated Watcher in the barbarous shortness of the language called Trade. "I am ashamed that I allowed myself to become so unnerved by the behavior of the persons to whom you found yourself indebted to the extent that they might claim the use of— of our ship—that I offered violence to a creature—a being—so much weaker than myself—"

"Cease."

Watcher obeyed and stood silent, striving to maintain personal dignity while the *T'carais* stared at him.

In the fullness of time, Edger spoke again. "It would perhaps be instructive for you to tell me further of the persons who came and claimed our vessel for their use. Do so."

"They came together, *T'carais:* one dark-furred, the other bright; both very small. The dark one interrupted me as I began to introduce myself, saying it was in too much haste for the exchange of names and that I must instruct it—"

"The proper syllable is 'he' in this instance, as the

person you speak of is a male of the human species. The brightly-furred companion is a female of the same species and shall be referred to as 'she' or 'her' in accordance with rules of grammar applied to this tongue. Continue."

Watcher clenched himself in mortification—to be instructed so, as if he were an eggling!—and took up the thread of his tale.

". . . that I must instruct him, *T'carais*, in the piloting skills necessary to take the vessel where he desired. This I did and set in coordinates for the planet named Volmer or V87350273, as he instructed. Then did he bid me to say to you this. . . ." He paused, awaiting permission.

It came: a flick of the hand.

Scrupulously adhering to the original phrasing and inflection, Watcher repeated: "I would that you say to my brother Edger. . . ." He paused once more when he reached the end of it. The *T'carais* waved at him to continue.

"Then he bade me go, saying that I must do so in the greatest of haste, as he would cause the ship to enter into labor within five of Standard minutes. At no time, kinsman," Watcher cried, unable to contain himself longer, "was I treated with courtesy or consideration by this person, who offered neither his name nor that of his companion nor asked after mine. Nor did he—"

"You will be silent," Edger commanded. He closed his eyes and, after a time, re-opened them.

"You are young," he said, "and it is perhaps possible that you have no knowledge of the person of whom you speak. This might account for something of your discontent with his behavior, though I feel that the fact that he is my brother should have borne more heavily with you.

"Know then, Uninformed One, that this person is named, in present fullness: Val Con yos'Phelium Scout, Artist of the Ephemeral, Slayer of the Eldest Dragon, Knife Clan of Middle River's Spring Spawn of Farmer Greentrees of the Spearmaker's Den, Tough Guy. Know also that I make no being my brother who is not worthy. And know at last that the person who tends this name is yet—*even yet*—of an age where he would not have attained the first of his shells, were he of our race." He paused, allowing Watcher time to think on what he had heard.

"Further reflect," he continued, "that the tenor of his message indicates that my brother was in danger of his life. Appreciate now that he paused in doing that which was necessary to preserve himself and his companion to make known to me his death desire, as is fitting between brothers, and to assure me of his honor and affection. I fail to find in this action discourtesy or aught less than what might be expected of an honorable and great-hearted person of any race. I am ashamed that one of my Clan should be so far lost to propriety that he could fail to see and understand this."

Watcher bowed his head. "I will think much on what you have said, T'carais."

"Do so. For the moment, however, continue with your accounting. How came it to pass that Herbert Alan Costello has been maimed by a member of my Clan?"

"After your brother dismissed me, T'carais, I passed down the tunnel at a rapid rate, sealed the inner door, and signaled that I was without. I felt the vibration of the vessel entering drive and at the same moment heard a person shouting in Trade. The words were 'Hey, you!' I did not understand that they were addressed to me until this person who is Herbert Alan Costello laid his hand upon my arm." Watcher could not quite control his blink of revulsion at the memory. Edger motioned for him to continue.

"He asked where your brother and his companion had gone and, when I did not answer, he spoke words which I feel were threatening, stating that, should I not say where these two had gone, that there were ways to make me do so. I was at that present upset by my inability to appreciate your exalted brother and when Herbert Alan Costello said these words and pushed his fingers at my face, I bit him." Watcher bowed his head. "That is what transpired, T'carais. I am ashamed."

"As is proper. You will now present yourself to your kinsman Selector and make known to him my desire that you serve him as he requires. Also, think on what I have said to you, as I will think upon what you have said to me. We will speak of your punishment at another time."

"Yes, T'carais."

HE WAS IN the atrium, lying on his stomach on a patch of springy blue grass, chin resting on his folded arms. If he heard her approach, he gave no sign.

Looking down at him, she considered slitting her own throat, but rejected that as a coward's answer and sat cross-legged at his side, where he might see her if he chose to turn his head.

He did not so choose.

Miri pinched herself to make sure she was really there, and wet her lips. "It is my sorrow to have caused you sorrow," she began in stumbling High Liaden, "and my pain to have incurred your displeasure. In my need to say that which I felt to be of importance, I wounded you. That my motives were of the highest does not excuse me." She took a deep breath and concluded in rapid Terran, "I'm a rude bitch."

His shoulders jerked and he turned his head to look at her. "Miri. . . ."

"Hey, I'm sorry! But you could cut me some slack, y'know? I didn't expect you to fall for it! Could've knocked me over with a snowflake—"

He was laughing. "Miri, how can you be so absurd?"

"I practice," she told him earnestly. "Every day. Even when I don't feel good." She held out the mug. "Here's your wine."

He made no move to take it, though he rolled into a cross-legged seat facing her, arms resting on his thighs. "Liz *did* say that you were less than wary of beauty."

"Yeah, well, at least she didn't tell you I was good," she said, frowning down at the mug.

"Most likely she felt I would see that for myself."

She snapped her eyes to his face, unsure of the expression there. "Now you *are* laughing at me."

"Am I? Terran is a hard language in which to make a compliment."

"Not like Liaden," she agreed, "which it's impossible to make sentences in."

"The High Tongue can be inflexible," he conceded

thoughtfully. "But that is because it's very like Terran in its purposes: imparting information, dealing with technical and trade concerns, keeping people at a polite arm's length. The Low Tongue is for expressing feelings, relationships—human things. Much of the meaning is in the inflection—something like working the sound stops on a 'chora, to get more mileage out of the words."

"Sounds hard to learn."

"Easier to learn than to explain, I think. Anne found that. I believe that is the reason she never finished her second grammar."

Miri shifted, irritably conscious of the mug she held. "Edger has her book on High Liaden in his collection. Thought I'd learn the language right, since I got almost three weeks to kill."

He looked at her closely. "Will you go to your family, then?"

"I ain't got—Oh. You mean Clan Whoever-they-are." She shook her head. "They ain't family."

"Erob is your Clan, Miri. I am certain they'd be honored to learn of a child such as you."

"Well, I don't know why they should be," she said, puzzled. "They don't know me from Old Dan Tucker."

He lifted a brow. "From who?"

"See? And we were even introduced."

He shook his head, frowning. "You are a daughter of the Clan, one who is courageous and strong, quick in perception and thought. I know of no House so wealthy in its members that it would shun you. You would be an asset to Erob. They would welcome you and provide you your birthright."

"It don't figure," she told him. "I don't know them and they don't know me. I sure wouldn't go to them if I was in trouble. I'd go to Edger before them."

There was a small silence. "Perhaps it would be best," he said softly, "to go to Edger, were you in trouble."

Miri set the mug carefully on the grass between them. He did not appear to see.

"How'd you get to be Edger's brother?" she asked, more because she was uncomfortable with the lengthening silence than because she had planned to ask the question.

He lifted a brow. "By right of the dragon we slew between us."

"Dragon?"

"Grant me some knowledge of the species; a dragon figures prominently in Korval's shield."

"And it breathed fire and everything?"

"It is possible," he admitted, "that we struck it down before it had completed its graduate work. Indisputably, however, a dragon. I believe it compensated for any handicap attendant to an inability to breathe flame by growing at least three times more teeth than were necessary, and growing them three times longer than I feel was strictly required. Quite terrifying."

She studied his face, sensing a joke of some kind; she caught the barest gleam of what might have been— mischief? "So you and Edger killed it between you," she guessed, "with just a crystal knife and a handful of pebbles."

"No, Edger had a lance. I had a pellet gun, of course, but the thing was so large that it was simply a waste of time to shoot it." He shook his head. "I was stupid with fear and reached for my belt, feeling for a bigger gun. The best thing I had was a flare gun, so I fired at its face. That distracted it long enough for Edger to make the kill. Luck."

"Some people got it all," she agreed, unconvinced. "You sure you're not leaving something out? Or making something up?"

"It happened exactly that way," he said, eyes wide. "Why should I invent it? Edger will tell you the same tale."

"Why do I doubt that?" she wondered and held up a hand. "Never mind. I'd hate for you to perjure yourself." She pointed. "You want that wine or don't you?"

"I would very much like to have the wine," he said, making no move to take it or, indeed, even looking at it. His face was completely sober now, and he kept his eyes on hers. "Miri. Why?"

Ah, hell, she thought. "Why which?"

Val Con pushed the hair off his forehead, brows up. "Shall I determine the order of the explanation, then?" He waited, but she waited longer, and his mouth twitched slightly.

"Very well. Why did you push, not to say entrap me?"

She hesitated, hearing his voice in memory: "It is my intention to tell you the truth. . . ." So many debts, she thought suddenly, all to be paid in kind.

She licked her lips, and tried to explain.

"I wanted to make the point—to make sure you understood—that it might be true that you ain't the person you used to be. But I don't think you're the person you *think* you are, either." She paused, fighting for clarity.

"Everybody who *does* things, sometimes does things they ain't proud of. It's just that you gotta—gotta learn from it and get on with things and try not to make that mistake again." She took a breath and resisted the temptation to close her eyes.

"And it ain't—*right*—for you to take the whole blame for the things you did 'cause somebody else forced you. 'Specially not," she concluded in a rush, "when it's clear they've been walking inside your head with combat boots on and screwing around mightily with the wiring!"

His smile flickered. "Why take the burden of proving this point upon yourself? When, whether you choose to believe it or not, I am dangerous and unpredictable?"

"I don't—I don't want you to die . . . Being made over to somebody else's specs—that's dying, ain't it?"

There was a small pause. "Perhaps. But why do you care?"

She moved her head, not quite a shake, not quite breaking eye contact. "You said you'd been a Scout— *First-In* Scout. . . ."

"Yes."

She felt herself tensing and tried to ignore it. "You remember what it was like—being a Scout?"

His brows pulled sharply together. "How could I not?"

"Just checkin'." She kept her voice matter-of-fact. "Scouts ain't the same as spies."

"True," he said calmly. "A Scout must complete quite a bit of training in order to become a spy." He paused, then continued gently, "I have completed *all* of that training. Miri."

"So you said. But you remember what it was like when

you were a Scout and that's more'n I expected—" She cut herself off and began again, on what seemed a tangent.

"You know about friends—there's Edger—and about partners . . . okay," she said, apparently now having it sorted to her satisfaction. "I care because you're trying to be my friend. Maybe you don't even know why—that's okay, 'cause I'm your friend and I'm damned if I know why I should be. And we're partners—though it don't look like either one of us is very good at it.

"People," she continued, as one spelling out basic truths, "help their friends. That's what holds it all together. If people didn't help their friends, then everything would fall apart. I'm in favor of holding things together, so I help my friends." She looked at him closely, wondering at the unease she saw in his face. "You understand all that, Tough Guy?"

He closed his eyes and bowed his head.

"Do I lose?" she asked after what her stretched nerves insisted was a very long time.

His shoulders jerked and he looked up. "I hope not," he murmured. He straightened abruptly, smiling into her eyes.

"It is good to have a friend." Picking up the mug, he drank deeply and offered it to her.

She paused with her hand half-extended to take it, searching his face. His smile deepened, lighting the depths of his eyes, and he nodded slightly.

Stomach fluttering, she took the mug and drank what was left, returning his smile.

He grinned and snapped to his feet, bending to offer her his hand. She slid her hand into his.

"Do you think dinner is ready by now?" he asked as they went down the garden pathway toward the flower-shrouded doorway.

"I think dinner's ruined by now," she said. "I never was a very good cook."

THE DRIVE HAD kicked in half an hour before. Val Con paused as he reached for his mug, his attention captured by a movement behind Miri's shoulder.

The floor was beginning to ripple, shading from brown toward purple. Sighing, he closed his eyes.

"Starting up already? Didn't it take closer to an hour last time?"

His eyes flicked open. "You, too?"

"Think you're special? Though I'm not getting any—oh-oh, here we go." The wall directly behind his head flared orange. "Ugly. Orange never was one of my favorite colors." She sighed. "Damned silly way to make a space drive, anyway."

Val Con sipped wine. "It seems I should have paid more attention in school." He gestured with the mug, encompassing the room at her back. "This is an effect of the drive, you think?"

"Have it on the best authority," she assured him. "*Space Drives for Dummies* says that the Electron Substitution Drive works on a principle that involves the ability of an electron to arrive in a new orbit before it leaves the old one. So the ship and everything in it—that includes us—must be in two places at once all during the time we're in drive." She took a drink and ignored the fact that the table was beginning to pulse and shimmer.

Val Con was staring, a look of stark disbelief on his face. "Correct me if I'm in error. That means that every electron in the ship and everything in it—including, as I am reminded, us—is firing *twice* for each individual firing in normal space?"

"Sounds right to me, but I'm a soldier, not a physicist."

He looked over her shoulder at the control room. The floor was flashing wildly now, torn by dark lightnings, while the board oozed violet and magenta vapors, and the pilot's bench glowed blue with serpentine streaks.

Taking a deep breath, he expelled it and said something softly in a language that sounded like glass breaking around a steel maul.

"Come again?" Miri asked, interested.

"Never mind. It is not fitting that the youngest of Edger's siblings hear his brother speak of him so."

"I was thinking about that," she said, finishing off her wine setting the mug on the shimmering table with care. "How different is Edger from us in how he—thinks about—things? Maybe all this stuff happens too fast for him to notice. Or maybe he can't see it at all." She frowned slightly. "Do *we* see it?"

He moved his shoulders. "If the mind processes something as experience, then it is experience. Reality is perhaps more difficult to define than truth. . . ."

"The visuals ain't so tough," Miri offered after a minute. "Best thing seems to be to concentrate on something else and let 'em fade into the background. Or we could sleep for the next three weeks—maybe not. Had some real weird dreams last sleep. How 'bout you?"

He was contemplating the navigation tank, which

seemed at this moment to be filled with busy multicolored fish of varied sizes. "I don't dream," he murmured absently, then shook his head slightly and returned his gaze to her face. "It is my feeling that—delicious though it is mushroom soufflé will become just a bit boring in three weeks. Would you care to help me concentrate on a tour of the ship? Perhaps we can find a storeroom containing different kinds of human food."

Her eyes lit. "Coffee!"

He grinned and stood, stretching. "Stranger things have happened."

YXTRANG COMMANDER KHALIIZ considered the scan-tech's data: A single ship, poorly shielded, with three life-forms showing. No doubt Terran, and normally not worthy of the hunt, but booty had been scarce thus far, and the crew was hungry.

"Enter normal space."

The quarry was abruptly before them: a private yacht, with speed alone to its credit. The Commander had seen two of these in the past; both had been personal spacecraft, owned by individuals rather than a Troop. They'd had no weapons and only pitiful shields.

"Scan contact," the Adjutant announced as the low gong sounded. A moment later, he added, "Intruder scan. We are seen."

In the screen the vessel was turning and beginning to accelerate.

"Local radio," the Adjutant reported. "It seems they are calling for aid!"

"Signals responding?" Khaliiz asked.

"None." The Adjutant's voice was filled with the joyful anticipation of battle.

Khaliiz found an answering joy within himself. "Pursue."

EDGER HIMSELF ANSWERED the comm and inclined his head in recognition of the caller. "Xavier Ponstella Ing. A pleasant day to you."

"And to you, sir," Ing replied, bowing his head deeply. "I have the information you requested concerning Herbert Alan Costello."

"You are kind. Is there further news, also, of this person's physical state?"

"The fingers have been replaced and the nerves are disposed to grow and the bones to knit. Another few days will tell the whole tale, of course, but the physician is most optimistic."

"This is welcome information. I shall inform my kinsman, who will rejoice."

Ing doubted it, but neglected to say so; it wouldn't do to offend the old gentleman. "In terms of the other things you wished to know: Herbert Alan Costello is employed by a man named Justin Hostro, who is a private businessperson in Econsey. I am sorry that I have been unable to ascertain from Mr. Hostro's assistant the precise amount of Herbert Alan Costello's wages—"

"This person Hostro is known to me," Edger said, cutting him off in a most un-Clutchlike manner. "We have done business together. I shall myself treat with him on this matter. Yes, I believe that will be best." He inclined his head once more to the man in the screen. "Xavier

Ponstella Ing, you have been most helpful and courteous. I thank you for your care of my kinsman and for your willingness to allow us our customs. My Clan will not forget."

"It is mine to serve," Ing assured him, "and I rejoice to have served well."

"Joy to you, then, Xavier Ponstella Ing, and a good, long life."

✦ CHAPTER NINETEEN ✦

THIS, VAL CON TOLD himself sternly, must stop. There was no indication, however, that it would do so in the near future.

The visuals, as Miri had said, were easily ignored. One simply concentrated on the next order of business and refused to be turned from one's chosen course by fuzzy doors, edges, or ceilings, or by flaring colors. Such things could not be happening. Thus, one walked through them.

The physical effects were more difficult.

His shirt caressed chest and arms with every move as he delightedly slid his palms down leathered thighs. When he put up an exasperated hand to push the hair away from his eyes, the feel of the thick, silky stuff slipping through his fingers nearly had him weeping in pleasure. Irritably, he put his hand to the flickering wall and dragged it along for several paces before admitting defeat there, as well.

Everything felt so nice!

There was worse. At the moment, Miri was walking ahead, allowing him a fine view of her strong, slender shape and the tantalizing hint of sway to her hips. It was a sight that gave him delight, which was not of itself surprising. He had been aware for some time of taking a certain satisfaction in contemplating Miri's physical self; he had, indeed, noted a tendency to allow his eyes to rest upon her more and more frequently. It had not seemed particularly worrisome.

Now, with the beat of the drive calling forth multiple songs of sensuality from body and mind, it was very worrisome, indeed.

There was an inward flicker, and hanging before his mind's eye was the equation showing him how he might take her to his own—though not their mutual—pleasure. CMS wavered between .985 and .993.

Go away! he snarled silently, and it faded, leaving a taste of metal in his mouth.

A position of less jeopardy was required. Stretching his legs, he came alongside her, which put them both in greater safety—he hoped. She looked up at him, grinning, allowing a glance of the sweet curve of her throat down to what lay hidden by the lacing of the snowy shirt.

He slammed to a halt, eyes closed and teeth gritting. Wrong again, he thought. This is getting to be a habit.

Her hand was warm on his arm, and he snapped his eyes open to find her standing closer than he liked, yet not close enough, looking up at him. Sympathy seemed at war with laughter in her face.

"Little bit of lust never hurt anybody."

He shook his head, as if the motion would clear his brain. "It's been a long time."

"With a face like that? Don't lie to your grandmother."

Laughter triumphed over sympathy. "Bet the galaxy's full of green-eyed kids."

"Countless numbers," he agreed. "None of them mine."

"Real waste," she murmured, slipping closer until her hip touched his. Slowly, seeming to take as much pleasure in the sensation as he did, she slid her hands up his arms to his shoulders. "It'll give us something to concentrate on."

His hands of themselves had settled around her waist, holding lightly; he noted that he was trembling. Yes, he thought suddenly, with the surety of a well-played hunch, with no taint of drive-effect attached. Yes and yes and—

No.

Easing back a fraction, be searched her face and found what he sought in the soft curve of her mouth and deep in her eyes. It had been there for a while, he realized with startling clarity, yet she had no notion. For all her life, Miri had played single's odds, and if she could deny what she was feeling before it was conscious, dismiss it as drive-induced pleasure. . . .

He pulled back another inch. "Wait."

She stiffened, mouth tightening. "Guess I'm as bad as Polesta, huh?" Hurt showed on her face—but also relief.

"Oh, Miri. . . ." He dropped his face to her warm, bright hair, rubbing cheek and forehead in its wonderful softness, rumpling her bangs and half unmooring her braid. His retreat was timed to a millisecond; and taking his hands from around her waist required more disciplined timing than the throw that had not broken Polesta's back.

"Well—" Her mouth twisted, and she half-turned away.

He caught one small hand and waited until she turned again to look at him. "When the drive goes off," he said.

She frowned. "What?"

"When we are again in normal space, let us speak of this." He tipped his head, half-smiling. "Don't be angry with me, Miri."

The ghost of a laugh eased the tightness of her face as she pulled her hand away and moved on. "You're a mental case, my friend."

"WATCHER."

"Yes, *T'carais*?"

"Extend to our kinsman Selector my regret for any inconvenience I may cause him by requiring you to accompany me to the place where Justin Hostro conducts business."

"Yes, *T'carais*."

"Say also to our kinsman that, should he have heard nothing from us—either by comm or by our return to this place—within three Standard hours, he must inform my brother the *T'caraisiana'ab* of this event, instructing him in my voice that he is to act as he knows is proper in the case, always keeping in his thoughts that Justin Hostro has been adjudged by our failure to return guilty of capturing the knives of four of our Clan."

"Kinsman?"

"Such may overstate the case," Edger said more gently. "But when one deals with the Clans of Men it is well to be prepared for ill-thought action. Do as I have asked. We depart in fifteen of these things named minutes."

THE MEAT had been easy, the pillage of no great worth. But the kill had put fresh heart into the crew, and Commander Khaliiz, satisfied that the luck of the hunt had changed, gave the order to take the ship into the underside of space.

"WHICH WAY NOW?" Miri asked at the branching of the corridors.

Val Con considered it with his new sense of clarity and gestured to the right. "There."

"You're the boss." She followed him down the indicated hall, grimly looking at the tricksy walls, which was not a good idea. Her eyes slid to Val Con, ahead of her. In some ways, that was not much better an idea, though it offered a more pleasing aspect than the walls. Vividly, she recalled the warmth and the slim strength of him and his hands curved with promise around her waist—and bit her lip hard enough to draw blood as she strove to keep her walk even, though she was shaking with desire.

He'd stopped and was bent close to the wall, seeming to study something. Though how anybody could study *anything* in the present sense-storm was more than Miri could fathom. She leaned against the opposite wall and waited.

Val Con had put his hands against the wall and seemed to be trying to square something off. After a few minutes of effort, he shook his head and straightened.

"What's up?" she asked.

"This is the storeroom we want," he said, not turning to look at her. "But it's locked, and I can't see the keyplate properly—it keeps running and shifting."

This was absurd! There was food and drink and music on the other side of the door—he knew it! To be thwarted now by something so minor as an inability of physical eyes to perceive—

The answer formed just behind his eyes, in the space reserved for Loop phenomena, and hung there, glowing, its aura strongly reminiscent of hunch. The keyplate configuration was clear. He thought of the pattern he saw, and the door slid open, untouched.

He stood staring.

"I didn't know you could do that," Miri commented from across the hall.

"I can't," he said and stepped forward. The open door to the storeroom was not an illusion. He walked through.

A moment later, Miri pushed away from the support of the wall and went after him.

That proved to be a mistake. The moment she crossed the threshold, odors of every kind assailed her: spices, wood-shavings, wool, mint, musk. Added to the visuals and the textual and the need, it was too much. Much too much.

She sat down hard on the first thing that looked like it might be real. Arms wrapped in a tight hug around her own chest, she hunched over, eyes closed, shaking like a kid in a fever.

She would never make it. Eight hours? Impossible!

"Miri. Miri!"

"What?" The word was a hoarse gasp.

"Put out a hand and take this. *Miri.* Put out a hand and take this. Do it now."

Obviously, she was not going to have any peace until she did what he said. She managed to get one arm unwrapped and, after a hard struggle, opened her eyes.

Val Con sat on the shifting floor at her feet, holding out an open bottle of wine. She took it from him, blinking.

"Now what?"

"Drink."

"Drink? Out of the *bottle?*" Her laughter sounded shrill in her own ears, but any joke was better than none.

"It was difficult enough finding wine without wasting time looking for glasses," he said repressively. "Drink."

She shook her head. "Always telling me what to do. No *reasons*, just—"

"Alcohol depresses the senses," he said. "Drink your wine."

"You go to hell!"

He drank. "I suppose," he murmured pensively, "I could pour it down your throat."

"Bully." But she took a pull, drinking it like *kynak*, not for taste, but to get drunk.

After a time she paused for breath, grinning and shaking her head. "And I had you figured for a kid from the right side of town."

He lifted a brow. "As distinct from the left side of town?"

"As distinct from the wrong side of town." She paused to gulp more wine. *"I'm* from the wrong side of town—no money, no prospects, no education, no brains."

"Ah. Then you figured correctly. Clan Korval is very old; we've had a great deal of time to amass wealth. Quite likely money accounted for the excellence of my education, which made it easier to qualify for Scout training." He took a long drink. "I don't think brains are the sole property of people from the—right side of town, however."

"Yeah?" She leaned forward, which was taking a risk, even though the shakes had largely departed. "Why'd you say no, back there?"

Both brows raised. "Enlightened self-interest. The drive is still engaged."

"Could've fooled me." She sat back and drank deeply. "How'd you pull that gimmick with the door?"

He took a slow swallow and set the bottle on the bucking floor at his side. "When I became halfling it was seen that I had an ability to—pick up objects—without physically touching them. Within my Clan, such abilities are not unknown. However, testing found my talent too insignificant to train, though I was given instruction in its control, so it would not affect my normal activities.

"The talent neither grew nor disappeared, merely remaining at the same level into my adulthood. I played with it occasionally, but it was too much of an effort to use seriously. By the time I had reached forth with my mind and brought a cup to myself from across the room, I could have walked the distance, picked the cup up in my hands, sampled the contents, *and* been much less tired." He paused to retrieve his bottle and drink.

"Then it vanished. I—" He took a breath, reviewing sequences in his mind. Yes, the timing was correct. There was much there that required Balance. . . . "I believe that the—energy—generated by certain nonsurvival functions is what fuels the Loop."

Miri was not shaking anymore, though she was exceedingly cold. "Nonsurvival functions? Like, maybe, dreaming? Or sex-drive?"

He closed his eyes, nodding. "Or music. Or the very faintest of—paranormal talent." He opened his eyes. "The night we met was the first time I had made music in nearly four years."

She tipped her head. "If you didn't have it and now you do—does that mean the Loop's bust? Or—is it a machine or something in your head? What'd they do?"

"What they did—" he shrugged. "I am fairly certain it is not a physical artifact implanted in my brain—that would be inefficient, since the tissue tends to reject an implanted machine eventually." He drank, considering the problem.

"I believe that it must be more like a—master program, superimposed—" He stopped, aware of something akin to anger building in him, except that it was a thing of surpassing coldness, rather than flame.

"Superimposed and overriding," Miri continued, eyes focused tightly on his face, "that set of programs named Val Con yos'Phelium."

He did not reply. They had both found the correct conclusion.

"Val Con?"

"Yes."

"I don't much like your bosses."

His smile flickered briefly. "Nor I."

"But it's bust now, right?" she insisted again.

Was it? he asked himself. He was immediately answered by the flare of an equation, elucidating the latest figures for his survival. Thirty-day CPS was at .06 now.

"No."

"What then? Something's got to be causing—oh." She closed her eyes and reopened them immediately. "The drive."

He drank the last of his wine and stared at the writhing bottle for a moment before setting it aside. "It seems likely. Apparently I've enough ability to balance everything—that which was originally mine and that which has been forced on me—when the ship is in drive and every electron in my head is firing twice.

"Even more. I was never able to see with wizard's eyes so well that I could have picked up the image of the keypad and the pattern of the lock."

She finished her own bottle and put it down. "What's going to happen?"

"The ship will continue to labor yet awhile and then it will rest." He looked up at her, smiling slightly. "Do you feel better?"

"Better. Beat up. Knocked down. Stomped on. And rode over. But definitely better. What now?"

He rolled to his feet, remembering at the last instant not to offer her his hand. "I suggest we gather food and whatever else we can use from what is stored, while I have extra eyes to see with."

THE JUNTAVAS HIT planet brief hours after Port clearance, despite the high rates of cumshaw required for such speed. Once on-world, money was spent with astonishing open-handedness for the purchase of clearance lists, ships parked, new arrivals, visas issued, and papers filed.

"They ain't here," Jefferson said some hours later, throwing the last fan of printout from him in disgust.

"Whaddya mean, they ain't here? Where else would they be? Maybe they hit and Jumped out again—you check that?"

Borg Tanser, second-in-command of the project, was a tight, smallish man, given to nagging; he was a good gunman and a quick thinker in a jam, and Jefferson was fortunate to have him along. He reminded himself of that now.

"We checked. No Clutch ships in or out of system for nearly six months. They ain't here. And they haven't been here." He shook his head. "Beats hell out of me."

"Yeah? Well, how's this, then? Let's split the team. Half checks the planet inside-out. Other half takes the ship and backtracks. Could be they're hanging a Jump or two back, waiting for the heat to cool."

Jefferson thought about it, reaching for the printouts and stacking them neatly together. "Yeah—we'll run it that way. The boss was real anxious to have both of 'em. Impolite, they were."

But Tanser was not a man known for his sense of humor. He snapped to his feet, nodding sharply. "Okay, then, I'll take the crew and get out of here. See ya." He was gone.

"See ya," Jefferson said absently. He sat for a moment, staring sightlessly at the stacked sheets, then pushed away from the table and went over to the bouncecomm to make his preliminary report to the boss.

MATTHEW LOOKED UP from his study of the latest data and regarded the two Clutch members expressionlessly.

"I am very sorry, sirs, but Mr. Hostro has given orders that he is not to be disturbed for any cause. I will be happy to give him a message—"

"I have no message to leave," Edger interrupted. "My business with Justin Hostro is of an urgent nature and will brook no further delay. Please allow him to know that I am here and must have speech with him now."

"I am very sorry, sir," Matthew repeated, "but I am not allowed to disturb Mr. Hostro for any cause."

"I understand," Edger said. "Therefore shall I interrupt him." He turned, moving around the comm station with a speed astonishing in someone so large, paused at the locked door long enough to extend a hand and push the panel—which screamed in protest—along its groove and into the wall, then stepped royally across the threshold into Hostro's office, Watcher at his back.

Justin Hostro was behind his rubbed steel desk, absorbed in a sheaf of papers. At the scream of the forced door, he looked up. At the advent of Edger, he stood.

"What is the meaning of this intrusion?" he demanded. "I left strict orders not to be disturbed. You will forgive me, I know, when I say that I have urgent business—"

"I, also, have urgent business," Edger said. "And it must be settled with you in this time and place." He moved over to the only Clutch-sized piece of furniture in the room, signing to Watcher with a flick of the hand to stay by the door.

Justin Hostro hesitated a heartbeat before sitting down also and folding his hands atop the desk with a creditable semblance of calm. "Very well, sir, since you are here and have disturbed me, let us settle your urgent business."

"I have come to speak with you," Edger announced, "concerning the proper bloodprice owed by our Clan for the damage we have done to Herbert Alan Costello."

"Costello?" Hostro frowned. "It is of no matter, sir; we shall take care of his expenses. I am sorry, however, if he has offended you."

"Ours was the error," Edger said, "and ours the payment. Our Clan is honorable. We pay what is owed."

"My clan is also honorable," Hostro snapped, striving to keep hold of his fraying temper, "and we take care of our own. Pray think no more of the matter, sir. The Juntavas shall care for Herbert Alan Costello."

"The Juntavas? This is the name of your Clan, Justin Hostro?"

"It is. A very powerful clan—one that spans planets and star systems. We count our members in the hundreds of thousands and we care for each of them, from the lowliest to the most high."

"Ah," Edger said. He inclined his head. "This gladdens me, Justin Hostro. It is true that I have not previously heard of your vast Clan—and I beg pardon for my ignorance. Happily, you have enlightened me and we may now deal together properly. Do you not feel that this is correct?"

"Of a certainty," Hostro agreed, forcing his hands to relax from the clench he had abruptly found them in.

"Know then, as an Elder of your Clan, that it has come to my attention that your kinsman, Herbert Alan Costello, has offered threats of physical harm—and perhaps termination—to three of my own kin." He waved a huge hand, indicating Watcher.

"That this my kinsman did grave harm to Herbert Alan Costello is not forgiven, and shall in the fullness of time be punished. However, the threat of danger was offered before he struck, which circumstance alters the punishment that must be meted. I ask. "He concluded, "if you have knowledge of the nature of the disagreement existing between your kinsman and the two of my Clan who are not present."

Hostro took a deep breath and let the rein on his temper out just a bit. "If one of those with whom you claim kinship is the woman known as Miri Robertson, then I must tell you that Costello was acting in accordance with my instructions to him that she be detained, and also her companion, if he still traveled with her."

"Ah. And, if one Elder may ask it of another, in the interest of an equitable solution after fair judging: Why did you so instruct your kinsman?"

"The woman is declared outlaw by my Clan and has recently, along with her companion, been responsible for the deaths of some of my kinsmen—as well as causing discontent between my Clan and the—Clan of policemen." Briefly, he considered the pellet gun in the top drawer of his desk; recalled the ruined door and sat still.

Edger was puzzled. "Was Miri Robertson then a member of your Clan? I would know the laws she has broken, that she adds 'outlaw' to her name while her life is made forfeit. Surely one or the other were sufficient punishment?"

"She hired herself as bodyguard to one who was himself outlawed, slaying in this capacity many of my kin. Her life is ours to take, though she was never a member of the Juntavas."

"She is not your kin, Justin Hostro, yet you pass judgment and seek to mete punishment?" Watcher looked at the *T'carais* worriedly: he did not like *that* note in the old one's voice.

"That is true," Hostro said.

Edger moved his massive head back and forth. "You baffle me, Justin Hostro. It is not so that we deal among Clans. Let me be plain, that there be no tragic misunderstanding between us: The woman Miri Robertson and the man Val Con yos'Phelium are adopted of the Clan of Middle River's Spring Spawn of Farmer Greentrees of the Spearmaker's Den. It is true that they are young and sometimes over-hasty in their actions. Possibly, they have wronged you in some manner. As Elders of our Clans it is our purpose to determine what harm has transpired and what balance may be made. My Clan is an honorable Clan; we pay what is owed. We are a well-traveled Clan and as such have found it good to allow other peoples their customs.

"But know, Justin Hostro, that whatever wrong they may have done you, the knives of these two are not yours to take. If they are judged after deliberation to deserve death, their own kin shall deliver that punishment, not the Clan of the Juntavas. Is this thing clear to you?"

"The Juntavas," Hostro snapped, "is a mighty Clan. We take what we will, as we see fit. Including the knives of the kin of the Spearmaker's Den."

Majestically, Edger rose from the chair. Watcher dropped his hand to his blade.

But the T'carais inexplicably stayed his hand. "You are of the Clans of Men," he boomed, "and thus hasty. Hear me further: In our history was there a Clan that meted judgment to a member of the Spearmaker's Den, against all tradition and without justice. Two persons from our Clan were thus dispatched to construct balance with this renegade family." He paused, taking the half-step that put him at the edge of Hostro's desk.

"The name of that Clan is not now written in the Book of Clans," he said slowly. "Nor is that combination of traits any longer available to the gene pool. Think, Justin Hostro, before you take the knives of any of the Spearmaker's Den."

Hostro did not speak. Wipe out an entire family? And he had claimed the Juntavas as family—countless thousands, yes. But those of the Clutch lived two thousand years and more. . . .

"Have you heard me, Justin Hostro?" Edger asked.

"I have heard you."

"It is good. However, it has come to my notice that those of the Clans of Men have memories shorter even than the span of their years. Allow me to leave you a reminder of our talk." The Clan Blade was then in the hand of the *T'carais*, flashing down—to slice clean into the steel of Hostro's desk and stand there, quivering.

Justin Hostro managed to stare calmly at this for a moment before raising his eyes to Edger's.

"As Edger for my Clan, Justin Hostro, I know that our blades are worthy—the youngest no less than the eldest." He reached forth a hand, plucked the knife from its nesting place, and returned it to its sheath.

"Think on what we have spoken of, Justin Hostro. I shall return to you in one Standard hour and you may tell me what you have decided, so that we may talk further. Or begin to feud." He turned toward the door. "Come, Watcher."

Abruptly, they were gone, leaving Mr. Hostro to gingerly finger the razor-edged gash in his desk.

ONE JUMP BACK from Volmer, a dead ball of dust circled a cold sun, bands of rubble marking the orbits of what had been three—or even four—additional worlds. The sensors reported nothing else.

Borg Tanser gave the order to initiate second Jump.

✧ CHAPTER TWENTY ✧

THEY EMPTIED A box containing dehydrated escargot and filled it with dried eggs, vegetables, a quarter-wheel of cheese, dried fruits, and tea. There was, to Miri's vast disappointment, no coffee.

"What's wrong with Edger, anyhow?"

Val Con grinned. "Possibly he did not expect you—and I don't like coffee."

"Don't know why you didn't take him up on that offer and stay," she said, shaking her head. "I'd sure hang onto anybody took that much care of *me.*"

He bent to add a package of cocoa and another of dry milk to their supplies. "I didn't become a Scout in order to stay in one place all my life."

Miri shut up. She knew she was on dangerous ground and she wasn't feeling up to any danger just then. "See any bread?" she asked.

He straightened, frowning at the boxes piled high on all sides. "I don't think—" The frown lightened, and he pointed at a carton by her right hand. "Will crackers do?"

"Suits." She pried open the top, hauled out a metal tin,

and handed it to him, trying to not see that yellow and turquoise sparks were raining over her hand. "That okay for awhile?"

"It seems to be enough food for a day or two," he said dryly. "Do you mind waiting here a moment? There is something else. . . ."

"No problem." She waved him off, retrieving the bottle they had been sharing from beside a case of sardines. "But if I'm drunk when you get back, you gotta carry me home."

He grinned. "A fair bargain," he said, and then the towering boxes swallowed him.

Miri settled on the floor next to their supply box and closed her eyes, wine bottle forgotten in her hand. The ship had been in drive for—what? Four hours? There were only another four to live through. *You're that tough, ain't you?* she said to herself.

Her thoughts settled on Val Con, where they tumbled like the colors in floor and walls. *Talk to me when the drive goes off, huh?* she thought. *What the hell does that mean? Damn Liadens. Never straight with anybody . . .* She shifted sharply, setting the bottle aside without opening her eyes, and revising her opinion of whether she could sleep for three weeks.

She might even have drifted off, for she was not aware of his return, nor of the hand that hovered for an instant over her bright head before he took it away and sank to his knees before her.

"Miri?" He spoke softly, reluctant to disturb her, but she started violently, eyes snapping open, shoulders tightening—and relaxing instantly.

Silently, he offered three things for her inspection.

The first was recognizable through its flowing iridescence as a portable 'chora. The colors of the second thing writhed and shimmered too much for her to wrest sense from them. And the third—

She took it from him, shaping her hands around it to be sure, then brought it to her mouth, blew a ripple of notes, and sawed them back and forth. She looked up to find him grinning, and she grinned back.

"I ain't asking, notice, how you knew I play harmonica."

"Is that its name? I had never seen one before. I thought perhaps you might know. . . ." He was still smiling, delight showing in his bright green eyes.

"Harmonica," she affirmed, rubbing her fingers over the smooth metal sides. "Also, mouth organ." She squinted at the unidentifiable something. "What's that?"

He turned it over in his hands. "A guitar. I think. Something with strings and a soundboard, at least." He came smoothly to his feet and slid the two instruments into the food box. "Would you like to put the harmonica in here as well?"

"Do—" She frowned at him, loath to give the mouth organ up. "It's Edger's, ain't it? I better put it back."

Jerkily, she came to her knees, then stopped, because he was in front of her, hands out, inches from disaster.

"Miri, if it gives you pleasure, keep it. Edger named you kin, and this ship is Clan property, belonging to all equally. If you would repay Edger for the gift, play for him when next you meet."

"I don't steal from my friends," she insisted. "And Edger only said I was his sister because of—" She caught herself, dropping her head into her hands. "If this ain't the *stupidest* damn way to make a space drive!"

"Because of?" he asked, though he knew what the answer would be.

"Because of you," she said, and he longed to touch her, so worn did she sound. "He made a mistake. Said the knife you gave me—back in Econsey . . ." She couldn't finish it.

Val Con took a breath and let it out, very gently. "Edger thought I had knife-wed you," he said, keeping his voice even. "A reasonable assumption, from his standpoint, though I had not spoken to him, as would have been proper in a young brother. The fault is mine. I did not think. And I am sorry to have caused you pain."

He balled his left hand into a fist to keep from touching her and continued. "Of this other thing: Edger would not have named you sister only to rescind the honor. He has accepted you into his Clan. Whether we are wed or no, you carry a blade given you by one of his kin and he considers you worthy of it." He sighed when she still did not uncover her face, and tried once more.

"I can attempt to explain all I know of the tradition and customs of the Clutch and of Edger's Clan, though it will take a bit longer than either of us might find comfortable sitting on the floor here. Will it suffice you at this moment to know that Edger does not allow unworthy persons into his family; and that being named kin is a great burden and a great joy?" He bit his lip and leaned back, wondering if she had heard him at all.

"What this means in practical terms, right now, is: Does the harmonica please you? If so, you must take it

and strive to master it, to the betterment of the Clan
no less than your duty."

"Yaaah!" Her whisper carried the inflection of a scream. She looked up suddenly and shook her head. "Well, it just goes to show you that things're never as bad as they look. When I started this run, I didn't have anything—no unit, no money, no place to go. Now, when I think I got even less, it turns out that somewhere along the line I picked up a husband, a family and a—what? hundredth share?—in a space rock powered by the looniest drive going. *Two* families," she amended and snapped to her feet, harmonica gripped tightly in her hand.

"Maybe they oughta lock *me* up, 'cause I sure don't know what I'm doing." She looked down at him for a moment, then waved her hands helplessly and spun away, marching unsteadily out of the storeroom.

Val Con came to his feet slowly and bent to retrieve the box.

"*Three* families," he murmured.

THE BOUNCECOMM began to chatter, bringing Jefferson, cursing and on the run.

He scanned Hostro's incoming instructions and jabbed the button for a hardcopy. Cursing ever more fluently, he cleared the board and warped a message to Tanser. The machine chattered, went silent, and chattered again before spitting back the message he wanted to send. The ship was in drive.

Curses exhausted, he set the comm to resend the message every ten minutes until received by Tanser's ship, and then sat staring at the screen, stomach tight.

ght of his son; and, shaking his head,
mself that the message would reach
r reached the prey.

THE STUFF EDGER used for soap *was* sand. Miri used it liberally, relishing the minor pain, then unbraided her hair and washed that, too.

Music filled the poolroom, though she hadn't thought a portable 'chora had that kind of range on it. There was, as far as she could tell, no order to the play list. Terran ballads mixed with Liaden chorales mixed with bawdy spacing songs mixed with other things the like of which she'd never heard mixed with scraps of see-sawing notes that sounded like the melodies of children's rhyming games.

On and on and on and on it went: Val Con playing every shard of music he'd ever heard. In some ways, it was worse than the drive effects.

The music broke and came back together, jagged-toothed and snarling, reminding her of the language he'd cursed in. She struck out for the edge of the pool as he added a new element to the sounds he was making—a high-pitched, whispery keening, twisting and twining through the hateful main line, sometimes louder, sometimes not, resembling, it seemed to her as she levered herself onto the lawn, one of the Liaden songs he'd played earlier.

And then it changed, shifting louder, intensifying until the breath caught in her throat: a wail that rattled the heart in her chest and the thoughts in her head.

She reached her piled belongings and crumpled them

to her chest. Slowly, bent as if against the stormwinds of Surebleak's winter, Miri sought refuge in the bookroom.

THE SHIP had been at rest for perhaps fifteen minutes when she entered the control room, her hair still loose and damp from her bath.

"I give you good greeting, Star Captain," she told Val Con's back in what she hoped was much improved High Liaden.

"Entranzia volecta, cha'trez," he murmured absently, his attention divided between board and tank.

Miri wandered over to the map table. Avoiding the silent 'chora and the guitar, she set down the cheese.

"How," she wondered, pulling out her knife, "am I gonna learn High Liaden if you keep answering in Low?"

"Do I? I must be having trouble with the accent."

Her brows rose. "You got the makings of a nasty temper there, friend."

He leaned back, hands busy on the board and eyes on the tank. "I am usually considered patient," he said softly. "Of course, I've never been tested under such severe conditions before."

She laughed and sliced herself a sliver of cheese. "Very nasty temper. Sarcastic, too. It ain't my fault you don't remember your milk tongue."

He made two more adjustments to the board and stood, then came over to the table. She whacked off a slab of cheese and offered it to him on knife point. He took it and sat down on the bench near the 'chora, one foot braced on the seat.

"Thank you."

"No problem." She sliced a piece for herself and sat astride the second bench. "What did you say, just then?"

One eyebrow lifted. "Are the roots so different?"

"Oh, I got 'good greetings' okay, but there was another word—sha . . ."

"Cha'trez," he murmured, nibbling cheese.

"Right. What's that?"

He closed his eyes, frowning slightly. When he finally opened his eyes, he sighed a little. "Heartsong?" He shook his head briefly. "Not quite, though it has the right flavor."

She blinked and changed the subject. "How many languages you speak?"

He finished his cheese and dusted off his hands. "At the level at which I speak Terran—five. I know enough of nine more to ask for meat and bed. And Liaden. And Trade."

"All that?" She shook her head. "And you speak Terran better'n most born to it. Little weird, though, you not having an accent."

He shifted, reaching to take up the guitar and fidgeting with the knobs projecting from the top. "I had one once," he murmured, turning a knob and plucking a string, "but when I was put on—detached duty—it was not considered politic for me to speak Terran with a Liaden accent."

"Oh." She took a breath. "My friend, you ought to chuck that job."

"I am considering it."

"What's to consider?"

"How it might be done." He plucked another string. *Twong!*

She stared at him. "Tell 'em you're all done now, detached duty is over and you'd like to go back and be a Scout, please."

Plonk! He shook his head, listening to the vibration of the string.

"It is not possible they would agree to that. I've lived too long, learned too much, guessed a great deal. . . ." *Bong.*

"They'll kill you?" Plainly, she did not believe it, and he cherished the effort she made to keep her voice matter-of-fact.

He ran his fingers in a sweep across the strings near the bridge and winced at the ensuing discord. Numbers were running behind his eyes: He should not be having this conversation; he should not have helped Miri in the first place; he should not have gone back for her—that was what the numbers seemed determined to say. And now his life was forfeit. He tried to ignore the numbers. CMS was at .08.

"Val Con."

He looked up, holding the guitar across his lap by its fragile neck. The numbers were running faster, switching from one Loop to the other, almost too rapidly for him to scan.

Death and danger. Disgrace and death. Dishonor and destruction. . . .

His muscles were tightening, his breathing quickened—and still the numbers raced.

"Val Con." Rising concern was evident in her voice.

He shook his head, struggling for words. "It is most likely that they will kill me," he managed, fascinated, watching the numbers flash, reverse themselves, and flash again as they counted the reduced chances of his living out the month, the week. . . . "Though it is true that my Clan is a powerful one, which reduces somewhat—" It was hard to breathe; he seemed to hear himself *out there* somewhere, while back here, where the truth was, where *he* was, he felt heat and a need to hide. "—the chance that they would kill me outright." His mouth was too dry; the rushing in his ears amplified the sound of his heart pounding against nearly empty lungs.

He tightened his grip on the guitar and sought out Miri's eyes.

"They would not want trouble . . . trouble with Korval. So it is—possible—that they would only . . ." He was sweating, but his hands were cold.

"Only?" Her question was barely a whisper.

"Only wipe me . . . and let my body go home."

The air was too hot and too thin, but it wasn't happening to Miri; he needed to run from her to get out *get out—look at the numbers!*

CRR-RACK! The guitar's neck snapped in his grip and he jumped back, dropping it and gasping, looking for a way out. His shirt was choking him and the numbers were glaring behind his eyes: dead, dead, zero percent chance of survival. He grabbed a wall and held fast.

"No! No! Not here! Dammit, not here!" I won't die here! I'll get out. . . .

"Val Con!"

The scream penetrated his panic, piercing the terror for an instant. It seemed so sure a name—Val Con. In fact: Val Con yos'Phelium Scout, Artist of the Ephemeral, Slayer of the Eldest Dragon, Knife Clan of Middle River's Spring

Spawn of Farmer Greentrees of the Spearmaker's Den—
and from somewhere her voice added, "Tough Guy!"

He sobbed and held on, then found himself gasping
against the strong stone wall. Several feet away, hand
outstretched and terror in her eyes, was Miri. He brought
his breathing down slowly and calmed himself, feeling the
air cool him as his hands began to warm.

The numbers were clear: zero and zero. No chance of
surviving the mission. The mission itself a failure.
Accordingly, he was dead.

He took another breath, leaned back against the wall,
and accepted the slow slide to the floor as natural, even
comforting; the sound he made verged on laughter.

"Val Con? You there?"

He nodded. "Here," he said raggedly.

She approached cautiously and knelt by his side, gray
eyes intent on his face.

"Miri?"

"Yo."

His breath was still slowing; his lungs ached from the
hyperbreathing he'd done, but he was calm. He knew his
name and with that he knew he was safe. "Miri, I think I
died just then."

Her brows twitched upward and she reached out to
lay cool fingers on the pulse at the base of his throat.
Shaking her head, she removed them.

"Sergeant Robertson regrets to report a glitch in the
system, sir."

He laughed, a jagged stone of sound, then lifted both
hands and ran them through sweat-soaked hair.

"Dead," he said. "The Loop showed me dead at the

moment I told you I would be wiped." His breath was nearly back, and he felt at ease, though drained in a way he'd never been drained before. "I think I believed it— panicked or—something. I *believed* them. . . ."

"The Loop," Miri asked, hoping. "It's gone? Or busted?"

"No . . . . Still there. Not, I think, broken. But it may have been programmed to lie to me—do *you* understand?" he asked her suddenly. "They took so much—so I would survive, they said. Surely it's important to survive? My music, my dreams—so *much*—and all to give life to a thing that lies. . . ." He rubbed his hands over his face. "I don't understand. . . ."

Miri laid a wary hand on his arm; his eyes were on her face instantly, noting uncertainty and strain.

"Yes."

She bit her lip. "What's—wiped—please?" Her voice was small and tentative, most un-Mirilike.

He shifted slightly, bumping a leg against the fallen guitar. Awkwardly, he retrieved it and cradled the splintered neck. "Ah, poor thing. . . ."

Looking up, he half-smiled. "Wiped is . . ." He shook his head, keeping a wary eye out for phantom equations. "A machine was made in answer to the thought that it would be—convenient—if, instead of impersonating someone, an agent could *become* that person. It was thought that this could be accomplished by—smoothing out the agent's own personality and overlaying a second." He saw nothing. The screen behind his eyes was blank. "When the mission was done, the second personality would be removed and the agent allowed to reemerge."

He paused for breath. Miri was watching his eyes closely, the line of a frown showing between her brows.

"It didn't work out very well. The only thing the machine did was eradicate, totally, the prime personality. No other personality could be grafted on to what remained. Nor could more conventional learning take place. The person was gone, irretrievably, though the body might live on to a very respectable old age."

A shudder shook her violently and she bent her head, swallowing hard and screwing her eyes shut against the sudden tide of sickness.

"Miri." Warm fingers brushed down her cheek, then slid under her chin, gently insisting that she raise her face. She gave in, eyes still shut, and after a moment felt him brushing away the tears.

"Miri, please look at me."

In a moment she opened her eyes, though she couldn't manage a smile.

His own smile was a better effort than the last; he shook his head. "It would be wisest not to mourn me until they bring the body before you."

"They bring me a zombie, I'll shoot it dead!"

"I would appreciate it," he told her gravely.

She dredged up a lopsided grin, looking closely into his tired eyes and grim face and hoping that this last little scene was the final drama his unnamed bosses had engineered. It had been ugly enough—and, potentially, deadly enough. What if he'd been in a shoot-out or one of the other tight spots he seemed prone to when that damned—panic—had hit?

Murder by extrapolation? She shook the thought away.

"How are you now?" she ventured, aware that he had dropped his hand and twined his fingers lightly around hers.

He smiled. "Tired. It is not every day that one dies and lives to tell the tale."

She grinned and squeezed his hand. "Wanna get up? Or should I get you a blanket?"

"Up, I think." But that was easier said than done. Somehow, they both managed to rise; they stood close, leaning against each other.

Val Con moved, surprising them both as he hugged Miri to him and dropped his face to her hair, murmuring something that did not sound like Terran or Trade. Holding her away, he looked seriously into her cautious face.

"There are many things for us to talk about—but there are many things I must first say to myself, to hear what the answers may now be. I require time—perhaps a day, perhaps two—by myself. I will take food, find another room to be in. . . ."

She stiffened. "Ain't no reason to run away from me—"

He laid light fingers over her lips, cutting her off. "Not *away* from you. But think: Twice in two days I have frightened us both—badly. I must take time—while there is so much time—to find the man I am, now that there are two I am not." He unsealed her lips and touched her cheek. "It is something we both should know, I think."

Not trusting her voice, she nodded.

"Miri Robertson." There was a glimmer of ritual in his voice. "Consider please if you wish to become my partner—to remain my partner. We will speak in a few days."

Quickly, he bent and kissed her forehead, then released her and turned to gather food for his time away. The broken guitar he left on the map table. One day, he vowed, he would repair it.

✧ CHAPTER TWENTY-ONE ✧

FOR THE FOURTH TIME Miri sneaked back to the bookroom after having peeked in at her partner. She felt like a spy herself after having agreed that he should have his time to himself. But, despite her great joy at having all the marvels of Edger's library at her command, she discovered in herself a need to be sure that Val Con was all right.

For the second time, she was confused by what she'd seen: Val Con standing in the center of the large room, moving slowly, eyes closed. He would stop for a minute, two minutes, three—and then she'd realize that he'd done a half-turn in that time. His movements had been sinuous and twisting, like a dance, but so *slow*, as if he were Edger imitating a flower growing.

In the midst of this, he would suddenly run or jump or sit to relax or concentrate, and then get up and try the same thing again. Or maybe not *quite* the same thing.

That there was method here, she was certain. She refused to think that it could be madness, as well.

To pass the time, she did more ordinary calisthenics,

making sure her body was in shape to fight, to act, when this time of fairy-tale safety was over.

And the books! She worked her way through the High Liaden grammar, then devoured, in rapid succession, a small book of poems by someone named Joanna Wilcheket, a rather longer volume illuminating the intricacies of a team game called bokdingle—which she thought sounded more like pitched battle than a game— then learned the proper way to veri-date Qontikwian tree carvings. She finished up with a history of some place called Truanna, which had self-destructed back in Standard 250.

She spent an entire rest period wandering through a Terran dictionary, wondering at all the words she'd never heard of—and this was her milk tongue! An hour was given to an adventure novel by an ancient Terran writer; her sides hurt from laughing when she finished, but she searched the shelves for more.

Hiking through the ship, she noticed that the weird effects of the drive seemed much less distracting at the ship's stern, where the cargo holds were. The bookroom wasn't too bad, once she adjusted. The control room was worst.

She filed that away to mention to Val Con.

The ship's labors ended and began again. At the end of three days, Miri was worried, visions of him lying rigid and trapped intruding between her and the words in the reader—but then she caught sight of him working very hard, doing exercises she was familiar with.

That's okay, then, she thought in relief, and continued on her way to the pool.

✧✧✧

THE SHIP was between labors, and Miri woke. Stretching, she realized that this wasn't what had awakened her; it was the crisp smell of breakfast hanging in the air, odors tantalizingly close to coffee and—*coffee?*

She sat up on the shelf—sleeping in the library had become a habit; it was too depressing to sleep all alone in one of the Clutch's big beds—and, weaving her hair into a single loose braid, she considered what her nose was telling her.

Coffee, she decided. She went to investigate.

Val Con was sitting crosslegged before a portable camp-stove in the center of the wide hallway, watching the entrance to the bookroom. A pan on the left burner held meat and pancakes; on the right steamed a ceramapot of dark, brown coffee.

"Good morning, *cha'trez*."

"Morning," she returned, staring at him from the doorway.

"You will join me for breakfast, I hope?" He waved a hand at the places set, camp fashion, with plates, cups, disposable napkins, and utensils.

"Is that *real* coffee?" she asked, coming closer.

"You tell me, my friend. The pack said something like 'Certified Brazilian,' I believe."

She grinned and pushed a cup at him. "Pour, dammit."

"Yes, Sergeant," he murmured, nodding at the pad he'd laid out for her to sit on.

She folded her legs and sat, studying his face. He turned, offering her the full cup, and lifted an eyebrow.

"Have you a problem, Miri Robertson?"

She took the cup. Gods, but real coffee smelled so good!

"You look—different," she told him.

"Ah." His shoulders dipped in the gesture she never quite understood. "I am sorry."

"I ain't." She sipped, closing her eyes to savor the taste and to buy herself time. Different, yes. Alive? His eyes were vividly green; his face in general was less haggard, less—prisoned.

She opened her eyes to find him watching her and smiled. Yes. It was as if his energy filled him joyfully now, rather than pushing him on past endurance.

"Where'd you get the goodies?" she asked, indicating the meal cooking on the small stove. "I thought we decided there wasn't any coffee."

"I was not—thinking properly," he explained, "when we looked before. Edger is nothing if not thorough, and so I looked for camp sets. He'd seen me use them when I stayed with the Clan." He grinned.

"There is approximately an eight years' supply of camp sets in the second storage compartment. Terran sets, so it seemed safe to assume there would be coffee."

She stared at him. "Not thinking properly? I'd like to know why not! You couldn't have had anything else on your mind."

He laughed as he turned the meat and the flapjacks.

She took another sip of coffee. "Val Con?"

"Yes."

She frowned slightly, watching his face. "How are you, my friend?"

"I am—well. Not very well. Nor even completely well. There was much—damage done, with little care taken. It was not expected that I would live quite so long." He shook his head. "I will have to work hard, to be certain that all heals rightly."

She hesitated. "I—needed to make sure you were okay, so I—spied—on you. That *slow* stuff you were doing—is that to make sure that all—heals rightly?"

He nodded. "It is called *L'apeleka*—a Clutch thing. It is—" He paused, eyes half-closed, then laughed softly, spreading his hands, palms upward. "The best I can do in Terran is that it is a way of—reaffirming oneself. Of celebrating proper thought."

"Oh." She blinked at him.

He laughed fully. "Forgive me, *cha'trez*, but Terran will not bend so far. I *do* know what *L'apeleka* is and I am certain that I could explain it to you, but you must tell me which you desire to learn first—Low Liaden or Clutch?"

She laughed, then sobered. "The Loop?"

"Exists." He looked at her closely. "The Loops are tools, Miri. They do not demand a course of action, only elucidate it."

She drank coffee. "But *you* ain't a tool."

His face hardened momentarily. "I think not." He turned his attention to the pan as she watched.

Funny, she thought, she felt warm, though she hadn't felt cold before. And she felt comforted. She wondered if she'd been sad without realizing it.

He divided the contents of the pan evenly between the two plates.

He did look well, she decided. Sure of himself, not just sure of what he could do.

Offering her a plate, Val Con tipped an eyebrow at her cup. "More coffee, *cha'trez*? It would be a shame to waste what is in the pot."

"Never happen." Laughing, she held it out for a refill. "Thanks, partner."

"So it runs that way?" He looked at her speculatively as he picked up his own plate. "I had thought the question not properly asked." He paused, watching her as she began to eat.

"And the other?" he asked softly.

She frowned, puzzled. "What other?"

"Ah, *that* question was not asked so well," he murmured, seemingly to himself. Picking up his fork, he began to eat.

Miri shook her head and returned to her breakfast, savoring tastes, smells, and silent comradeship.

Val Con ate his own meal with relish, his eyes on her. She had rested, he saw; the lines of strain that had been in her face since they'd met were gone, and she seemed easier within herself, as if she, too, had reaffirmed who she was. Her eyes, when they rested upon him, were unguarded. He hugged that small warmth to him and dared to hope.

In a short time, he set his plate aside and leaned back to watch her where she sat, her back against the wall and the cup cradled in her hands.

"Breakfast was fine." She smiled at him. "Thank you."

"You're welcome," he replied. "Miri?"

"Yo."

He shifted, and brought his gaze to meet hers. "Only if *you* wish it, Miri . . . ."

She set the cup down, giving him her whole attention. "Okay."

"It would please me very much," he said, choosing each word with care, "to allow the—fact—of our marriage to endure."

She blinked. She blinked again and broke his gaze, looking down and groping for her cup.

Val Con held his breath.

"You got a family and stuff, doncha?" she asked, head bent. "They probably wouldn't be . . . overjoyed . . . about you marrying somebody who—somebody like me. 'Specially when you don't—" She swallowed, hard. "Partners are lovers, sometimes."

Slowly, he let his breath go. "There are," he told her softly, "several answers to be made. The first is that whom I wed is *my* choice, not the choice of the Clan." He paused, then dared to add, "*I* wish us to be wed."

Her shoulders twitched, but she did not look at him. After a moment, he continued. "It is unlikely that I will return to Liad, *cha'trez*."

Her eyes flicked to his, warm with pity. "You mind?"

"I mind," he admitted. "But I feel certain I would mind being dead much more." He smiled. "Understand that it is no great bargain I offer you: A short, skinny man with only the money in his pouch and a certain ability on the 'chora to recommend him—"

"So much?" She grinned. "Short and skinny?"

"Thus was I described to your friend Liz—"

She laughed, tossing off the rest of her coffee as he grinned. "Is Edger an honest man?"

"None more honest."

"And our—marriage—stands up to laws and stuff?"

He considered it. "I believe so. The post that Edger holds—*T'carais*—is somewhere between that of father, captain, priest, and mayor. If we are wed by custom—partnered as well, if you like—and it is certified and witnessed by the Clutch, there are few who would question it. The Clutch, like the mythical elephant, never forgets. Nor does it remember wrongly. If you will—if you truly desire it—then it is done."

She took a breath. "It's real?" she asked quietly. "Not something you're doing 'cause it's—expedient?"

He looked at her sharply, then smiled ruefully. "To the Clan of Middle River, the Spearmaker's Den, it is fact. It is something that I wish for completely: That you be my partner, that we be mated for life."

Miri picked up her cup and found it empty. "Is there more coffee?"

"I can make more if you wish."

"But?"

"But I would rather fill a cup with wine that we share."

She slid across the rock floor until she was next to him. "You have wine?"

"It is here," he said. "Though I should tell you that it is Green Nogalin. A large bottle of it."

Her brows rose. "That's the aphrodisiac? The one banned on about three-quarters of the Terran worlds?"

"So it is."

She shook her head. "And I thought Edger was an innocent." She paused. "Husband?"

Thank you, gods, he thought. "Yes, my wife?"

"Please open the wine."

He smiled and leaned close. "In a moment—"

Miri was on her feet, gun in hand, with the first siren shriek. Val Con was already far down the hall, strobe beams throwing his shadow crazily over the rock walls.

"The control room—quickly!"

They ran.

"What *is* it?" she demanded, braking to a halt just inside the door.

"Distress beacon." He was at the board, hands busy, head tipped up at the tank. "But I don't see—ah."

He upped the magnification and Miri saw it, too: a drifting bulk that could only be a ship. Keeping her eyes on it, she slid her gun back into its holster and went slowly toward the board.

Val Con moved his hand and began speaking in slow, distinct Trade. "This is Scout Commander Val Con yos'Phelium on Clutch vessel in tangential orbit. We hear your distress signal and will attempt a rescue. Reports required: damage and personnel." He touched the pink disk, listening.

Miri came up behind him. "You can't bring non-Clutch people onto this ship with its goofy drive! It'll make 'em crazy!"

He shook his head, frowning at the tank. "Isn't that better than being dead?"

She put her hands on his shoulders, her eyes on the

ship drifting in the tank. "How come I gotta answer all the hard questions?"

TWO THINGS HIT ship's comm as they dropped into normal space: the keening wail of a distress beacon and a clear, measured voice announcing name, location, and intention to rescue.

Tanser leapt out of his chair, swearing at the pilot. "Get me some magnification! Where're they coming from—*there!*"

A mid-sized asteroid floated to their starboard, oriented above them and the wreck. The pilot increased mag, as ordered, then did a doubletake and ran the screen as high as it would go.

Without a doubt, a smaller rock had separated from the larger, falling as if thrown toward the wreck.

Tanser grinned. "Hide us," he snapped.

"Huh?"

"Hide us! Hurry up, asshole! You know what's on that thing?"

The pilot was making rapid adjustments, nervously edging the ship into a flotilla of space junk. "No, what?"

"Them kids Hostro wants."

"How you figure that?" the pilot muttered, sweat dripping like icicles down his face as he matched speed with the junk and eased into the center of the drift.

"That's a Clutch ship, right?" Tanser asked, purely to draw out the revelation of his genius.

"Yeah," the pilot allowed.

"Well, Scout Commander Val Con yos'Phelium don't sound Clutch to me. Ten'll get you one the only people on that rockship out there is one little girl and her boyfriend. Real nice folks, they are, coming down to help out somebody in trouble." He settled back into his chair, sighing in self-satisfaction.

"So what're we gonna do, Borg?" the pilot asked, since the question seemed to be expected.

"We wait till they're on that wreck and then go get 'em." Tanser sighed again and permitted himself the luxury of a grin. "Caught like rats, Tommy. Gonna be so easy, it's almost a shame."

JEFFERSON SAT BY the bouncecomm, staring at it in frustration. It had stopped sending fifteen minutes before, and a cursory inspection of its innards had failed to provide him with a clue as to this malfunction. He slammed the lid down and went to the local unit to summon a comm-tech, on the bounce.

His fingers were shaking so badly, he had to punch the number twice.

⋄ CHAPTER TWENTY-TWO ⋄

VAL CON MATCHED speed and drift, fastened their pod to the entry port of the disabled vessel, and traded air.

The sensors, as near as Miri could tell, showed that the air in the other ship was good; no leaks were detected. Terrific. They were going to *have* to go inside. Because there might be survivors, too hurt or too scared to answer; or the board might be blown. . . . Miri put a hand to her gun, making sure it was loose in the holster.

Val Con locked the board and turned to grin at her. "Ready?"

"Never readier," she lied. She didn't like it. Not at all. It smelled. It reeked.

He went first, rolling through the matched locks and into the unknown. There was a minute's silence before his voice drifted back to her. "All right, Miri."

She gulped air and rolled through, landing on her feet, gun out, in the hallway beyond. Illumination was provided by emergency dims, and gravity was a shade light. The only sound was the hum of the life-support system.

Val Con was moving silently down the hall. She saw with a certain amount of relief that his gun was out, as well. Following him reluctantly, she considered whether it was worthwhile mentioning that there was no one alive on this tub.

Robertson, she asked herself, very earnestly, you psychic?

No, Sarge, she replied.

Good, she approved. Now, get the lead out and cover your partner's butt.

THE INFORMATION that a half-hour's intensive research had provided on the Clutch was clarifying, but not encouraging.

Hostro's lawyer, when appealed to, gave him to understand that the word of a Clutch person in matters of contract was considered wholly binding. In the nine hundred Standards that Terrans had been dealing legally with the Clutch, the Clutch had never broken their word in any matter.

"I wouldn't worry about it, Justin," his lawyer told him comfortably. "The Clutch promises, the Clutch delivers. Never known to be an exception; no one's ever heard one lie. . . ."

Justin Hostro thanked his man of business cordially and cut the connection, turning his attention to the files that the efficient Matthew had so rapidly obtained for him.

There was a great deal of speculation regarding the exact social structure of the Clutch—it was generally felt to be highly complex and extremely competitive. Justin

Hostro scanned the data rapidly, searching for he knew not what.

Fact: At one time the warlike Yxtrang had considered the Clutch fair game. There were many documented attacks of Yxtrang upon Clutch vessels as late as eight hundred Standards before.

Then, the attacks ceased. It was observed to be the general rule that, given a Clutch vessel and an Yxtrang chancing across each other in normal space, no incident occurred. The Yxtrang passed on, as did the Clutch.

Justin Hostro had an uneasy feeling that he knew why this was so. And if the *Yxtrang* were afraid of the Clutch . . .

He closed the file and sat quite still, his hands folded precisely before him, his eyes regarding the scene just beyond the edge of his desk.

He was still lost in that regard when Matthew announced Edger and Watcher's return.

THE ONLY PERSON left on the Terran ship was in no condition to be rescued. In fact, Miri thought dispassionately, about the only thing he *was* in condition for was colander duty. Whoever had shot him had been insanely thorough about it.

Val Con straightened from his examination of the body, shaking his head. "Yxtrang," he said. The word told a wealth of stories, none of them happy.

"How do you know?"

He waved a hand. "They use tiny pellets with fins on them to cut as they enter; their guns are bored for maximum spin. . . ."

She sighed. "Think I'd learn not to ask you these questions." She spun slowly, checking out the storage hold in which they stood. "How'd they get in?"

"Matched speed and latched on." He shrugged. "It would be easy to force a storage hatch, since the mechanism is built not to withstand abuse—"

The ship shuddered with the impact of a locking magnet on the hull, and from the next hold came the anguished groan of machinery being forced against its will.

"Oh, *hell*," Miri breathed.

Val Con was moving, swinging back toward the hallway. "Go!" he snapped. "Get back to the pod!"

She stared at him. Run? It was no good to run from Yxtrang.

He grabbed her arm, pivoted, and let her go with a push. "Go! Get the hell out of here!"

She ran, sensing him, swift and silent, at her right shoulder, and was absurdly relieved.

Suddenly she realized that Val Con was no longer with her.

Miri braked, cursing, and flattened her back against the wall, trying to see in both directions at once. Two feet downhall was a side corridor. She forced herself to think back: When exactly had he vanished?

It was impossible to know: He had been there, and then he had not. But he'd been gone *before* she'd passed that intersecting hallway, or so she thought.

From the holding section came the voices of men and the sound of boots against metal floors. Miri bit her lip. If she managed to top the best spurt of speed she'd ever had, she *might* reach the pod in time to figure out how to seal the latch against them.

Val Con's back there, damn his eyes! she cursed silently.

Miri unglued her back from the wall and moved cautiously down-corridor. She was four or five feet farther from the pod when the first shot was fired. She froze, listening to the sounds of confusion and voices yelling— *Terrans!*—and heard another sound that he could not have anticipated.

Several pairs of footsteps were still bearing down on her position.

Miri spun and dove for the cross-corridor.

JUSTIN HOSTRO rose and bowed to Edger, then indicated a seat.

The *T'carais* inclined his head in response and remained on his feet. "The decision I am here for as a simple one," he told the man. "I expect that you will be able to tell me what you have chosen in very few words. It is hardly worth the effort to sit, in such a case."

Hostro bent his own head and cleared his throat. "It is my decision, as an Elder of the Juntavas, to let your kin go with their lives. A message to this effect has been relayed to those I sent to search.

"I should, however, inform you that I am the most minor of Elders of my Clan and cannot, therefore, speak for the more senior Elders. It was their word that set me and my—immediate family—to work on the apprehension of these members of your Clan. The— eldest of our Elders is most anxious to obtain certain information from Miri Robertson, and it is reasonable to expect that such inducements to speech as he would employ would render her unlikely to live long.

"Thus, you should understand that, though I have agreed to let your kin retain their knives, Miri Robertson is still considered an outlaw by the eldest of our Elders. There is a price upon her head—small, should she die in the capturing; larger, should those who trap her be skilled enough to keep her alive. The man who is also your kin is of no importance to the Eldest. But, if he is still with her when she is taken his life will be forfeit."

Edger took several Standard minutes for consideration.

"I understand," he said finally. "It is enough for now that the immediate threat posed by you and your close kin is removed. You will, of course, provide me with the name and planet of the eldest of your Elders, so that we may discuss the matter fully, for all the families of your Clan."

Hostro licked his lips. Ruin. Ruin and most likely death. He looked at that future and considered the other he had been offered; then he took a breath and performed what was perhaps the only act of heroism his life had encompassed.

"Of course," he told Edger. "I would be delighted to provide you with an introduction to the eldest of our Elders."

THEY'D MANAGED TO CUT Val Con off from the corridor. Four were in the ransacked far hold—three Juntavas and himself.

One of the three became a bit ambitious in his aim

and acquired a slug in the arm for his presumption, but that sort of thing could not continue long. He *had* to get out. Soon. Sufficient time had elapsed for Miri to have reached the pod and sealed it, though she could not pilot it—a lapse in her education he intended to rectify the moment current difficulties were resolved.

He cracked his gun, sighed, and reassembled it. He had to move soon, even if nothing—Across the room, there was an empty *click:* The man stationed near the door was temporarily out of ammunition.

Val Con moved.

He put his last two pellets into the man who had aspired to marksmanship, and lodged his throwing knife in the throat of his companion, who was so foolish as to rise above his cover to take aim. Reversing his gun, he used it as a club, smashing toward the shooting hand of the one survivor.

The man saw it coming and dodged—but lost his gun as it slid out of wet fingers. Val Con flipped the spent gun to his right hand and brought Edger's blade to his left; glittering and sharp and deadly, it flashed in toward the other's belly.

The man jumped back, rolling, and came up with a length of metal pipe in his hand.

Val Con slid to the left, but the Juntava was quick and swept out with the pipe, keeping him from the door.

Val Con dove forward, parrying with the gun—but the pipe shifted, snaking sideways and twisting, and the gun spun out of nerveless fingers as he danced clear, his face stinging where jagged metal had sliced it.

The Juntava sensed the advantage of his longer reach

and swung the pipe again. Reaction threw Val Con's left hand up to ward off the blow, crystal blade in his grip.

And his opponent leapt back, swearing, his advantage negated: The knife had shorn away nearly a third of his weapon.

SHE COULD SIT DOWN HERE and pick them off all day long and far into the night.

As a tactician, Borg Tanser admired her for it. As force leader, he hated her for the three men dead at the mouth of her snug little hallway. There were other alternatives, of course. For example, they could just leave and evacuate the air from the wreck.

He considered the various angles to that and decided against. The bounty was higher—a lot higher—if she was delivered alive. If only he could come up with some way of luring her out of that damn cul-de-sac!

Suddenly Tanser froze, head snapping back toward the holding bays. The gunfire had stopped. He crept several feet down-corridor to be sure.

Silence. And no hail from the men he'd left to take out the boyfriend.

Dropping back to the mouth of the corridor, he spoke into the ear of his Second and moved off with rapid caution, gun at the ready.

THE MAN SCREAMED as the blade sheared through the muscle and tendons of his upper arm, but he managed an awkward spin that sent him out of range and bought him time to take his weapon into his other hand.

Val Con flipped his blade, catching it by the point. It

was not a throwing knife, but when one had no choice . . .

`   The explosion and the pain were simultaneous—he was spun half-around with the force of the blast. He loosed the blade at the man who stood, gun in hand, in the doorway, before blackness claimed him. He never felt the second blow as the pipe cracked across his skull.

MOREJANT STOOD OVER the fallen boyfriend, pipe still at the ready, his arm bleeding badly. Tanser threw him a clamp from the kit on his belt.

"Where's Harris and Zell?"

"Dead." Morejant rasped, seeming loath to relinquish his guard over the figure on the floor. "Would've had me in another minute—sure glad you come along." He bent over the body, peering, then straightened and looked at Tanser.

"Boss, I think he's still breathing. You wanna finish 'im off?"

Tanser's attention was on the knife buried to the hilt in the steel wall two inches from his head. He levered it free and whistled softly: the crystal was unmarred, the edge unbroken. He thrust it in his belt.

"Boss?" Morejant repeated.

"Naw." Tanser holstered his gun and came forward. Leaning over, he got a grip on the back of the boyfriend's collar and heaved him up to hang like a drowned kitten, blood dripping off the front of his shirt and pooling on the floor.

"Wrap yourself up," Tanser snapped at the staring Morejant, "and get a gun. We're gonna talk to the Sergeant."

✧✧✧

THEY'D BEEN HANGING BACK for the last fifteen minutes—still there, but out of range. Every so often one of them would lob a shot inside, just to see if she was awake, she guessed. She didn't bother returning the favor.

The lull in activity had given Miri the opportunity to reload her gun, check remaining ammo, and think deeply on the inadvisability of disobeying a superior officer, not to mention straying one step from her partner's side when it looked like they were in for a hot time.

None of these thoughts were particularly comforting, nor were they useful. She banished them and shifted position; her attention was abruptly claimed by a movement at the mouth of the corridor.

Miri raised her gun, waiting for the man to get into range. But all he did was heave the bundle he carried in his arms forward, so that it struck the floor and rolled, well inside her range.

She sat frozen, gun still steady on the figure at the mouth, eyes on the man who lay too still, legs and arms every which way, graceless.

No, she thought. Oh, no, Val Con, you can't be . . .

"Sergeant?" boomed the sitting duck at the top of the hall.

She did not raise her eyes. "What the hell do you want?" she asked, her voice flat with hatred.

"I just wanted to tell you, Sergeant, that he ain't dead yet. We'll fix that, though, if I don't see your gun and your belt tossed up here within thirty-five seconds."

She licked her lips. "How do I know he ain't dead now? Take *your* word for it?"

"That's your gamble, Sergeant, not mine. You got another fifteen seconds."

Jamming the safety up, she snapped to her feet and hurled the gun with all her strength.

It hit a foot short and skidded to a stop against Tanser's left boot. A moment later, belt and pouch repeated the maneuver.

Tanser laughed. "Temper, temper. Now, you just walk on out here like a good girl—real slow. Don't want you to trip and get yourself shot 'cause somebody thought you were tryin' something fancy. We lost five men between you and the boyfriend, Sergeant. Proud of yourself?"

"Hey," Miri said, stepping carefully over Val Con's body. Blood was a darker stain on the dark shirt; there was no way to know if he was breathing. "Everybody's got an off day now and then."

✧ CHAPTER TWENTY-THREE ✧

TANSER HIMSELF FORMED part of the guard that took her across to the Juntavas ship. With his own hands he shoved her into the holding cell and set the lock.

Miri made a quick circuit of the cell: metal platform welded to the wall, sanitary facilities stark in one corner, a panel that looked like a menuboard. She approached this, asked it for water, and was surprised when it provided a pitcherful, chips of ice circling lazily within. She drank deeply.

Suddenly the door slid open, admitting a gaunt man with a wrap of healtape around his right forearm, dragging a limp, dark figure by its collar.

The man hauled his burden inside, apparently oblivious to the trail of red in its wake, and dumped it at Miri's feet.

"Sorry, Sarge, but we only got this one cell, so you gotta share. Wouldn't fret too much though," he confided, "'cause like as not the boyfriend'll bleed to death pretty soon and you'll have the place to yourself again."

If he had hoped for a show of emotion, he was

disappointed. Frowning, his eyes fell on the still, dark bundle and he drew back, aiming a kick at undefended ribs.

Her foot intercepted his, bootheel clipping ankle neatly and painfully. Morejant nearly fell, then caught himself and spun back to find her between him and the man on the floor, death in her eyes.

Snarling, he turned away to leave.

"Hey, hero."

"What?" He turned back, hackles rising at the look on her face.

She waved at the boyfriend. "What about a medkit? Happens I ain't in favor of my partner bleeding to death."

"Then strangle him," Morejant advised her. "Only one we *gotta* keep alive is you. Why haul more weight than we need?"

She shifted position and he jumped, scuttling through the door and slamming the lock in place.

THE TECH CLEARED the malfunction inside of five minutes and went away with her fee in cash and a fifteen percent tip for a job well done.

No sooner had she gone than the bouncecomm chattered and whirred and lit up the green light that was Tanser's crew acknowledging receipt of the message.

Jefferson sighed and turned away, intent on soothing his frazzled nerves with a few swallows of local brew— and spun back, nerves fraying even more.

The bounce-comm chattered and rattled merrily, purple eye lit: Stand By For Message Incoming. . . .

✧✧✧

"BORG?"

"Yah?" Tanser looked up from his meal to find Tommy holding out a sheet of hardcopy.

"Message from Jeff," the pilot said. "Just come in. Thought it might be hot."

Tanser put down his fork and took the sheet. "Thanks."

A minute later, he swore loudly and pushed back from the table, leaving the dining hall at a determined half-run.

IT WAS DARK and cold and it hurt to breathe the air. It was bad air: he could feel the pain of it sliding in and out of his lungs like knives. He should stop; it was wrong to breathe such air. Yet another wrong added to a long list of them. . . .

Drifting there in the cold and dark, it seemed that he moved away from the necessity of air, for the pain receded somewhat. Drifting still more, he perceived himself above a tunnel of even greater darkness than that in which he traveled. This new tunnel seemed to be lined with dark fur, promising warmth, and the diamond tips of the fur glittered and beckoned like stars.

Yes, he thought. I should go there, where there is warmth and stars and good, sweet air to breathe. . . .

It seemed to him that he drifted nearer this place of warmth and stars, and he was content.

Suddenly a flare of living fire crossed the darkness and the moment was lost—he was drifting upward, toward lightening blackness and the pain that cut at him like crystalline knives. . . .

✦✦✦

MIRI HAD DONE what she could with water and a makeshift bandage torn from her shirt. The pellet had entered and exited cleanly, barely nicking a lung. With a medkit, he would have mended without trouble in a couple of days. But with only water and cloth, he would die. There was no way to stop the slow, stubborn flow of blood.

Wearily, she rubbed a bloody hand across her cheek and used her damp scarf to dab at the gash across his face. Not a serious wound, though it would have scarred—she killed that thought instantly.

His brows twitched, and she froze as he passed a tongue across dry lips. "Who?"

"Miri."

"Not dead?" His lashes fluttered, as if he were struggling to lift their great weight.

"Not yet," she told him, somehow keeping her voice light and easy. Gently, she brushed the hair from his eyes. "You got a little beat up, though. Just lie there and rest, *accazi*? Don't try to talk. We'll talk later, after you rest."

He had won the battle with his lashes and was watching her face, his green eyes lucid. "Poor liar, Miri."

She sighed and shook her head. "Think I'd be better, wouldn't you? Guess I ain't practiced enough lately."

Something flickered across his face—a smile, perhaps; it was gone before she was certain. "Is there any water?"

She helped him drink from the second pitcher, the already-soaked bandage absorbing more than he swallowed, and eased him back. He captured her hand and wove their fingers clumsily together, then closed his eyes and lay still, so she thought he'd passed out.

"Where?"

She sighed. "Juntavas ship."

"Forgive me. . . ."

"Only if you forgive me," she snapped. "I didn't go back to the pod. Useless damn thing to do. Can't pilot it."

"I know." He paused, and she saw the ghost of the ghost of a smile. "Miscalculation. . . ."

She was wondering how to answer this when the lock jiggled. Rolling, she was on her feet between Val Con and the door when it slid open.

"How's the boyfriend, Sergeant?" Borg Tanser stepped cautiously into the room, medkit in one hand, pellet gun in the other.

"What's it to you?"

"Boss wants both of you alive," Tanser said. "New rules. Was just you. Seems Scout Commander Val Con yos'Phelium owns some stock now, too." He threw the box in a sharp underhand, and she caught it without a flinch.

"Well, whaddya waiting for, Sergeant?" He waved the gun. "Patch him up!"

THE PILOT BLINKED at the screen, swore, and upped mag. The big asteroid—the Clutch vessel—was behaving in a most peculiar manner, stuttering across the screen, phasing in, phasing out—in, out, in, out—going somewhere. . . .

Gone.

Tommy rubbed his eyes and hit the inship, demanding strong black coffee, on the bounce.

Then he looked back at the screen. Gone, all right.

Sighing, he cleared the board and began to run check calibrations. It seemed like a good idea.

JEFFERSON GAVE A couple of minutes' frowning thought to the newest message from the boss before keying in the relay to Tanser, adding a rider that he should hang where he was until things were settled. It didn't seem like a good time to be out of touch with each other.

SHIRTS WERE PROVIDED, as was a pad and blanket for the bed, and the menuboard supplied Miri with a hot meal. Val Con had passed out sometime during her ministrations with the medkit and hadn't come round yet. She carried her second mug of coffee over and sat on the edge of the bed, watching him breathe.

His chest rose and fell with the rhythm of sleep; his breathing was no longer labored or shallow. The pulse that beat at the base of his throat was a little rickety, but hardly dangerous—nothing a day's rest wouldn't cure.

It had taken her over an hour to stop the bleeding from the pellet wounds, with her sweating and swearing, and Tanser holding the gun and snarling at her not to botch the job.

She'd had a go at patching the gash on his face. The pipe had just missed his eye, slicing diagonally across the high line of the right cheek. She'd done her best; the scar would be even, anyway, and it would fade in time from angry red to pale gold.

His lashes fluttered and his eyes were open, his wide mouth curving in a soft smile. He moved his hand to touch her knee.

"What are you thinking?"

She blinked. "That I love you," she said and dropped her hand over his. "Stupid damn thing, but what're you gonna do?"

"Accept it?" he guessed. Then he said more softly, "I may now tell you the same—that I love you—and you will believe me?"

"Yeah," she said, staring, "I guess so." She laughed. "Saving me from my lust to keep me for my love? Melodrama, Star Captain!"

"Scout Commander is sufficient," he murmured, shifting slightly. "How does one obtain dinner here?"

She finished her coffee and grinned at him. "One tells the nurse—that's me—that one is hungry. Then one is served something healthy. Like soup."

He sighed, closing his eyes. "In spite of this I feel I should inform you that I am very hungry."

Miri stood up. "Okay, pal, but remember: You asked for it!"

✧ CHAPTER TWENTY-FOUR ✧

JUSTIN HOSTRO LAID ASIDE the three-page printout that was Borg Tanser's report and sat, his hands in a pyramid before him, his eyes on the gash in his desk.

Both were alive; though the man had taken some damage, it appeared that he would mend. So the letter of Edger's bargain was met. The problem now remained of how to exact punishment and yet make it appear that the hands of the Juntavas were clean. So might he yet come out of this with his life and his business intact.

An idea forming in his mind, he found the description of the wrecked yacht and reread it carefully. Then pushing back from his desk, he strolled to the comm unit by the far wall and punched in the code for Edger's rooms.

The shell-less one answered the call, bowed in recognition, and begged Hostro not to sever the connection while he went to fetch the *T'carais*. He vanished without waiting for an answer, leaving a garish abstract design on-screen for his caller's contemplation.

Hostro shuddered and turned his eyes to the

Belansium planetscape above the comm. He was still absorbed in its study when Edger's voice roused him.

"Justin Hostro? You wished to speak with me?"

He bowed. "Indeed, sir. I am calling to inform you that your kin were overtaken by those of my family to whom I assigned this task. Happily, both are well, though presently not at liberty. I also wished to inform you of my intention to allow them to go free, returning their weapons and giving them a ship in which to continue their journey, since the ship they had been traveling in has, according to the pilot's report, gone into drive spontaneously and vanished."

There was a long pause. "I am pleased that you have given me these tidings, Justin Hostro," Edger said finally, "and would ask that you grant another request."

Hostro bowed. "If it is within my power. sir, certainly."

"I long to hear the voices of my sister and my brother. I would ask that you arrange to have them speak into a recording device before they are restored to liberty and that your kin bring this tape to me when they return."

Justin Hostro smiled. "Nothing could he easier, sir. It shall be done exactly as you have said."

VAL CON AND MIRI sat on the floor under the menuboard.

"What do you suppose they're waiting for?" he asked, carefully balancing his glass of milk as he eased his back against the wall. "We've been hanging in normal space for days. If the two of us are so valuable, it seems Borg Tanser should waste no time taking us to his boss."

"I don't care if we never go anywhere," Miri told him. "Even if the view is monotonous. Better a little monotony than gettin' hauled up before the big boss. I don't think she likes me too much. Or he. And Justin Hostro don't like *either* of us. And that's who Tanser works for." She sipped her coffee. "Maybe we'll get time off for good behavior, huh?"

He raised an eyebrow. "I doubt that anyone who knows you would grant such a thing."

"You," she said with deep sadness, "are gonna be an *evil* old man."

"I certainly hope so. . . ."

The door opened, and Borg Tanser strode into the room, gun ready, voicecorder over one shoulder. He dumped the 'corder beside Val Con, who looked up, one brow quirked.

"You know a turtle named Edger?" Tanser demanded. "Claims to be related to you."

"Yes."

"Good, 'cause Hostro's got a deal with the turtle. Includes giving you your weapons and lettin' you go. Seeing as how the rock you were on is gone, we're even gonna give you a ship. Sweet deal, huh?"

When neither of them answered, Tanser shook his head. "Turtle don't trust Hostro. Wants to hear your voices. Wants to hear how nice we been to you and how you're not hurt and how we're gonna let you go, all fair and square." He pointed at the 'corder.

"So you're gonna tell 'im that. Now. In Terran." He pointed his gun at Miri's head. "I said *now*, Commander!"

Both brows lifted and Val Con set the glass aside,

pulled the 'corder onto his lap, and touched the GO button.

"I greet you, brother, and thank you for the lives of myself and the youngest of your sisters. I am to say to you these things, which are true: We are alive and have been well treated, having received food, a place to sleep, and medical aid. I regret that the ship of the Clan has continued its voyage without us. It was undamaged when it left us and should achieve its destination as planned, as it kept course without fail during the seven seasons of its labor." He glanced up, encountered Tanser's glare, and bent again to the device.

"I am also to say that we will be returned our knives and given a ship in which to continue our travels.

"My thanks to you, again, brother, for your care of two of your Clan who are foolish and hasty." He thumbed the OFF stud and looked at Tanser inquiringly.

"Your turn, Sergeant. Sweetness and light, remember."

Miri took the 'corder and punched it on. "Hi, Edger," she began in a singsong monotone completely unlike her usual manner of speaking. "Everything's fine. Wish you were here. Love to the family and see you soon." She banged the OFF switch and shoved the device at Tanser.

He took it by the strap, shaking his head in wonder. "Sergeant, it beats hell out of me how you ever lived this long." He waved the gun at them. "Okay, let's go."

"Go where?" Miri demanded.

"Didn't you just hear? We're givin' you a ship and turnin' you loose. Free citizens, see? The Juntavas keeps its word." He moved the gun again. "Move it."

✧✧✧

MIRI STOOD IN the control room of the wrecked yacht, weaving her belt around her waist and watching the viewscreen. The Juntavas ship was just at the edge of her sight, dwindling rapidly until it disappeared.

Sighing, she turned from the screen to where Val Con was lying on his back, fidgeting under the piloting board.

"They're gone," she told him.

He didn't answer, but continued his work. Miri sat on the floor to wait.

Presently, he emerged and sat up, the hair across his forehead damp with sweat.

"Well," she asked, "what's the bad news? We sit here for a couple days till we get bashed by low-flying junk? Or go on at sublight for Volmer?"

He gave her a tired grin. "And arrive as skeletons? The bad news could be worse, in fact. I can do some illegal things with power shunts and cross-currents and get up enough power for one modest Jump."

"One Jump?" She lifted her eyebrows.

"One *modest* Jump. We won't raise Volmer."

"Well," she said, bumping her elbow on the knife in her belt and frowning. "One Jump's better'n no Jumps. I guess. What do I do to help?"

THE HUNTING had been good since the taking of the Terran yacht, and Commander Khaliiz was pleased. Now it was time to collect the prizes, to return home, to report, and to receive the payment of bounties and the accolades of success.

Commander Khaliiz issued his orders and the ship slid

away into the underside of space. Perhaps, he thought, he would allow the new Adjutant the honor of bringing the Terran prize home.

MIRI SIGHED AND DRAGGED a sleeve across her forehead, surveying the pile of junk she had assembled in the forward hold. Val Con was still in the control room, rearranging the innards of the ship's drive. Miri's task was to lighten the mass they had to move when the time came.

She sighed again as she remembered the location of another useless bit of mass and moved off in that direction.

The dead man weighed a lot, even in the light gravity, and it took her longer than she liked to move him up with the rest of the items to be spaced. Finally, she let him slip gently to the floor and stood, breathing hard, looking down at him, wondering who he might have been, and whether he had had a family.

Family meant something to some people. Like Val Con. And Edger. This man had been Terran, and Terrans did not form into clans. Still, she thought suddenly, turning the new idea around in her head, there might be somebody around who would want to know what had happened to him.

She bent and went through his pockets, removing papers, coins, a flat, flexible metal rectangle that looked as if it belonged in a computer, and a folder of holos featuring a woman and two little boys. Bundling it all together she dumped it in her pouch, then went in search of other junk to space.

✧✧✧

VAL CON WAS AT THE BOARD, his hands moving in measured control as if he were playing the 'chora. Miri slid into the copilot's chair and watched the side of his face as he ran through his rituals and read the responses in the board's flickering lights.

After a time he leaned back and smiled at her.

"Everything that can be spaced is spaced," she told him, with a mock salute. "How's life in the clean world?"

He waved a hand at the board. "We have power. We have fuel. Where would you like to go?"

She tipped her head. "What're we near? What's a 'modest' Jump?" She shrugged her shoulders, half-smiling. *"Piloting for Dummies . . ."*

Frowning, he suddenly leaned forward and felt around on the short shelf under the pilot's board; he slid out of his chair and peered inside, pushing his arm way back.

"What?" she demanded.

"Coord book." He sat back on his heels and looked at her. "Miri, when you were gathering things together, did you come across a book, about so—" He shaped it in the air with quick golden fingers. "—probably bound in leather, containing many thin, metallic pages? It would have been in this room."

She shook her head. "Would've showed you something like that first, in case it was important."

He snapped to his feet and made a quick circuit of the room, checking behind and under every instrument panel and chair. Miri got up, pushed at the cushion in her chair looking for large lumps, but found none; she gave the pilot's chair the same treatment, then shook her head. Nothing.

She turned to say so and froze. Val Con was standing in the center of the room, staring at the screen. There was no particular expression on his face.

"Coord book's pretty important?" she ventured, coming to his side and laying a cautious hand on his arm.

He moved his eyes to her face. "Without coordinates, there is no Jump. Coordinates define direction, shape, location."

She considered the implications of his words. "Think Borg Tanser knows that?"

"Yes," he said grimly. "I do."

"Can't Jump without coords?" she persisted. "Take luck of the draw?"

He shook his head. "I could invent some coordinates, just to initiate a Jump, but the chances are very, very good that we'd leave drive to find ourselves inside a sun, or a planet, or an asteroid belt, or another ship, or—"

She laid her hand over his mouth. "Got it." She closed her eyes to think. Thin metallic pages? She had seen something, just recently. Not a book, but something. . . .

"Like this?" She snapped open her pouch, pulled out the dead man's effects, and held out the metal rectangle.

Val Con took it, his eyes questioning.

"The guy in the hold," she explained. "I thought— maybe somebody might want to know what happened."

"Ah." He nodded. "We will tell his family, then." He turned his attention to the rectangle. "Why carry it with him?"

"Will it work?" she demanded.

He was on his way back to the board. "We will see what the computer thinks." Sliding into the pilot's chair, he inserted the page in a slot near the top of the board, flipped two switches, and hit a button.

Lights began to flicker and displays glowed to life. Miri settled back in the copilot's chair to watch.

"Perhaps a student?" Val Con murmured, more to himself than to her, his eyes on the readouts. "A smuggler?" He shook his head as the board flickered into stillness and the slot allowed the metal page to rise to convenient gripping height.

"Will it work?" she asked again, trying to keep the edge out of her voice.

He spun the chair to face her. "There is one set of coordinates within our range," he said slowly. "This particular page holds four. I am familiar with only one set—far out of range. It is for orbit around a planet called Pelaun, an inhabited world that has achieved the technical expertise necessary to establish electronic communication, transworld."

She blinked. "Spaceflight?"

"None."

"And the other coords? The one that's in our range?" She had a feeling she knew what the answer was going to be.

"They are not familiar to me," he said. "The only reason I recall the coords for Pelaun is because I was first Scout in-system."

"Well, I don't know as how I can think of anything *much* worse than being stuck for the rest of my life on some podunk world that thinks a planet-wide comm-net's a big deal."

He smiled slightly. "It's a bit less spectacular than a comm-net," he said gently. "Voice transmission only; no image. And the reception is horrible."

Miri stared at him, but he seemed to be serious. She shifted her eyes to the screen—and sat frozen for a long heartbeat while her mind scrambled to find words for what her eyes were seeing.

"Val Con?" her voice rasped out of her tight throat.

"Yes."

"Something worse," she told him. "There's Yxtrang, just Jumped in-system. . . ."

✧ CHAPTER TWENTY-FIVE ✧

THE YXTRANG PILOT stared at the readout in disbelief, upped the magnification, and checked the readings once more, cold dread in his heart.

"Commander. Pilot requests permission to speak."

"Permission granted," Khaliiz said.

"The vessel which we captured on our last pass through this system is moving under power, Commander. The scans read the life forces of two creatures."

"Pilot's report heard and acknowledged. Stand by for orders. Second!"

"Commander."

"It was reported to me that none were left alive aboard yon vessel, Second. Discover the man who lied and bring him to me at once."

His Second saluted. "At once, Commander." He turned and marched from the bridge.

Khaliiz eyed the screen, perceived the ship-bounty slipping through his fingers, and was displeased.

"Pursue."

✧✧✧

VAL CON cursed very softly, then snapped back to the board, slapped the page into its slot, and demanded coords, position, speed, condition of power in the coils.

They were moving at about one-quarter the speed they could muster, locally. The Yxtrang were pouring on speed, moving to intercept.

"Could we leave now?" asked a small voice to his left.

He turned his head. Miri was sitting rigidly in the copilot's chair, her eyes frozen on the screen and the growing shape of the Yxtrang vessel. Her face was the color of milk; her freckles stood out vividly.

"We must wait until the power has reached sufficient level and the coordinates are locked into the board," he said, keeping his voice even. "We will leave in a few minutes."

"They'll *be* here in a few minutes." She bit her lip, hard, and managed to drag her eyes from the screen to his face. "Val Con, I'm *afraid* of Yxtrang."

He was aware of the tightness of the muscles in his own face, and did not try to give her a smile. "I am also afraid of Yxtrang," he said gently. His eyes flicked to the board, then to the screen. "Strap in."

"What're you gonna do?" She was watching him closely. Some of the color had returned to her face, but she was still stiff in every muscle.

"There is a game Terrans sometimes play," he murmured, dividing his attention between board and screen, his fingers busy with his own straps, "called 'chicken' . . . Strap in, *cha'trez.*"

Moving like a manikin, she obeyed; she forced herself to lean back in the chair, her eyes on his profile.

He flipped a toggle. "I see you, Ckrakec Yxtrang. Pass us by. We are unworthy to be your prey."

There was a pause for transmission, then a voice, harsh as broken glass, replied in Trade. "Unworthy? Thieves are always worthy game! That ship is ours, Liaden; we have won it once."

"Forgive us, Ckrakec Yxtrang, we are here by no fault of our own. We are not worthy of you. Pass by."

"Release my prize, Liaden, or I shall wrest it from you, and you will die."

Miri licked her lips, steadfastly refusing to look at the screen. Val Con's face was smooth and calm, his voice nearly gentle. "If I release your prize, I shall die in any case. Pass by, Hunter. There is only I, who am recently wounded."

"My scans show two, Liaden."

Miri closed her eyes. Val Con, measuring board against screen, eased the speed of the ship higher, toward the halfway point. "Only a woman, Ckrakec Yxtrang. What proof is that of your skill?"

There was a pause, during which Val Con slipped the speed up another notch and pressed the sequence that locked in the coords.

"Will it please you, when you are captured, Liaden, to watch me while I take my pleasure from your woman? Afterward, I shall blind you and give you as a toy to my crew."

"Alas, Ckrakec Yxtrang, these things would but cause me pain." Coils up! The Yxtrang were finally near enough, beginning the boarding maneuver, matching velocity, and direction. . . .

"It would give you pain!" the Yxtrang cried. "All things give Liadens pain! They are a soft race, born to be the prey of the strong. In time, there will be no more Liadens. The cities of Liad will house the children of Yxtrang."

"What then will you hunt, O Hunter?" He flipped a series of toggles, leaned back in the pilot's chair, and held a hand out to Miri.

Slowly the ship began to spin.

There was a roar of laughter from the Yxtrang, horrible to hear. "Very good, Liaden! Never shall it be said, after you are dead, that you were an unworthy rabbit. A good maneuver. But not good enough."

In the screen, the Yxtrang ship began to spin as well, matching velocity uncertainly.

Miri's hand was cold in his. He squeezed it, gave her a quick smile, and released her, returning to the board.

He gave the ship more spin, and a touch more speed. The Yxtrang moved to match both. Val Con added again to the spin, but left the speed steady.

"Enough, Liaden! What do you hope to win? The ship is ours, and we will act to keep it. Do you imagine I will grow tired of the game and leave? Do you not know that even now I might fire upon you and lay you open to the cold of space?"

"There is no bounty on ruined ships, Ckrakec Yxtrang, nor any glory in reporting that a Liaden outwitted you. But," he said, sighing deeply, "perhaps you are young and this your first hunt—"

There was a scream of rage over the comm, and the Yxtrang ship edged closer. Val Con added more spin; ship's gravity was increasing, and lifting his arm above the board the few inches required to manipulate the keys was an effort. His lungs were laboring a little for air. He glanced over at Miri. She grinned raggedly.

"How much faster will you spin, Liaden? Until the gravity crushes you?"

"If necessary. I am determined that you will collect no bounty on this ship, Ckrakec Yxtrang. It has become a matter of honor." He increased the spin. He paused with his hand on the velocity lever.

"Speak not to me of honor, animal! We have toyed long enough. We shall—"

Val Con shoved the velocity to the top, slammed on more spin, hesitated, counting, eyes on the board—

Jump!

✧ CHAPTER TWENTY-SIX ✧

THE BLAST HIT like a tsunami, rocking the Yxtrang ship. Overloaded equipment sparked and smoked; crew members not firmly tied down joined other loose debris thrown against walls, floor, and ceiling.

The spin made it hard to stand, to move, to understand what had happened. For the moment, chaos held the ship in its grip and squeezed lungs tight, nerves tighter.

"Report! Report now!"

Reports began to trickle in. The pilot was dazed beyond sense, his Adjutant thrown against the wall. . . .

The crew slowly pulled themselves together. Khaliiz took over the pilot's chair, read the impossible readings, and used emergency rockets to slow the spin. The Adjutant came to and began his work; he found whole compartments which refused to answer in the near darkness of the emergency lighting.

It became obvious that there was no such thing as a system: Individual processors still carried out their work, but the command computers were out, as were the backups.

Gravity came back to near normal as Khaliiz gained more and more control of his vessel. A technician managed to get one screen working, though Khaliiz was forced to rotate the ship to achieve a full 360-degree view capability.

"Commander, what happened?" ventured the Adjutant.

"Work! We speak of this later."

THEY HIT NORMAL space spinning. Hands flickered over an alarm-lit board, easing acceleration, killing spin, slowing all systems back to normal.

Val Con, shivering with reaction, drooped in the pilot's seat and turned his head, mouth curving in a smile. Then he gave a start.

Miri hung limp in the copilot's chair, held erect by the webbing, head lolling, face too white.

His fingers fumbled with the straps and he was out of the chair, kneeling before her to seek the fragile pulse in the throat. "Miri?" he whispered.

Her pulse was strong, her breathing deep. He closed his eyes in relief, then snapped to his feet and gathered her in his arms. He curled her on his lap, her head resting on his shoulder, and sat listening to her breathe and watching the unfamiliar pattern of light that was the system they were bound for.

After a time she stirred, muttering something unintelligible, and raised her head to stare into his face, her eyes slightly narrowed, as if she were looking into too bright a light.

"What'd you do?"

He lifted a brow. "When?"

She raised a hand to gesture vaguely, then allowed it to find a resting place on his chest. "With Yxtrang. Why'd they have to be so close? And the gravity—" She shuddered and his arms tightened momentarily.

"I *am* sorry," he said, "about the gravity. For the rest—" He grinned. "Allow me to give you your first lesson in piloting, which is this: Never, under any circumstances at all, take a ship into drive when there is another ship or mass closer than one thousandth of a light-second in any direction. It is a very dangerous thing to do. On the occasions when it *has* been done, one of two things occurred.

"Sometimes *both* objects go into hyperspace where it was planned only one would go. Neither comes out.

"The second possibility is that—if you are lucky, or foolhardy, or afraid—you will do everything perfectly for your ship and make the Jump without mishap." He sighed. "But the ship that remains behind is then immediately caught in a hysteresis energy effect proportional to the velocity and spin of the vessel that Jumped. . . ."

Miri stared at him. "Poor Yxtrang," she said, her tone belying her words. "And we're okay? On course? Whatever that means."

He nodded. "The ship is intact and we are proceeding at moderate velocity toward an unfamiliar planetary system. We should reach scanning range in—" He glanced at the board. "—seven hours."

She sighed. "Time for a good, long sleep. Or something."

"Or something," he agreed, lifting a hand to trace the line of her cheek with a light fingertip.

She grinned, then her smile faded and she pulled away from his caress, using the hand that rested on his chest to emphasize her words.

"I want you to understand one thing, okay? No distress beacons. It goes off *five feet* from us, we ain't moving from this ship, *accazi*?"

"Yes, Miri," he murmured penitently, unable to control the twitch at the side of his mouth.

"Ah, you—" She leaned forward to kiss him.

THE THIRD PLANET had possibilities, he thought some while later. Too far out for decent scanning yet— not that this brute had anything like the instrumentation a Scout ship carried—but it definitely seemed the most likely of the five.

"They're all dead, ain't they?" said a voice at his elbow. "No stations, no traffic, no orbitals. . . ." Staring at the screen, her face bleak, the glow of lovemaking gone out of her, she was shaking her head at the five little planets and their lovely yellow sun. "We're stuck in the back end of nowhere and we ain't never gettin' out." Her mouth twisted and she turned to look at him. "You think there's any people?"

He suddenly recalled the training she had not had. "Many people. At least on the third planet. See that silvery shimmer over the land mass that looks like a wine bottle?"

She squinted. "Yeah. . . . What is it?"

"Smog." He smiled and took her hands in his. "Miri, listen: Where there is smog, there's technology. Where there's technology, there exists the means to build a transmitter. Where there's a signal, sooner or later, is a rescue." He lifted an eyebrow, winning a glimmer of her smile.

"You don't think Edger will let us stay missing, do you?" he asked. "He's bound to be along, in a decade or two. . . ."

✧ EPILOGUE ✧

THE ADJUTANT SAT with the Engineer and the Commander, apart from the crew.

"Report," Khaliiz ordered.

The Engineer reported that things were not well. The Adjutant reported that a number of men were dead, more injured: the ship would be hard put to resist a determined boarding party. The Engineer, quaking, reported that it might not be possible to have full power drive for home.

Khaliiz thought.

"It is apparent," he said. "that the vessel we approached had been badly damaged in the previous battle. It exploded, giving up what energy was left in its drive cells."

He pointed at the Engineer. "You will make the reports read so, as you value the air you breathe!

"Who swore the ship empty, Adjutant?"

"Sir, it was my Second, Thrik."

"You will shoot him, personally. You will then record your demotion to Assistant Cook. This will be your lifegrade. You failed in your choice of assistants."

"Yes, sir. Thank you, sir," the Assistant Cook said.

"Get out!"

Khaliiz played idly with the cover of the destruct switch, though he had made his decision when he ordered the man shot. If he had meant to destroy the ship, he would have ordered the Second Adjutant to push the button. But he played with the cover, anyway, wondering if he'd been tricked—wondering if the little Liaden had blown himself up on purpose. Or if it had been an accident.

A distant boom claimed his attention, the echo ringing as an explosive gunblast will inside a ship.

It had been an accident, the Commander decided. For centuries, Liadens had lacked the courage to emulate the Yxtrang—lacked the honor to be truly worthy opponents. That could not change.

An accident.

About the Authors

✧

Steve Miller's first professional sale was "Charioteer," to Ted White's *Amazing Stories*, in 1976.

"A Matter of Ceremony," was **Sharon Lee's** first professional sale—to *Amazing Stories* in 1979.

Steve and Sharon were each pursuing careers as writers when they met, in the late 1970s, realized that the sum of them was greater than the parts, and decided to pursue a partnership.

Some time after consolidating their books, music, typewriters, and cats into one central location, they accidentally collaborated on a short story, "The Naming of Kinzel: The Innocent."

And so a third writer—Sharon Lee and Steve Miller—was born.

The Worlds of
SHARON LEE & STEVE MILLER
Intrigue. Adventure. Romance.
Find Them Here.

Epic Urban Adventure by a New Star of Fantasy

DRAW ONE IN THE DARK

by Sarah A. Hoyt

Every one of us has a beast inside. But for Kyrie Smith, the beast is no metaphor. Thrust into an ever-changing world of shifters, where shape-shifting dragons, giant cats and other beasts wage a secret war behind humanity's back, Kyrie tries to control her inner animal and remain human as best she can....

"Analytically, it's a tour de force: logical, built from assumptions, with no contradictions, which is astonishing given the subject matter. It's also gripping enough that I finished it in one day."

—Jerry Pournelle

1-4165-2092-9 • $25.00